SOCIETY FOR NEW TESTAMENT STUDIES
MONOGRAPH SERIES

GENERAL EDITOR

MATTHEW BLACK, D.D., F.B.A.

ASSOCIATE EDITOR

R. McL. WILSON

30

THE MELCHIZEDEK TRADITION

THE MELCHIZEDEK TRADITION

A CRITICAL EXAMINATION OF THE SOURCES TO THE FIFTH CENTURY A.D. AND IN THE EPISTLE TO THE HEBREWS

FRED L. HORTON Jr

Associate Professor of Religion
Wake Forest University

CAMBRIDGE UNIVERSITY PRESS

CAMBRIDGE

LONDON · NEW YORK · MELBOURNE

Published by the Syndics of the Cambridge University Press
The Pitt Building, Trumpington Street, Cambridge CB2 IRP
Bentley House, 200 Euston Road, London NWI 2DB
32 East 57th Street, New York, NY 10022, USA
296 Beaconsfield Parade, Middle Park, Melbourne 3206, Australia

First published 1976

Printed in Great Britain
at the
University Printing House, Cambridge
(Euan Phillips, University Printer)

Library of Congress Cataloguing in Publication Data
Horton, Fred L.
The Melchizedek Tradition.

(Society for New Testament Studies. Monograph series; 30)

Bibliography: p.

Includes index.

1. Melchizedek, King of Salem. 2. Bible. N.T.
Hebrews – Criticism, interpretation, etc. I. Title.
II. Series: Studiorum Novi Testamenti Societas.
Monograph series; 30.
BS580.M4H67   221.9'2[B]   75-32479
ISBN 0 521 21014 3

CONTENTS

PREFACE

This study originated in a short paper which I presented to Professor W. D. Davies' seminar on the Epistle to the Hebrews in 1968 which dealt with the relationship between Qumran and Hebrews. That paper dealt at length with a fragmentary document from the Dead Sea which treated Melchizedek as a divine figure, and at the time the parallels between Hebrews and that document seemed irresistible to me. To find a definite parallel to Hebrews at Qumran which was not also to be found in other forms of the Judaism of the period opened the possibility for a new way of understanding Hebrews and suggested some new answers to old questions about the origin and background of the Epistle.

The first task, it seemed to me, was to establish the parallel between Qumran and Hebrews as to Melchizedek, and it was to this task that I turned when I began research for this present work which was to be my dissertation. In the fall of 1969 I presented another paper to the Biblical Studies Seminar at Duke University in which I attempted to give further evidence for the association of Hebrews and Qumran on the basis of the Melchizedek fragment from Qumran. Simply to have expanded this study, however, would have been to assume the correctness of my assumptions, and it was for that reason that I decided that I should attempt to show the development of Melchizedek speculation through the early centuries of the Christian era in an effort to relate Hebrews to an independent development of thought. In particular, I hoped to show a continuity of development which extended from the Old Testament, through Qumran, to later Christian, Jewish, and Gnostic thought. This would show clearly what I supposed to be the very close relationship between Hebrews and Qumran, at least on the subject of Melchizedek.

The scheme decided on at the beginning of my work has been retained, but the assumptions which lay behind it have been abandoned. As regards my initial assumptions the results of my study have been largely negative, but as those assumptions were being discarded, another result emerged which is described in the last chapter.

The scope of this book is greater than is usually the case for a New Testament work, but I have benefited from having a perspective, limited as it is, from which to view some of the important debates in early Christianity, Gnosticism, and Rabbinic Judaism. Also the work has allowed me a much needed review of the major emphases of the so-called Myth and Ritual School. Nevertheless, my final aim has been to produce a book which will clarify a major issue in the study of the Epistle to the Hebrews. I hope at a later time to continue the present work and apply it even more directly to Hebrews.

I should like to thank the Danforth Foundation and Duke University for providing me with the funds necessary to stay in residence while I completed the original version of this book as a dissertation. I do not have enough words of gratitude to express my appreciation for the help and encouragement given me by my research director, W. D. Davies. His abiding interest in his students is altogether remarkable, and I have benefited immeasurably from my association with him. I also appreciate deeply the great interest which Professor Orval Wintermute took in my work. Without his help the investigation of several topics dealing with Qumran and Gnosticism would have been greatly hampered. Professor Franklin Young was kind enough to read the portion of the dissertation dealing with the church fathers and to point out certain of the weaknesses in that section. Finally, I am greatly in the debt of Professor A. S. Van der Woude and Professor R. McL. Wilson who read the manuscript and offered many suggestions for corrections and additions. The many errors in this work are my own, but without the help of those named above those errors would have been much greater.

During the fall semester of 1971 Wake Forest University was privileged to have Dr Matthew Black as Visiting Professor of Religion. I am most grateful for this opportunity to know that great scholar and am grateful for his encouragement of my presenting this work for publication. Also I must thank Wake Forest University for providing me with funds to have the manuscript typed for the press.

PREFACE

I have benefited greatly from the editorial abilities of my student assistant, Cathy L. Martin, who assisted me in correcting the master copy of this book for submission to the press. I am also indebted to her for suggestions as to how some of the material could be clarified.

Last of all I have to thank my wife Patricia, who more than once interrupted her own academic work to help me with the preparation of this study. Also I must thank my daughter, Christina, who spent so much of her time sitting on the sofa of my study, hampered by a broken leg and playing quietly while I worked on this book. To them this work is gratefully dedicated.

F.L.H.

Wake Forest University
Winston-Salem, N.C.

ABBREVIATIONS

*ANET*² *Ancient Near Eastern Texts Relating to the Old Testament*, 2nd ed.

ARN *Aboth de Rabbi Nathan*, ed. Schechter

BA *Biblical Archaeologist*

BASOR *Bulletin of the American Schools of Oriental Research*

Bauer, *Lexicon* Walter Bauer, *A Greek–English Lexicon of the New Testament and other Early Christian Literature*, trans. Arndt and Gingrich

BDB F. Brown, S. R. Driver, C. A. Briggs, *A Hebrew and English Lexicon of the Old Testament*

BZAW Beihefte zur *Zeitschrift für die Alttestamentliche Wissenschaft*

BZNW Beihefte zur *Zeitschrift für die Neutestamentliche Wissenschaft*

CBQ *Catholic Biblical Quarterly*

Ep. *Epistula* (in Latin titles)

G.–K. *Gesenius' Hebrew Grammar*, ed. Kautsch

HE Eusebius, *Historia Ecclesiae*

HTR *Harvard Theological Review*

HzNT *Handbuch zum Neuen Testament*

IEJ *Israel Exploration Journal*

Jastrow, *Dictionary* Marcus Jastrow, *A Dictionary of the Targumim, the Talmud Babli and Yerushalmi, and the Midrashic Literature*

JBL *Journal of Biblical Literature*

JJS *Journal of Jewish Studies*

JSJ *Journal for the Study of Judaism in the Persian, Hellenistic, and Roman Periods*

JTS *Journal of Theological Studies*

L.–S. Liddell–Scott, *Greek–English Lexicon*

m. Mishnah (before the name of a tractate)

Moore, *Judaism* George Foot Moore, *Judaism in the First Centuries of the Christian Era*, 3 vols.

MSG Migne, Series Graeca

MSL Migne, Series Latina

For MSG and MSL the volume number is given in Arabic numerals followed by the page number. Example: MSG 94, 712 is MSG vol. 94, page 712.

MT Masoretic Text

NTS   *New Testament Studies*

R.   *Rabbah* (in reference to the Midrash Rabbah)

RB   *Revue Biblique*

RGG   *Die Religion in Geschichte und Gegenwart* (Tübingen)

RSV   Revised Standard Version

Str.–B.   Strack–Billerbeck, *Kommentar zum Neuen Testament aus Talmud und Midrasch,* 4 vols.

USQR   *Union Seminary Quarterly Review*

VT   *Vetus Testamentum*

ZAW   *Zeitschrift für die Alttestamentliche Wissenschaft*

ZNW   *Zeitschrift für die Neutestamentliche Wissenschaft*

/ /   phoneme (a distinct class of sounds in a single language)

CHAPTER I

INTRODUCTION

THE SCOPE OF THIS INQUIRY

The purpose of this work is to investigate the tradition about Melchizedek from its setting in the Old Testament through roughly the first five centuries of the Christian era. This is a rather complex undertaking in several ways. The sources themselves are sometimes quite difficult to disentangle and interpret. For instance, one of the more important texts, a text from Qumran, throws new light on the understanding of Melchizedek in the first century A.D.[1] One is disappointed, therefore, to find that this text is so fragmentary that less than half of what was at least a two-column work can be read; furthermore, the reading itself depends upon a piecing together of the text which may or may not be correct. The Old Testament sources are very difficult to interpret. In Gen. xiv. 18–20 we have a passing mention of Melchizedek as a priest-king who brings refreshment out to Abram who is just returning from battle, and in Ps. cx. 4 we have a mysterious formula by which the king in Jerusalem is declared to possess a priesthood 'according to the order of Melchizedek'. These two passing references provide no clear grounding for our inquiry in the Old Testament, and much work has been required to make any sense out of these two Old Testament sources.[2] Both Philo and Josephus deal with Melchizedek and throw some light on the development of tradition from the first century B.C. to the first century A.D. Further, we possess two documents from Qumran which give us information for that same period. Nothing, however, adequately prepares us for the extraordinary use to which Melchizedek is put in the Epistle to the Hebrews.

Even in our own day opinion among scholars is divided as to whether Melchizedek in Hebrews is an angelic being or a mere man whose record in the Old Testament has certain exegetical advantages for the purpose of the author. We are not surprised

---

[1] See below, Chapter 3.
[2] I have devoted all of Chapter 2 to this topic

to find that the early church was similarly divided, and those who considered Melchizedek to be an angelic or divine being often went to extremes sufficient to call forth condemnation from anti-heretical writers in the early church. From these refutations of what we might call Melchizedekian heresies[1] we gain some insight into the growth of Melchizedek speculation in the first five centuries of the church's life. We shall also deal with the figure of Melchizedek in Rabbinic and Gnostic literature.

This inquiry will end with the situation in the first part of the fifth century A.D. This is a natural point of division from the point of view of the sources and my intentions. The fifth century A.D. would be a natural starting point for an investigation of the Melchizedek tradition in the middle ages since it is only after this time that the numerous legends about Melchizedek began to grow among both Jews and Christians. Further, Melchizedek came to play an important role in the thought of the Ishmaelite sect in the thirteenth century A.D.[2] I, however, have found no way short of pure conjecture to make a connection between the sources discussed in this study and the later Melchizedek legends. A full-scale study of the legends might point to some areas of contact, but that would be another thesis, possibly in another discipline.

I have divided the sources into what I have called the 'background sources' and the 'later sources'. The point of division is the Epistle to the Hebrews, a partition which begs the question of the date of the Epistle. I believe the Epistle belongs roughly in the last part of the first century A.D., but it would be improper to go into the date of the Epistle from such a narrow perspective as the Melchizedek tradition. I have, consequently, decided to discuss Hebrews at the end of my work.[3] There are several good reasons for this procedure. It is certainly true that Hebrews stands with Philo, Josephus, Qumran, and others as a witness to the growth of the tradition about Melchizedek in the first five centuries of the Christian era. To that extent there is no justifi-

---

[1] This is a term of convenience and has little value apart from convenience. The Melchizedekians, to be discussed in Chapter 4, are one of the sects included here under the designation 'Melchizedekian heresies'.

[2] Georges Vajda, 'Melchisédec dans la mythologie ismaélienne', *Journal Asiatique*, CCXXXIV (1943–5), 173–83.

[3] Chapter 6.

cation for failing to place it in its proper chronological position. However, two considerations led me to the placement of the chapter on Hebrews at the end of this book. (1) Most of the material with which we shall deal from the early church represents attempts by the church to come to an adequate understanding of Melchizedek in Hebrews. Methodologically we cannot approach these sources with the problem already solved in our minds since this would cause us to do violence to the later Christian sources. (2) Should some line of development come to light between the background sources and the later sources we would then be in a position to relate Hebrews to that development without arguing in a circle.

I have my own theory about the ultimate source of Melchizedek speculation which has grown out of this study, but the reader will find no reference to this theory until the last chapter. I believe this work will have more value for the reader if no theoretical solution to the perplexing question of why so much should be said about such a minor Old Testament figure is imposed upon the sources themselves. I hope that the reader who disagrees with me on my solution to this problem might find something helpful in the other chapters. I have attempted in Chapters 2–5 to discuss each source presented in a manner which adequately relates it to its historical and literary setting. This involves from time to time a conjecture or a theory, but the reader will find that such conjectures or theories are limited to the single area of concern for which they were fashioned.

I have dealt exhaustively with the background sources insofar as that material is known to me, and I have dealt with all the published Melchizedek material from Gnostic sources. I have not been able to deal exhaustively with the early Christian sources nor with the Rabbinic sources since these sources in terms of quantity more than equal the amount of material dealt with otherwise and would extend this study beyond reasonable limits. It was not difficult to select the Rabbinic material and except for repetitions I have given what I believe to be a full review of Rabbinic thought about Melchizedek in the period under discussion. The task was not so simple with regard to the Christian sources, but in dealing with the Melchizedekian heresies, I found that a normative position from the church fathers seemed to emerge in their rebuttal of these heresies.

3

Further, Christian thought about Melchizedek was to a large extent shaped by the reaction of the church to heretical thought about Melchizedek. Jerome's *Epistle LXXIII* which is central to our study is also a summary of orthodox opinion about Melchizedek.

THE OCCASION FOR THIS STUDY

There is no need to justify the study of any problem within the Biblical field, and the question of the identity of Melchizedek and the growth of tradition around him is without doubt a classical problem in Biblical studies. It would be untrue, however, to claim that this study has no setting in current thought within the community of Biblical scholars. There is no harm, and there is potentially great benefit in relating one's work to a current fashion in the field since many persons will be addressing their energies to the same general problem in the same period of time. On the other hand, it is dishonest not to acknowledge one's indebtedness to such current fashion in an effort to escape the criticisms which will eventually show us the weaknesses of that range of inquiry. Here I do not propose to review all the literature on Melchizedek, as this would be almost impossible. Instead, at this point I shall attempt to focus on the main features of Melchizedek research in the past fifty years, concentrating on the recent revival of interest in this figure. Some of the most important literature is discussed in the following chapters, and this section is designed only as a brief synopsis.

The brevity of the Old Testament records concerning Melchizedek has not been matched by an equal restraint on the part of modern scholarship. The person who hopes to review the modern literature on Melchizedek undertakes to examine the commentaries on Hebrews, Psalms, and Genesis. In addition, histories of Israel seldom omit reference to Melchizedek, an important exception being Noth's *The History of Israel*.[1] The references to Melchizedek in the Old Testament occur in two very difficult chapters, and several studies have been made of these individual chapters which one who is interested in

[1] Trans. P. R. Ackroyd (New York and Evanston: Harper & Row, Publishers, 1960). As we shall see in Chapter 2, Noth in other publications does assign some historical value to Gen. xiv. 18–20.

Melchizedek cannot neglect. None of these modern sources, however, deals specifically with Melchizedek. Nevertheless they make up the largest body of secondary literature on the subject. Interest in the figure of Melchizedek as an object of scholarly investigation *per se* has received much less attention. During the period of the 1920s, however, several works arose which have had importance for later studies. One of the first was an unpublished dissertation dealing with the history of speculation about Melchizedek and the application of that speculation to Hebrews.[1] About the same time an altogether remarkable study by G. Bardy[2] of the patristic literature on Melchizedek appeared in two installments. Not only did Bardy try to review the speculation about Melchizedek throughout the patristic period, he also included an introduction which dealt with the Jewish background[3] and a conclusion which traced the later Melchizedek legends, beginning in the sixth century A.D. To my knowledge there is no better review of the subject available to the reader. His treatment of the sources is quite balanced, and although he makes the Melchizedekians a figment of Epiphanius' imagination,[4] this represents a weak conclusion drawn from an excellent collection of data. Bardy deals mainly with the Melchizedekian heresies in the early church, and owing to his influence, I have decided that the Melchizedekian heresies provide a good base on which to build a view of the thought of the church about Melchizedek, though in terms of material cited and conclusions there is a wide difference between his work and mine.

A third work appeared in 1927 by a student of Dobschütz, Gottfried Wuttke, at that time Domhilfsprediger at Magdeburg.[5] This work attempted to trace the history of exegesis of Melchizedek in the Old Testament from the Epistle to the Hebrews right up to the modern period, although in point of fact the

[1] J. Jérôme, 'Das geschichtliche Melchisedech-Bild und seine Bedeutung im Hebräerbrief' (unpublished doctoral dissertation, Freiburg University, 1927).

[2] 'Melchisédech dans la tradition patristique', *RB*, xxxv (October 1926), 496–509; xxxvi (January 1927), 25–45.

[3] The section devoted to this is based mainly on secondary sources as is proper to the type of study Bardy undertakes.

[4] 'Melchisédech dans la tradition patristique', p. 509.

[5] *Melchisedech der Priesterkönig von Salem: Eine Studie zur Geschichte der Exegese* (*BZNW*, vol. v; Giessen: Alfred Töpelmann, 1927).

author's real expertise is in the field of patristic literature, and the bulk of the work centers around that literature. Unlike Bardy, Wuttke is not satisfied to deal mainly with the heretical opinions in the early church. Section 7 in his monograph[1] is a study of the treatment Melchizedek received at the hands of Greek and Latin writers right up to the middle ages. This is where the real value of Wuttke's work lies for the modern reader, especially the Biblical student whose acquaintance with the later fathers is something less than complete. On the other hand, his work is rather weak in certain vital areas. Remarkably, his treatment of Philo covers barely four pages which do little else than paraphrase the sources.[2] The review of the Rabbinic material[3] is done on the basis of the available German translations and is consequently rather selective, though correct in essence. Josephus is dealt with in two pages.[4] In his discussion of the Melchizedekian heresies,[5] Wuttke repeatedly calls them 'Gnostic' without offering any real proof for his contention. This causes him to conflate the Christian heresies with the Gnostic treatment of Melchizedek found in the Pistis Sophia and the Second Book of Ieû, leaving a totally unsatisfactory treatment of these two vital problems. Nevertheless, Wuttke's monograph is an achievement. He has brought together a great deal of material into a brief seventy-six pages and has thrown light on one area of thought about Melchizedek seldom handled by scholars. There is great value in simply viewing all of the sources together in one work, and for that reason alone one has grounds to be grateful for Wuttke's contribution.

In 1928 Hellmuth Stork wrote a short monograph[6] in which he attempted to deal at length with the Melchizedekians referred to by Hippolytus, Pseudo-Tertullian, and Epiphanius, reaching at the end conclusions as regard the historicity of the sect not too different from those of Bardy.

By the end of the decade of the twenties, the materials for an understanding of the figure of Melchizedek from the first

---

[1] *Ibid.* pp. 43ff.   [2] *Ibid.* pp. 14–17.
[3] *Ibid.* pp. 18–27.   [4] *Ibid.* pp. 17–18.
[5] *Ibid.* pp. 27ff.

[6] *Die sogennanten Melchizedekianer mit Untersuchungen ihrer Quellen auf Gedankengehalt und dogmengeschichtliche Entwicklung* ('Forschungen zur Geschichte des neutestamentlichen Kanons und der altkirchlichen Literatur', vol. VIII/2; Leipzig: A. Deichert, 1928).

century B.C. through the first few centuries of the Christian era were available to scholarship. This was dependent to no small extent on the publication of some of the original sources in more accessible form. One might mention, for instance, the excellent text of Epiphanius' *Panarion* edited by Karl Holl of which the first two volumes were available in the twenties. Vol. II of this work contained Epiphanius' treatment of the Melchizedekians.[1] In addition, in 1925 the Coptic text of the Pistis Sophia was published in a definitive form by C. Schmidt,[2] and Schmidt's translations of the Pistis Sophia and the Books of Ieû made these Gnostic sources available to all who could read German.[3] Interest in the history of the development of the figure of Melchizedek in Christianity, Judaism, and Gnosticism which characterized this period began to flag in favor of interest in the historical Melchizedek which had already been given impetus by Sigmund Mowinckel.[4]

Since the relationship of the theory of divine kingship in ancient Israel to Melchizedek in the Old Testament is discussed in the next chapter at some length, I shall not repeat myself here. Melchizedek became an important point of connection for those who saw in the kingship a western form of a common Near Eastern kingship ideology. How was it that Israel progressed so rapidly from a tribal confederation under the leadership of a charismatic leader to a dynastic state which showed definite connections with the kingship patterns of neighboring nations? Some found a partial answer in Melchizedek. Following ancient exegesis of Gen. xiv, the identification of Salem with Jerusalem

[1] Karl Holl, ed., *Epiphanius*, vol. II (Die Griechischen Schriftsteller der ersten drei Jahrhunderte; Leipzig: J. C. Hinrichs'sche Buchhandlung, 1922). Epiphanius treats the Melchizedekians in *Panarion*, LV.

[2] *Pistis Sophia* (Coptica: Consilio et Impensis Instituti Rask-Oerstediani, vol. II; Hauniae: Gyldendalske Boghandel-Nordisk Forlag, 1925).

[3] C. Schmidt, *Pistis Sophia: Ein Gnostisches Originalwerk aus Koptischen übersetzt* (Leipzig: J. C. Hinrichs'sche Buchhandlung, 1925); and Carl Schmidt, *Gnostische Schriften in Koptischer Sprache aus dem Codex Brucianus* (Texte und Untersuchungen zur Geschichte der altchristlichen Literatur, vol. VIII, Nos. 1–2; Leipzig: J. C. Hinrichs'sche Buchhandlung, 1892). These are but two of Schmidt's excellent editions of these texts.

[4] *Psalmenstudien* II: *Das Thronbesteigungsfest Jahwäs und der Ursprung der Eschatologie* (reprint from the first Oslo edition; Amsterdam: P. Schippers Verlag, 1961). We shall attempt to differentiate between Mowinckel's work and that of the 'myth and ritual school' in the next chapter.

became a commonplace, and Melchizedek achieved a new importance as a pre-Israelite king of ancient Jebus in the patriarchial period. Attempts were even made to reconstruct the theological foundations of the Jebusite kingship on the basis of clues to be found in Ps. cx and Gen. xiv. We shall see in the next chapter that even though many of the results of this kind of investigation have come to be questioned seriously in recent times, many of the assumptions about Melchizedek's supposed kingship in Jerusalem which were associated with these results have not always been as critically handled. We shall in the next chapter undertake to examine how much we really can know about Melchizedek as a historical figure and what justice there is in the belief that he was seen as a divine priest-king or in the view that it is possible to reconstruct the Jebusite theology which underlay that priest-kingship.[1]

The reason for current interest in Melchizedek, however, is not directly related to either of these two veins in older scholarship. Rather, interest stems from the publication in 1965 of a fragmentary text from the eleventh Qumran cave which treats Melchizedek as a divine, heavenly figure. This publication came just at a time when New Testament scholarship was completing the first phase of a discussion of the relationship between Qumran and Hebrews.[2] Parallels between Hebrews and Qumran had been noted in 1958 by Y. Yadin as to angelology and eschatology.[3] Yadin claimed that the Epistle to the Hebrews shows signs of being a polemical work addressed to a group of Christians in danger of slipping back into a form of Judaism much like that of Qumran. C. Spicq soon thereafter[4] contributed a longer study in which he claimed that the Epistle to the

---

[1] For a short but balanced review of recent research in this vein see Ignatius Hunt's article, 'Recent Melchizedek Study', in the collection of essays in honor of Michael J. Gruenthaner, *The Bible in Current Catholic Thought*, ed. John L. McKenzie, S.J. (New York: Herder & Herder, 1962), pp. 21–33.

[2] Herbert Braun, 'Qumran und das Neue Testament: Ein Bericht über 10 Jahre Forschung (1950–1959) – Hebräer', *Theologische Rundschau*, xxx (June 1964), 1–38.

[3] 'The Scrolls and the Epistle to the Hebrews', *Scripta Hierosolymitana* iv (1958), 36–55.

[4] 'L'épître aux Hébreux, Apollos, Jean-Baptiste, les Hellénistes et Qumrân', *Revue de Qumrân*, i (1958–9), 365–90.

Hebrews was written by the Apollos known to us from Acts, an Alexandrian who had contacts with Jerusalem. In that article Spicq tried to do justice to the parallels between Hebrews and Qumran while still holding to Alexandrian influence on the Epistle. Hans Kosmala in 1959 wrote a study in which he held that Hebrews was written to a non-Christian, Jewish community which had definite connections with Qumran.[1] None of these works relates directly to our concern with Melchizedek, for during that period only one text from Qumran, the Genesis Apocryphon, mentioned Melchizedek at all and that only in a rather literal Aramaic rendering of Gen. xiv. 18-20. Braun, in fact, could conclude that Melchizedek held no interest for the Qumranites in his review of the studies made up to 1960.[2] Thus it was very difficult to explain, if Qumran and Hebrews were really related, why so much would be made of Melchizedek in Hebrews. Further, the paucity of references to Melchizedek at Qumran could be explained on the basis that Melchizedek as a priest-king represented to the Qumranites the claims of the hated Hasmonaean priest-kings which had been rejected by the sect.[3] Braun concluded that there was little positive evidence for a connection between Hebrews and Qumran and preferred in general to account for common elements on the basis of their being shared by all Judaism in the period.[4] One might judge from the dearth of studies after 1960 that Braun's position on the relationship between Qumran and Hebrews had won the day.

The publication in 1965 of the 11Q Melchizedek by A. S. Van der Woude[5] gradually set in motion a revived interest in the question of Qumran and Hebrews which is just now becoming quite important. Also in 1965 Van der Woude collaborated with M. De Jonge[6] to write an important article in which the first edition of the text was revised and some suggestions were

---

[1] *Hebräer-Essener-Christen* (Studia Post Biblica, vol. 1; Leiden: E. J. Brill, 1959).

[2] 'Qumran und das Neue Testament', p. 20.

[3] Cf. Frank Moore Cross, *The Ancient Library of Qumran* (2d ed., rev.; Anchor Books No. A272; New York: Doubleday & Company, Inc., 1961), pp. 135ff. [4] 'Qumran und das Neue Testament', pp. 37f.

[5] 'Melchisedech als himmlische Erlösergestalt in den neugefundenen eschatologischen Midraschim aus Qumran Höhle XI', *Oudtestamentische Studiën*, xiv (Leiden: E. J. Brill, 1965), 354-73.

[6] '11Q Melchizedek and the New Testament', *NTS*, xii (1965-6), 301-26.

made for the application of this text to the New Testament and especially to Hebrews. Still, no real interest was taken in this important document by the majority of scholars, especially American scholars. With the publication of the text in 1967 by Joseph Fitzmyer, attention of American scholars was drawn to this remarkable document.[1] It is fitting that it was Joseph Fitzmyer who brought forth the 11Q Melchizedek in this country, for only a year previously his commentary on the Genesis Apocryphon, which contained the only other reference to Melchizedek at Qumran, had been published.[2] This, combined with a long article on Melchizedek in 1963,[3] easily made him the most knowledgeable person in this area in America.

At this time of writing the full weight of the meaning of the 11Q Melchizedek has yet to be felt, but clues to its future use are provided by James A. Sanders of Union Seminary. Since his commentary on Hebrews is still in preparation, we can only repeat clues to its content provided by Sanders in other writings.[4] Sanders informs us that Hebrews is a document relating to the revolt against Rome in the first century and was probably written in A.D. 69 or 70.[5] The combination of new insights furnished by the 11Q Melchizedek and the older studies produced in the nineteen fifties promises to make a compelling case for the dependence of Hebrews upon Qumran and to locate its point of composition of Palestine. Sanders' reasons for dating the composition around the time of the destruction of the Temple are not yet known, and we must await his commentary. Sanders' recent article on the hymn in Phil. ii. 1–11 gives us some idea of the way in which the information which has come to us about the angelology of Qumran may be applied to the New Testament.[6] In fact, Sanders in the summer of 1970 taught a course

---

[1] 'Further Light on Melchizedek from Qumran Cave 11', *JBL*, LXXXVI (March 1967), 25–41.

[2] Joseph A. Fitzmyer, *The Genesis Apocryphon of Qumran Cave I: A Commentary* (Biblia et Orientalia, No. 18; Rome: Pontifical Institute, 1966).

[3] Fitzmyer, 'Now this Melchizedek...', *CBQ*, XXV (July 1963), 305–21.

[4] Some of Professor Sanders' work has appeared in popular form as a series of tape recordings entitled *Letter to the Hebrews*, published by Alba House of Ohio in their series *The New Testament Today*.

[5] 'Outside the Camp', *USQR*, XXIV (Spring, 1969), 240 and 240 n. 1.

[6] James A. Sanders, 'Dissenting Deities and Phil. 2₁₋₁₁', *JBL*, LXXXVIII (September 1969), 279–90.

at Union Seminary on angelology, suggesting something of the importance which he attaches to the subject.[1]

I was first introduced to the 11Q Melchizedek at Union while enrolled in Professor Sanders' course on the Qumran literature in 1967, but I have had no direct relationship to the subsequent development of scholarly discussion. The original plan for the present study depended more heavily on the 11Q Melchizedek and was more restricted chronologically than the work as it stands now. The results of the study are different from those I expected or wished for and this difference required an expansion of scope to confirm the unexpected results achieved. Chapter 3 contains my examination of the 11Q Melchizedek, and in Chapter 6 I have tried to say something about the importance of the document for future study.

FINAL INTRODUCTORY STATEMENT

The material dealt with in this book covers Melchizedek speculation carried on by many different persons who belonged to different racial, linguistic, and cultural groups. The primary materials are in several different languages and dialects. The historian knows the difficulty of adequately understanding the thought of any one person within any one historical setting in a single language. To attempt to trace the tradition about Melchizedek over the centuries through different communities of belief and thought leaves much room for error. One corrective for this is the presentation of as much of the primary material as possible, but because of printing costs it has been necessary to present most of the primary material in English translation. Unless otherwise specified all translations are my own. I have tried to indicate the place where each text translated may be found.

[1] Since this work was first presented as a dissertation (1971) several articles have appeared dealing with the 11Q Melchizedek. In the main most of these make adjustments in the text of that document, and I have tried to take account of those changes in Chapter 3. A very important advance in research on the 11Q Melchizedek is represented in J. T. Milik's article, '*Milkî-Sedeq* et *Milkî-Reša'* dans les anciens écrits juifs et chrétiens (I)', *JJS*, XXIII (Autumn, 1972), 95–144, which I shall deal with at some length below. Unfortunately the second part of this article had not appeared at the time this book was completed.

CHAPTER 2

THE BACKGROUND SOURCES I:
THE OLD TESTAMENT

INTRODUCTION

By 'background sources' I mean to indicate those sources for the figure of Melchizedek which may be dated in or before the first century A.D. and are, therefore, either earlier than, or roughly contemporaneous with, the Epistle to the Hebrews.[1] I do not mean to imply that all of these sources were used by the author of Hebrews, but wish, rather, to put all of the evidence together in such a way as to make the growth of the Melchizedek traditions clear. For convenience I have divided this material into two chapters, but in principle chapters 2 and 3 belong together as one.

Melchizedek[2] is mentioned only twice in the Old Testament[3] in passages involving extreme difficulty in text, language, and date. The difficulty in understanding the references to Melchizedek in these passages is further increased by the fact that in both passages primary interest does not focus upon Melchizedek but upon some other figure: Abram in the first instance, and the Jerusalemite king in the second. Nevertheless, these passing references to Melchizedek, partly because of their citation in the Epistle to the Hebrews, and partly because of their place within very important Old Testament texts, have produced an abundance of secondary literature.[4] The lack of certainty in the

[1] I have no desire at this point to enter into a discussion of the exact date of the Epistle, and such a discussion could only serve to exclude data which might otherwise be important. For the purposes of this section I shall regard the Epistle as falling in the last half of the first century A.D.

[2] On the form of the name cf. Martin Noth, *Die Israelitischen Personennamen im Rahmen der gemeinsemitischen Namengebung* (Beiträge zur Wissenschaft vom Alten und Neuen Testament, Ser. 3, vol. x; Stuttgart: W. Kohlhammer Verlag, 1928), pp. 114, 161, and 161 n. 4.

[3] Gen. xiv. 18 and Ps. cx. 4.

[4] For some indication of the extent of the literature, see Otto Eissfeldt, *The Old Testament: An Introduction*, trans. P. R. Ackroyd (New York and Evanston: Harper & Row, Publishers, 1965), pp. 109 n. 23, 210, 444, 737,

dating of these two passages, which has led to their being assigned variously to dates ranging from pre-Israelite times to the period of the Maccabees, has provided a fertile ground for theory-building and speculation. Yet, if they do nothing else, the volumes of secondary literature demonstrate that the Old Testament evidence may be pressed beyond all reasonable measure; this we must try to avoid. It will be my purpose in this chapter to deal with these two passages critically and exegetically, relating my conclusions to the general discussion about Melchizedek only insofar as it serves the total purpose of this study.

GENESIS XIV. 18–20

Analysis

We begin with Gen. xiv. 18–20 simply as a matter of convenience and not because we are to consider it logically or chronologically prior to, or of more historical value than Ps. cx as regards Melchizedek.[1] Although the passage is imbedded in a section of the Pentateuch thought by some to have a great historical value,[2] vss. 18–20 are an insertion into the text and do not necessarily share whatever historical value might belong to the rest of the chapter. That vss. 18–20 are an insertion into Gen. xiv is shown quite easily by placing vss. 17 and 21 together:

After his return from the defeat of Chedorlaomer and the kings who were with him, the king of Sodom went out to meet him at the Valley

745, and 763. Also cf. Karl-Heinz Bernhardt, *Das Problem der altorientalischen Königsideologie im Alten Testament* (Supplements to *Vetus Testamentum*, vol. VIII; Leiden: E. J. Brill, 1961), pp. 307–24.

[1] Indeed, it is held by some that Gen. xiv. 18–20 represents a *midrash* on Ps. cx. 4. Cf. H. H. Rowley, 'Melchizedek and Zadok (Gen. 14 and Ps. 110)', *Festschrift für Alfred Bertholet zum 80. Geburtstag*, ed. Walter Baumgartner, Otto Eissfeldt, Karl Ellinger, and Leonard Rost (Tübingen: J. C. B. Mohr (Paul Siebeck), 1950), pp. 461ff. Also cf. Charles Augustus Briggs and Emilie Grace Briggs, *A Critical and Exegetical Commentary on the Book of Psalms*, II (The International Critical Commentary; Edinburgh: T. & T. Clark, 1907), 374.

[2] For instance, cf. W. F. Albright, 'Abram the Hebrew: A New Archaeological Interpretation', *BASOR*, CLXIII (October 1961), 51ff. See also the extended remarks on the historical value of Gen. 14 made by John Skinner, *A Critical and Exegetical Commentary on Genesis* (2nd ed., 'The International Critical Commentary'; Edinburgh: T. & T. Clark, 1930), pp. 271–6.

of Shaveh (that is, the King's Valley)...And the king of Sodom
said to Abram, 'Give me the persons, but take the goods for yourself.'
(RSV)

Gen. xiv. 18–20 represents an intrusion into the text of chapter
xiv and has but the loosest connection with what precedes and
what follows.[1] The word חוֹצִיא presumes no particular previous
action nor geographical location and, although the reference to
the giving of a tenth within the context of chapter xiv does
suggest the tithing of the spoils of the war with Chedorlaomer's
alliance on the part of Abram, the wording of vs. 20 makes no
reference to spoils. In fact, we note that the antecedent of וַיִּתֶּן
is not specified and might just as well refer to Melchizedek's
giving Abram a tithe, perhaps as a tribute.[2] Even within the
context of chapter xiv this is not at all an unreasonable understanding of the text since it would be quite natural to have a
local king pay tribute to a warrior chieftain such as Abram is
portrayed as being in chapter xiv.[3] But the only direct connection between vss. 18–20 and the rest of the chapter is the

[1] Cf. Gerhard von Rad, *Genesis: A Commentary*, trans. John H. Marks
(The Old Testament Library; Philadelphia: The Westminster Press, 1961),
p. 174. Sellin suggested that vss. 17, 21–4 were the insertion, against which
Gunkel replied: 'Dagegen hat die Melchisedek-Episode weniger feste
Beziehung zum Ganzen, trennt das Auftreten des Königs von Sodom 17 und
Abrahams Verhandlung mit ihm 21–24, und mag also nachträgliche Hinzu-
fügung sein, aus mündlicher Überlieferung oder anderer Quelle hier hin-
eingestellt...' (*Genesis* (6th ed., Göttinger Handkommentar zum Alten
Testament', vol. 1; Göttingen: Vandenhoeck & Ruprecht, 1964), pp. 284–
5). For a source-critical study see Immanuel Benzinger, 'Zur Quellenscheidung in Gen. 14', *Vom Alten Testament: Karl Marti zum 70. Geburtstag*, ed.
Karl Budde (*BZAW*, vol. XLI; Giessen: Alfred Töpelmann, 1925), pp. 21–7.
[2] Note that Gen. xiv. 20b reads simply 'and he gave him a tenth of everything' which leaves it to the reader to supply the proper subject and indirect
object. This was taken by Sievers as reason for striking out all reference to
Melchizedek from the chapter. See the discussion by Gunkel, *op. cit.*, p. 290.
[3] For instance, in the Tell El-Amarna tablets we find references to the
threat of the '*Apiru* chieftains to the city-states of Syria–Palestine. The rulers
of the city-states often had no choice other than to seek some sort of an arrangement with these chieftains as did the princes Lab'ayu and Miliku, as
perhaps did also the prince of Jerusalem. Cf. tablets EA 244 and 254,
ANET², pp. 485–6. Miliku's letter to the Egyptian king (EA 271, *ANET²*,
pp. 486–7) gives a picture both of the internal and of the external pressures
brought to bear upon him as the result of the adventures of the '*Apiru*.

repetition of the formula אל עליון קנה שמים וארץ in vss. 19 and 22.[1]
This is held by some to be evidence for the unity of vss. 18–20
with the rest of chapter xiv,[2] but this does not necessarily follow.
All that is shown by the repetition of the formula in vs. 22 is the
dependence of the present form of that verse upon vs. 19,
where the formula must stand for poetic reasons. One possible
reconstruction would hold that the divine name El Elyon
originally stood at vs. 22. Since chapter xiv, as we shall see, is
not necessarily from the hand of J, E or P, it is quite possible
that El Elyon was the name preferred by the author.[3] This
would later be harmonized to agree with vs. 19. It is reasonably
certain that the name יהוה in vs. 22 is a later addition which
tried to identify El Elyon with Yahweh.[4] All of the evidence is
most easily explained on the assumption that the writer who
originally inserted the Melchizedek story in chapter xiv also
brought vs. 22 into harmony with the poem of vss. 19f. There is
also no reason not to suppose that this person is the one who put
chapter xiv into substantially the form in which we now have it.

Form

The most striking feature of the unit is, of course, the blessing
which Melchizedek utters over Abram in vss. 19b–20a:

> Blessed be Abram by El Elyon who creates the heavens and the
> earth
> And blessed be El Elyon who delivers your enemies into your
> hand.

---

[1] Gunkel, *Genesis*, p. 284, thinks that there is a pun on מעשׂה (v. 20) in the
word תעשׂרתי at vs. 23, but this ignores the fact that in Biblical Hebrew /s/,
/ś/, and /š/ are separate phonemes which would not be confused in such a
manner.

[2] As, for instance, Skinner, *Genesis*, p. 269.

[3] Cf. Eissfeldt, *The Old Testament*, p. 211, where he holds that this source
is dependent upon the language of P and is, therefore, quite late. The unique
position of chapter xiv as a separate source was recognized quite early. It is
discussed quite routinely by S. R. Driver, *An Introduction to the Literature of the
Old Testament* (Meridian Books, No. 29; Cleveland and New York: The
World Publishing Company, 1956), p. 15, a work originally published in
1897. Cf. Skinner, *Genesis*, p. 256.

[4] This addition is missing in the LXX which reads simply πρὸς τὸν θεὸν
ὕψιστον, ὃς ἔκτισεν τὸν οὐρανὸν καὶ τὴν γῆν. It is also missing in the Genesis
Apocryphon which in this chapter follows the Masoretic Text rather closely.

This blessing shows a definite 2 + 2 metrical structure as well as the more poetic צר for איב.[1] The poetic structure of this blessing, however, is far from perfect.[2] Although there is parallelism, the parallelism is not exact. In vs. 19b El Elyon is the 'efficient cause' in the passive construction[3] and antecedent of the participial phrase beginning with קנה. In vs. 20b, on the other hand, El Elyon receives the action of the passive verb and is antecedent of the following relative clause. In addition, the use of the relative אשר is rare in formal poetry.[4]

As to *Gattung* the passage is (following Eissfeldt's terminology) a 'cultic saying' of the 'third type' (lay saying!).[5] Skinner distinguishes between this formula and the 'blessings' or 'curses' which include a prophetic interpretation of a concrete event (cf. Gen. iii. 14ff.; iv. 11ff.; xxvii. 27ff.),[6] a distinction also recognized by Eissfeldt.[7] The promise involved in the blessing is the delivering up by God of Abram's foes into his hand, a promise made by Yahweh to David (2 Sam. vii. 9), and to the Jerusalemite king (Ps. cx. 1). The main interest of the entire unit xiv. 18–20 centers upon this blessing, and everything else is subordinate to it.[8] The thin narrative surrounding the blessing may well have grown up over a period of time, but even if vss. 18–20 are taken to be a literary whole, it is difficult to deny that

[1] G.-K., §2s. Gunkel, *Genesis*, p. 284, sees a 4 + 3, 3 + 3 meter in vv. 19b–20a, but 2 + 2, 2 + 2 is the meter found when only the stressed syllables are taken into account. Also the 2 + 2, 2 + 2 meter conforms more closely to the Masoretic accents.

[2] S. R. Driver, *The Book of Genesis* (5th ed., Westminster Commentaries; New York: Edwin S. Gorham, 1906), p. 165, is very close to the truth when he describes it as 'semi-poetical'.

[3] On this construction cf. G.-K. §121f.

[4] G.-K., §2s.

[5] Eissfeldt, *The Old Testament*, pp. 75f. Certainly the term 'lay saying' is a classic misnomer here as it is also in reference to Num. vi. 23–7; Deut. xxi. 5; xxvii. 14–26 which Eissfeldt also lists with the 'lay sayings'. What Eissfeldt means by the term is that sayings beginning with 'blessed' and 'cursed' are not reserved to priests. He points out, however, that such sayings gain force by being uttered by priests or charismatic figures. Gunkel, *Genesis*, p. 286, calls vss. 19b–20a a *Segen*, specifically a priestly blessing, but he gives no characteristic features other than poetic form.

[6] Skinner, *Genesis*, p. 269.   [7] *The Old Testament*, pp. 75f.

[8] Gunkel, *Genesis*, p. 289, holds that the intention of the entire chapter is the glorification of Abram, but he does not apply that insight directly to our passage.

the center of interest is Abram and not Melchizedek. Melchizedek brings out refreshments of bread and wine to Abram (vs. 18). Melchizedek blesses Abram (vss. 19–20a). Even if Abram is the subject of ויתן in vs. 20b (and that is not at all a certainty apart from later tradition), it would be to ignore all that has gone before to say that this is the central point of the pericope. As an action of Abram it would probably be an editorial link with the rest of the chapter. As an action of Melchizedek it would fall into the pattern of exalting Abram. This view, no doubt, will be unwelcome, since Gen. xiv. 18–20 supplies exactly half of the Old Testament evidence for Melchizedek, but we must be careful to separate our modern interests from the interests of the ancient author. Specifically, it has been held that Gen. xiv. 18–20 is an aetiological legend showing Abraham's submission to the Jerusalem (i.e. Salem) priesthood.[1] We shall deal with this position more carefully later in the chapter, but at this point we may make the observation that this position does not account well for the form of the pericope. The narrative portion of the unit serves the purposes of the blessing, not the other way around. To stress an obvious point, the blessing rises in value in proportion to the greatness of the one who delivers it.[2] Hence, Melchizedek is identified as a king[3] and as priest of

[1] So, for instance, Rowley, 'Melchizedek and Zadok', pp. 468–9, and Hans Schmid, 'Abram und Melchisedek, David und Zadok', *Kairos*, VII (February 1965), 149ff. Both see this passage as having reference to the taking over of the Zakokite priesthood in Davidic Jerusalem. The older view that the passage refers to the Maccabean priest-kings is represented by D. Bernhard Duhm, *Die Psalmen* (2nd ed., Kurzer Hand-Kommentar zum Alten Testament, vol. XIV; Tübingen: J. C. B. Mohr (Paul Siebeck), 1922), p. 400.

[2] *Ibid.* p. 59.

[3] Or is he? Winckler has suggested that 'king of Salem' should actually be read as מלכי שלם, a doublet of the name מלכי צדק, identifying Sedek and Shalem as Canaanite gods. On this see Rowley, 'Melchizedek and Zadok', p. 471. W. F. Albright, 'Abram the Hebrew', pp. 51–2, holds that the phrase ומלכי צדק מלך שלם הוציא... should actually be read (using his transcription) *ū-Malkî-ṣedeq melek šelom ⟨oh⟩ hoṣî'...*, 'And Melchizedek, a king allied to him, brought out...'. Compare *'iš šelômî* (Ps. xli. 10), *'anšê šelômᵉka* parallel to *'anšê berîtᵉka* (Ob. vii), *'anšê šelômî* (Jer. xx. 10), *'anšê šelômᵉka* (Jer. xxxvii. 22). The older /oh/ third masculine singular suffix, according to this view, was lost through haplography with the initial /h/ of *hoṣî'*. Even if Albright is correct as to the meaning of שלם here, it would not be necessary o posit a lost suffix. The word could very easily be used in an adjectival

El Elyon. The further information that he is priest of El Elyon instead of simply a priest as in Ps. cx. 4 may be due to the name El Elyon in the blessing. Melchizedek's titles in Gen. xiv. 18 are not the result of simple biographical interest, i.e., are not designed to exalt Melchizedek but are mentioned in the interest of the blessing which follows. The weakness of the aetiological argument is further shown by the fact that the city involved is not clearly identified.[1] Also, the action which should be of greatest importance according to the aetiological theory, Abram's giving of tithes to Melchizedek, is dealt with abruptly.

Date

On the date of this unit opinions vary. Obviously the *terminus ad quem* for the passage is the time of the final editing of Gen. xiv since, as we have seen, vs. 22b is literally dependent upon vs. 19b. If Eissfeldt[2] and others are correct in claiming that Gen. xiv shows dependence upon the P narrative of the Pentateuch[3] then *ipso facto* we must assign a date after that of P to the inclusion of chapter xiv into the Genesis narrative. As to the time of the first composition of chapter xiv, however, opinion differs and we must deal with some of the main alternatives.

E. A. Speiser[4] holds that the words בימי in xiv. 1 reflect the

construction meaning (on the analogy of the examples brought forward by Albright) 'allied'. Hence, we could read, 'And Melchizedek, an allied king, brought out... '. This position will be discussed in more detail later on in the chapter.

[1] Even if Salem = Jerusalem, as is suggested by Ps. lxxvi. 2, we cannot thereby assume that שלם was a common name for Jerusalem. It is difficult to avoid the impression that if the author were especially concerned with Jerusalem he could have written it out. Von Rad, *Genesis*, p. 174, suggests that the name Salem was an artificial name for Jerusalem, which raises then the question of how von Rad knows that this is an artificial name for Jerusalem and why the author used it.

[2] *The Old Testament*, p. 211.

[3] The word רכוש 'property', 'goods' (xiv. 11, 12, 16, 21) is used often by P and by later writers. The word נפש (xiv. 21) in the sense of 'person' also reflects the usage of P. Although these two words do not prove dependence upon P, they are at least suggestive of a direction in which we may look. Cf. Skinner, *Genesis*, p. 256. Now also see J. A. Emerton, 'The Riddle of Genesis XIV', *VT*, xxi (October 1971), 403–39.

[4] *Genesis* (The Anchor Bible, vol. i; Garden City, New York: Doubleday & Company, Inc., 1964), p. 104.

Akkadian conjunction e/inuma/i 'when', and notes other
places where he believes that the Akkadian illuminates the
Hebrew text (vss. 7, 14, 23).[1] Further, he claims that in chapter
xiv Abram is glimpsed through the eyes of outsiders. He is
'Abram the Hebrew' (xiv. 13) which is the usual designation
of an Israelite to a foreigner.[2] Thus Speiser thinks there may be
an Akkadian document behind Gen. xiv which represents a
non-Israelite view of the patriarch Abraham and may be the

[1] Gunkel, *Genesis*, p. 289, considers the construction ויהי בימי to be historical style, comparing Isa. vii. 1 which reads ויהי בימי אחז. Gunkel's
point is well taken, and one must strain beyond all reason to see any real
syntactical difference between Gen. xiv. 1 and Isa. vii. 1. At xiv. 7 Speiser,
Genesis, p. 102, compares the phrase וישבו ויבאו to the very usual expression
of Assyrian rulers 'on my return' as a reference to additional victories. It is
frankly very difficult to see any real parallel here. At xiv. 14 the word וירק
is rendered in the Samaritan version as וידק which may suggest the Akkadian
word *deku*, but he admits that this is rather fanciful. Unfortunately Gunkel,
op. cit., p. 283 adopted this correction as did BDB, p. 938, and Kittel's
Biblia Hebraica in a footnote to xiv. 14. Why an unattested Hebrew root
*dqh would be preferable to the well-known root *ryq* is far from obvious. To
be sure, the Aramaic דוק in the Aphel does mean 'to count or reckon
exactly' and may have been the understanding of the translator of the LXX
who rendered וירק as ἠρίθμησε, but once the error of reading /d/ for /r/
arose, any translation would have to take account of it. In Greek the verb
ἀριθμέω can have specific reference to numbering troops as in the *Odyssey*
x. 304, but it would be a mistake to read that feature of the Greek verb back
into Hebrew. There is no necessarily military connotation in the Aramaic
דוק. Actually, the supposed cognates, Hebrew *dqh, Aramaic *dwq*, Akkadian
diku, are impossible in that /q/ and /k/ in the Semitic languages are two
different classes of sounds, and there is no evidence that Aramaic /q/ and
Akkadian /k/ are related. If we must look for cognates, the Egyptian *rqi*
'incline', 'bend', 'turn' (= Coptic *rike* 'bend', 'turn') would work quite
well, producing the same consonants as are in the MT. We would then read,
'And (Abram) turned his experienced men...and pursued (them) as far as
Dan.' Rather than seeking obscure roots, however, it might be better simply
to accept the word וירק as coming from ריק and having an otherwise unattested meaning. Speiser's final parallel is to be found at xiv. 23 which
reads אם מחוט עד שרוך נעל. This he compares to the Akkadian *hamu u husabu
u mimma*, 'a stalk of straw, or a twig, or whatever', an idiom carried over
into Aramaic as אן חם ועד חוט. The Hebrew of xiv. 23 seems to be a paraphrase of this idiom as the proto-Semitic *ham was not current in Hebrew in
the Old Testament period. Another way of saying the same thing, however,
is to say that the Hebrew is just one form of a common Semitic idiom. Thus
of Speiser's four suggested parallels to Akkadian none are really very
convincing.   [2] *Ibid.* pp. 103–4.

closest thing we have to independent testimony about Abraham.[1] S. R. Driver, on the other hand, while admitting the affinities of chapter xiv with the Priestly strand, can only say that chapter xiv stems from a date not earlier than Ezekiel and the Exile.[2] Gunkel, interestingly enough, considers Gen. xiv to be a legend from the 'Jewish period' and compares it to literature such as Chronicles, Judith, Testaments of the Twelve Patriarchs, and Jubilees.[3] The same knowledge of things Babylonian and Assyrian which has led other scholars to assign Gen. xiv to an early date points Gunkel in the opposite direction so that he compares this knowledge to the world-wide, cosmopolitan interests of Daniel, Esther, and Judith. Skinner[4] points out that the cuneiform documents in which parallels may be found for three of the four names of the kings in ch. xiv actually date from only the fourth or third centuries B.C. This reminds us that Akkadian (East Semitic) languages were known until very late, and even if Speiser and others were correct in saying that the Hebrew of Gen. xiv needs illumination from Akkadian, this would not *per se* indicate an early date.

Are there any internal clues in xiv. 18–20 which might help us date that single pericope? One possibility is the use of the name El Elyon for the deity. Certainly it is well attested that El Elyon was a Phoenician deity.[5] At the same time, however, we note that the name El Elyon is also found at Ps. lxxviii. 35, and a near cousin אלהים עליון at Ps. lvii. 3. The Aramaic equivalent of the name, אלהא אליא, is to be found at Dan. iii. 26, 32; v. 18, 21. Use of the word Elyon alone to indicate the deity is quite extensive. Use of the name continued well into the Roman period, perhaps under the influence of the title ὕψιστος used for Hellenistic deities.[6] Although El Elyon may have been wor-

---

[1] *Ibid.*

[2] *Genesis*, p. 155. Presumably he leaves open a later date, but he fixes no particular date or period after which the chapter could not have been written.   [3] *Genesis*, p. 289.

[4] *Op. cit.*, p. 275. Driver, *Genesis*, p. 157, quotes from the relevant texts and assigns them, along with Pinches, to the third century B.C.

[5] Von Rad, *Genesis*, pp. 174–5. This deity is the same as the Ἐλιοῦν ὁ ὕψιστος mentioned by Philo of Byblos and Eusebius, *Praep. Ev.* i. 10, 11, 12.

[6] As, for instance, for Zeus. Cf. C. Roberts, T. C. Skeat, and A. D. Nock, 'The Guild of Zeus Hypsistos', *HTR*, xxix (January 1936), 39–88. Cf. also Bernhardt, *Das Problem*, p. 95 n. 4, whose conclusions on this matter are substantially the same as mine.

shipped in Palestine in pre-Israelite times, the evidence does not permit us to posit an early date, since in one form or another the name is used throughout the Biblical period.

Another possible argument might come from the use of the verb קָנָה in the sense of 'create' instead of the more usual sense of the word in Hebrew 'possess'. It has been held by some that the use of the word קָנָה to mean 'create' here reflects the Ugaritic *qny* which in the tablets from Ugarit is the usual word for 'create' as at Keret I. 11. 4 and Aqhat II. vi. 40, although the meaning 'possess' is also known as at Aqhat I. iv. 58. The noun *qny* means 'master' or 'owner' (cf. Baal IV. iii. 5). Apart from Gen. xiv the Hebrew word קָנָה means 'create' only at Ps. cxxxix. 13; Prov. viii. 22; and Deut. xxxii. 6, the passage from Deut. being recognized as one of great antiquity.[1] The Hebrew קָנָה and Ugaritic *qny*, therefore, have more or less the same range of meanings, although each language has its own preferred usages. The meanings of the Hebrew word are quite stable, and the verb has the same range of meanings in the Rabbinic writings that it does in the Old Testament.[2] Linguistically it is quite improper to claim, as does von Rad,[3] that קָנָה 'create' represents an intrusion from Canaanite religion. To convince ourselves further that arguments such as von Rad's are weak we see that in most Semitic languages the roots *qny* and *br'* are represented in one form or another whereas in Ugaritic the root *br'* does not happen to be attested and the meaning 'create' associated with this root is reserved for *qny*. We note, however, that the root *br'* is to be found in Phoenician and Punic, illustrating Gordon's assertion that Ugaritic is not always typical of the Northwest Semitic languages.[4] In any

[1] Although dates as late as the fifth century B.C. have been suggested for Deut. xxxii, scholars now place it much earlier, in the tenth or eleventh centuries B.C. Cf. Eissfeldt, *The Old Testament*, pp. 226–7 and 227 n. 14.

[2] Cf. Jastrow, *Dictionary*, pp. 1390–1.

[3] *Old Testament Theology*, trans. D. M. G. Stalker (New York: Harper & Row, Publishers, 1962), I, 142. See also the literature referred to p. 142 n. 11.

[4] Cf. Cyrus H. Gordon, *Ugaritic Manual*, vol. I (Analecta Orientalia, No. 35; Rome: Pontificum Institutum Biblicum, 1955), §14.4:
'The accumulation of the impressive number of Heb. parallels has further been facilitated by the fact that the O.T. is the most extensive and best-studied corpus of literature from the ancient Near East. If the Amorites, Arameans, and Arabs of the Amarna Age had left us Bibles,

event it is meaningless to think of *qny* as 'more Canaanite' or 'less Hebraic' than *br*'. The use of קנה at Gen. xiv. 19, 22 reflects nothing more than a possible meaning of the Hebrew verb.

Another possibility for finding at least a relative date for Gen. xiv. 18–20 is to find dependence in one direction or another with regard to Ps. cx. 4. When, in the nineteenth and early twentieth centuries Ps. cx was generally considered to stem from a late date, the mention of the priesthood of Melchizedek at Ps. cx. 4 was thought to depend upon Gen. xiv. 18–20, usually as a later insertion into the text of the psalm.[1] More recent scholarship, however, has tended to push the date of Ps. cx back beyond the Exile to the time of the United Monarchy, or, in some cases, back to pre-Israelite Jerusalem. This raises the possibility that Gen. xiv. 18–20 depends upon Ps. cx. 4 and is something like a *midrash* on a difficult psalm.[2] We must, however, take note of the fact that there are only two points of connection between the two passages. To illustrate we shall place them side by side.

Yahweh has sworn and will not repent: 'You are a *priest* forever in the manner of *Melchizedek*.'[3] (Ps. cx. 4)	And *Melchizedek*, the king of Salem brought out bread and wine, and he was a *priest* of El Elyon; and he blessed him and said... (Gen. xiv. 18–19a)

Apart from the name Melchizedek, the only point of contact is the word כהן, hardly enough to establish literary dependence. If one has borrowed from the other, it is probably Gen. xiv,

we should be able to check, and considerably revise our theories on the position of Ugar. among the Semitic languages.'
The fact that the Semitic languages do not, in fact, break down neatly into the simple divisions shown in the family charts of the Semitic sub-family but are, rather, mutually influential at particular points in history should teach us to be open as to what is 'good Hebrew' or 'good Ugaritic'.

[1] B. Duhm, *Die Psalmen*, p. 400, who holds a Maccabean date for the psalm sees the mention of Melchizedek as an insertion, in fact, a very late insertion, since he also sees Gen. xiv as being quite late. Although he does not give a date, the earliest the reference from Duhm's point of view would be some time in the first century B.C. Briggs and Briggs, *Psalms* (ICC), pp. 374ff., while holding that the psalm itself is from the period of the Monarchy, also see the reference to Melchizedek as an insertion depending on Gen. xiv. 18–20.   [2] *Ibid.*

[3] For a discussion of על דברתי see below, note 1, p. 52.

since the reference to Melchizedek's priesthood there reads very much like an insertion into the text, whereas at Ps. cx. 4 only great violence to the sense of the text could result from such an excision. There is, however, no compelling reason to accept this possibility. It seems impossible to establish any literary dependence between Gen. xiv and Ps. cx, and for that reason one may not give a relative date to Gen. xiv. 18–20 by positing such a dependence.

Results

To review briefly, I have found it very difficult to assign a date to Gen. xiv. 18–20 except to say that it is, in its present form, later than the rest of chapter xiv. I have examined certain historical and linguistic arguments for an early date and found that even though Gen. xiv. 18–20 could certainly have come from an early date, the passage could just as well have come from another, later time. Further, I found that, failing evidence of interdependence, Gen. xiv. 18–20 cannot be dated in terms of Ps. cx. 4. Our one real clue is the possible dependence of Gen. xiv on the Priestly strand of the Pentateuch. This, it must be admitted, is not very strong evidence, and, barring some new discovery, it seems probable that the actual date of Gen. xiv in general, and of our pericope in particular, will remain a mystery. With these reservations, however, and on the basis of the evidence actually present, we may perhaps view Gen. xiv. 18–20 as a traditional story of indeterminate origin and age, glorifying the patriarch Abram and promising him relief from his enemies. At a point in time not previous to the date of P, but well before the LXX Genesis and the Genesis Apocryphon, this story was taken over into a chronicle of Abram's victory over the Elamite coalition by the same editor who put Gen. xiv into substantially the same form in which we now have it.

PSALM CX

Lower criticism

Ps. cx is one of the most difficult of the psalms textually and exegetically. The interpretation of the psalm is complicated by its great importance for the New Testament where it is quoted at Matt. xxii. 44; Mk xii. 36; Lk. xx. 42–3; Acts ii. 34; Heb. i.

13; v. 6; xi. 21.[1] Because of its importance for the New Testament, literature on Ps. cx is massive,[2] and the time may be ripe for a new study of the psalm by an Old Testament scholar. We cannot attempt here to do anything like full justice to the psalm, considering the magnitude of the task. Our task will be the more modest one of exploring the main features of the psalm especially as they pertain to Melchizedek.

The most obvious problem which faces the would-be exegete of Ps. cx is that of lower criticism. It is perhaps fortunate for our purposes that Ps. cx. 4 is almost free of textual difficulties.[3] This is a mixed blessing, however, because other portions of the psalm are so beset with textual problems that one is sometimes tempted to ignore the context of vs. 4, a procedure which further isolates the figure of Melchizedek. Therefore, we cannot avoid making some judgements about the text of Ps. cx.

With one or two interesting variants the LXX translates the same consonantal text that is found in the MT. We are impoverished by the fact that to date no text of Ps. cx has been found at Qumran,[4] and hence we have little direct evidence for the pre-Masoretic text of the psalm. The main textual problems with which we shall be concerned are to be found in vss. 3,

---

[1] I have not included here the places where Ps. cx is simply alluded to nor the places in the Epistle to the Hebrews where κατὰ τὴν τάξιν Μελχισεδέκ occurs by itself.

[2] For the literature up to 1959 see Hans-Joachim Kraus, *Psalmen*, (Biblischer Kommentar: Altes Testament, vol. xv/2; Neukirchen/Moers: Neukirchener Verlag, 1960), II, 752. Cf. also Eissfeldt, *The Old Testament*, pp. 109, 109 n. 23, and 737. In addition to the literature listed in these places there are many studies of Ps. cx included in works on other subjects some of which we shall have occasion to mention.

[3] Except for texts which omit the י– ending on the word דברתי, but דברתי must certainly be the more difficult reading which explains the simplification to the construct form.

[4] In the spring of 1967 Professor James Sanders distributed a catalogue and index of pre-Masoretic Psalter texts to the members of his seminar on Qumran in which I participated. Using that catalogue as a check list it is to be noted that the following psalms are not attested at Qumran: Pss. iii, v, vii, viii, x, xi, xix, xx, xxi, xxiii, xxiv, xxix, xxxii, xli, xlvi, lv, lviii, lx, lxi, lxv, lxxii, lxxiii, lxxiv, lxxv, lxxix, lxxx, lxxxix, xc, cvi, cx, cxi, cxvii. Also Pss. xx, xxi, xli, lviii, lxxxix are reflected but not directly quoted in the manuscripts. Thus, 26 of the 150 canonical psalms are not attested at Qumran and no particular significance can be attached to the fact that Ps. cx has not yet been found.

6–7.[1] As vs. 3 now stands in the MT it is very difficult to translate.

עַמְּךָ נְדָבֹת בְּיוֹם חֵילֶךָ בְּהַדְרֵי־קֹדֶשׁ

מֵרֶחֶם מִשְׁחָר לְךָ טַל יַלְדֻתֶךָ:

Your people are a freewill offering in the day of your might.
In holy raiment, from the womb of the dawn, yours is the dew of
your young men.

This translation already assumes that the initial מ of the word
מטחר is a case of dittography from the מ of מרחם. The LXX
understands עמך as μετά σου and the entire phrase is translated
μετά σου ἡ ἀρχή ἐν ἡμέρᾳ τῆς δυνάμεώς σου. To view ἀρχή as a
translation of נְדָבֹת is difficult as it is also difficult to see it as
a translation of נְדַבַּת or נִדְבַּת, as is suggested in Kittel's *Biblia
Hebraica*. Although the LXX makes sense in its own right, it
does not direct us back to a pointing of נדבת, and the latter
possibly should be viewed as a corruption, but of what we cannot say. The reading בהדרי קדש is often corrected to בהררי קדש,
a reading supported by several Hebrew MSS, Symmachus, and
Jerome. This is certainly the easier reading, and there is no
difficulty in seeing how בהדרי would be changed into בהררי
with which it looks almost identical in most Hebrew scripts.
It is not clear why an original בהררי would be changed into
בהדרי, which reading is behind the LXX translation, ἐν ταῖς
λαμπρότησιν. The LXX does not translate the difficult לך טל,
and reads ילדתיך as ἐγέννησά σε,[2] i.e. as יְלִדְתִּיךָ (compare Ps. ii.
7, יְלִדְתִּיךָ). To accept this reading for the Hebrew one must
either omit לך טל or change the text to כטל as does Kraus.[3] With
all of the suggested changes, the translation of vs. 3 differs
markedly from the translation we gave above. Here I might
quote Kraus' rendering:

---

[1] We shall not be able to consider some of the more conjectural changes
such as those of W. O. E. Oesterley, *The Psalms* (2nd ed., London: SPCK,
1953), p. 463, who in vs. 2 reads the tetragrammaton as 'Elohim' so as to
have the king addressed as 'Elohim' (cf. Ps. xlv. 6).

[2] Codex א reads ἐξεγέννησά σε. This, of course, does not represent another
Hebrew text.

[3] *Psalmen*, II, 753. Also cf. the remarks of J. Coppens, 'Les apports du
Psaume CX (Vulg. CIX) à l'idéologie royale israelite', *The Sacral Kingship*
(Studies in the History of Religions (Supplements to *Numen*), vol. IV;
Leiden: E. J. Brill, 1959), pp. 337–8, 341.

Um dich her (stehen) Adlige
   am Tage deiner Macht.
Auf heiligen Bergen
   aus dem Schoss der Morgenröte
habe ich wie Tau dich gezeugt.[1]

If the test of lower criticism were only the production of a meaningful and easily read text, this translation would certainly substantiate the suggested changes. Unfortunately, this is not the only test, and, as we have seen, each of the suggested changes is questionable, making a composite text even more suspect. As to vss. 5–7 we need say very little here, as few of the suggested changes would make any difference from the standpoint of our interest of Melchizedek.[2] The text of the psalm is difficult, and even if it be accepted in essentially the same form in which it is found in the MT, its translation involves great doubt in certain verses. It may be reasonable to conjecture that most of the difficulties present in the text of the Masoretes, were already present in the text translated by the LXX with one or two exceptions. If the text is corrupt, and it almost certainly must be in some places, the corruptions must be very old and so deeply imbedded in the psalm as to preclude almost entirely the reconstruction of a completely reliable text of Ps. cx.

Literary and Form Criticism

There is, at present, almost general agreement among scholars to follow Gunkel[3] in calling Ps. cx a Royal Psalm along with

---

[1] *Loc. cit.* We may render Kraus' translation into English as:
   'About you stand the nobles
      on the day of your power.
   On holy mountains,
      out of the womb of the dawn
   have I begotten you as the dew.'

[2] For a summary of the possible changes cf. Coppens, 'Les apports du Psaume CX', pp. 337–8, 341. The difficult גּוִיּוֹת is read by Aquila, Symmachus, and Jerome as גֵּאָיוֹת. Briggs and Briggs, *Psalms* (ICC), pp. 373 and 381, replaces the word מְלָכִים so as to read, 'He executeth judgment on kings. He doth fill the valleys with nations.' It is difficult to see why this makes better sense than 'He will judge among the nations. He will heap up bodies.' Possibly the problem is not with the text here but with our understanding of the historical reference.

[3] Cf. Hermann Gunkel, *The Psalms: A Form-Critical Introduction*, trans.

Pss. ii, xviii, xx, xxi, xlv, lxxii, ci, cxxxii, and cxliv. 1–11. Particularly striking is the oracular element in Ps. cx introduced by the prophetic formula 'says the LORD'.[1] Although a prophetic note is sometimes to be found in the Psalms, especially the Royal Psalms, it is seldom so strong.[2] In Ps. cx there is no direct reference to the king other than the address 'my Lord' in vs. 1. At the risk of flying in the face of widely accepted results, we should note that the word, although often used in reference to the king (cf. 1 Sam. xxii. 12, etc.), may also be used of a master (Ex. xxi. 5), a husband (Gen. xviii. 12), a prophet (1 Kings xviii. 7, 13), a prince (Gen. xlii. 10), a father (Gen. xxxi. 35), Moses (Ex. xxxii. 22), and a priest (1 Sam. i. 15, 26) to mention but a few of its connotations.[3] In short, the address 'my Lord' is an address used by an inferior to a superior in any one of many contexts.[4] The speaker, at least through vs. 4, and possibly throughout the entire psalm, is a prophetic figure of some sort who delivers the address from Yahweh, sometimes with Yahweh as the speaker (vss. 1b, 3–5), and sometimes with Yahweh referred to in the third person (vss. 1a, 2, 6–7).[5] This

from vol. 1 of the *RGG* by Thomas M. Horner (Facet Books: Biblical Series, No. 19; Philadelphia: Fortress Press, 1967), pp. 23–4. See also his *Ausgewählte Psalmen* (4th ed., rev., Göttingen: Vandenhoeck & Ruprecht, 1917), pp. 157–62. For a full introduction to this category of psalms, cf. Hermann Gunkel and Joachim Begrich, *Einleitung in die Psalmen: Die Gattungen der religiösen Lyrik Israels* (Göttinger Handkommentar zum Alten Testament, Ergänzungsband zur II. Abteilung; Göttingen: Vandenhoeck & Ruprecht, 1933), §5.

[1] Only here in the Psalms is נאם יהוה to be found. Another usage of נאם is to be found in Ps. xxxvi. 2. Cf. Gunkel, *Ausgewählte Psalmen*, p. 157 and Oesterley, *The Psalms*, p. 463.

[2] For a discussion of the prophetic element in the Psalms cf. Gunkel and Begrich, *Einleitung in die Psalmen*, §9.   [4] Cf. BDB, p. 11.

[3] It is incorrect simply to identify 'my lord' as a royal title as does Coppens, 'Les apports du Psaume CX', p. 334, without some further qualification.

[5] As one might expect, there is anything but general agreement on this analysis. It is especially difficult to determine the subject in vs. 5. The Masoretic punctuation in pointing אֲדֹנָי and placing the *'Athnah* at יְמִינֶךָ suggests the translation, 'My Lord (i.e. Yahweh) stands at your right hand'. This allows the יום אפו to refer to the Day of Yahweh as would be expected. On the other hand, we make אדני the subject of vss. 6–7 mainly on the basis of vs. 7 where the subject cannot be Yahweh. Vs. 6 seems to be connected with vs. 7 as pointing to a concrete historical event. It would be foolish, however, to hold that this analysis is the only possible one.

variation in person has led to more than one theory of composition which sees Ps. cx as a composite of more than one psalm.[1]

As I have said, the expression 'my Lord' is not defined. In those poems recognized as Royal Psalms we find specific reference to the king as Yahweh's 'anointed' (Pss. ii. 2; xviii. 50; xx. 7; cxxxii. 10, 17), or some form of the word 'King' is used (Pss. xviii. 51; xxi. 2; xlv. 2; lxxii. 1; cxliv. 10). Only in Ps. ci do we find no direct reference to the king, but the identity of the speaker in this psalm, especially in vs. 7, leaves very little to the imagination. The situation is otherwise in Ps. cx. The only office mentioned by name is that of priest in vs. 4, an office which can take the address form 'my Lord'. That the psalm refers to the king at all can only be shown indirectly as we shall now proceed to do.

The reference to the enemies as being a 'footstool' suggests reference to the king as the motif is often held to be a common Near Eastern one. The understanding of the phrase 'footstool for your feet',[2] however, is very difficult. This is the only place

---

[1] So Duhm, *Die Psalmen*, p. 400. This old theory, frankly, has much to recommend it. In vss. 1–4 the emphasis is upon the submission of the enemies to Zion, the willingness of the people to do war, and the priesthood of Melchizedek. In vss. 5–6 we find reference to the fierceness of Yahweh's judgement in general (vs. 5) and in particular (vs. 6), as executed by the person addressed by 'my lord'. The meaning of vs. 7 is obscure, but it is difficult to see any connection between vs. 7 and the rest of the psalm. Especially to be noted is the difference between the שב לימיני of vs. 1, and אדני על ימינך in vs. 5. Rudolf Kittel, *Die Psalmen* (5th and 6th eds., Kommentar zum Alten Testament, vol. XIII; Leipzig: A. Deichertsche Verlagsbuchhandlung, D. Werner Scholl, 1929), p. 358, tries to harmonize the conflict here by suggesting that the king and Yahweh change places for the battle. However, Kittel fails to give any evidence for this view. It is doubtful, though, whether it is legitimate to break up this psalm into different psalms on no better criteria than these. Usually additions to a text may be excised on the basis of a clear understanding of the rest of the text and the demonstration that the conjectured addition breaks the thought and/or the syntax of the rest of the text. In the case of conflation it is best to be able to recognize the individual units clearly. It should be obvious to the reader that we are not operating here on the basis of such certainty. Although vss. 1–4 and 5–7 may come from different psalms, we are not in a position to understand why they should be put together by an editor. Hence, the exegete has solved none of his problems by breaking Ps. cx into two parts of different origin; in fact, he has made his task more difficult.

[2] Rendered by the LXX as ὑποπόδιον τῶν ποδῶν σου.

in the Old Testament where 'footstool'[1] is used in reference to anyone other than Yahweh. The 'footstool' of Yahweh is the sanctuary in Lam. ii. 1; Pss. xcix. 5; cxxxii. 7; 1 Chron. xxviii. 2, and the land in Isa. lxvi. 1. Leaving aside the problem of this referring to a human being in Ps. cx, we note that the emphasis is not on military victory and subjugation of enemies as in the equivalent motif in Egyptian wall painting.[2] Even when we are given Near Eastern parallels to ideas to be found in the Old Testament, it is wise to consider the usage in the Old Testament in its own right. Here we find as the result of such consideration that 'footstool for your feet' probably represents the presence of 'the Lord' with authority in the midst of his enemies, making vs. 2 exactly parallel:

> The staff of your power will Yahweh
> send abroad out of Zion.
> Have dominion in the midst of your foes!

Reconstructing the author's thought we may surmise that the expression 'footstool for your feet' suggests immediately Yahweh's authoritative presence in the land and specifically in the sanctuary, a usage extended here to refer to a human ruler's position of authority in the midst of hostile peoples. It seems impossible that this should refer to anyone other than the king, but we note for future reference the differences between this and the other Royal Psalms which we have noted. Whether or not this is an enthronement Psalm[3] must be discussed later so as not to prejudice the material on the sacral kingship.

Date

The question of the date of Ps. cx is especially involved since the only real clues for the date are to be found within the psalm

---

[1] Always joined with רגלים in a construct chain except here in vs. 1. For the same meaning in later Hebrew, cf. *b. Makk.* 24b. Cf. Briggs and Briggs, *Psalms* (ICC), p. 378.

[2] On this see the evidence brought forward by Hans Schmidt, *Die Psalmen* (Handbuch zum Alten Testament, First Series, vol. xv; Tübingen: J. C. B. Mohr (Paul Siebeck), 1934), p. 203. The sense of military victory often ascribed to this word may stem from the supposed Arabic cognate 'overthrow', 'overturn'. Cf. BDB, p. 213.

[3] Psalms used either at the coronation of the king or at a yearly enthronement festival. Cf. Gunkel and Begrich, *Einleitung in die Psalmen*, §5.

itself. Dates for the psalm have been posited for as early as the pre-Israelite period[1] and as late as the rule of the Maccabees.[2] The latter position, if sustained, would be important for the Qumran material to be presented in the next chapter, and we shall begin with that position.

Were we able to assign Ps. cx to the Maccabean period, the reference in vs. 4 to a priesthood 'according to the order of Melchizedek' would be perfectly understandable since the Maccabean princes were high priests as well. Ps. cx could be viewed as a psalm which justified this irregular situation whereby the ruler took over the cultic duties of high priest. In particular, the psalm has a striking similarity to what was said about Simon after he had come to terms with Demetrius II who had established his authority as high priest and 'friend' in 1 Macc. xiv. 41:

οἱ ἱερεῖς εὐδόκησαν τοῦ εἶναι αὐτῶν Σίμωνα ἡγούμενον καὶ ἀρχιερέα εἰς τὸν αἰῶνα ἕως τοῦ ἀναστῆναι προφήτην πιστόν.

Compare Ps. cx. 4 as translated by the LXX:

σὺ εἶ ἱερεὺς εἰς τὸν αἰῶνα κατὰ τὴν τάξιν Μελχισεδέκ.

The objection often raised to this comparison is that Simon, though high priest, was not king but only ἡγούμενος.[3] This may be met by the observation made above that unlike the other Royal Psalms, with the exception of Ps. ci, the ruler in Ps. cx is not identified specifically as king.[4] To these observations we may add the evidence of the acrostic found by G. Margoliouth and independently by Bickell and dealt with by Duhm.[5]

---

[1] Cf. H. G. Jefferson, 'Is Psalm 110 Canaanite?', *JBL*, LXXIII (September 1954), 152–6, who uses a statistical method to find a higher percentage of Ugaritic words (i.e. words found in both Hebrew and Ugaritic) in Ps. cx than is usual for the Psalms in general. My remarks, and those of Gordon, above (p. 21 and 21 n. 4) should serve to cast enough doubt on this method. There is no particular reason why this should suggest any Canaanite background. One wonders if it would not be possible to find passages in the Mishnah with equally high 'Ugaritic' content.

[2] Duhm, *Die Psalmen*, pp. 398ff.

[3] So, for instance, Schmidt, *Die Psalmen*, p. 204, and Oesterley, *The Psalms*, p. 461.

[4] A fact recognized by Briggs and Briggs, *Psalms* (ICC), p. 374.

[5] From whom the material for our discussion is taken, *Die Psalmen*, pp. 398–9.

Table 2.1

(vs. 1)	שב –	ש
(vs. 2)	מטה –	מ
(vs. 3)	עמך –	ע
(vs. 4)	נשבע –	נ
	=	שִׁמְעֹן

This acrostic suggests even more strongly the application of Ps. cx to Simon's acclamation as governor and high priest by the people. Attempts to discredit this as an acrostic have been shallow, such as the statement by Briggs and Briggs that the acrostic 'is based on arbitrary arrangement and is against the usage of the acrostics'.[1] In point of fact, any arrangement of a psalm into poetic format is arbitrary to some degree as is shown by the way in which the psalms were written in ancient texts.[2] There is no rearrangement of the text involved here, and Duhm's translation of the psalm shows that the arrangement which he uses is at least possible. Although in practice acrostics are built upon an alphabetical scheme, there is, in principle, no reason why an author might not have selected some other scheme. We must give this position its just due and say that there is a possibility from the evidence presented so far that the psalm might indeed be dated in the 170th Seleucid year (142–141 B.C.).[3]

There are, however, excellent arguments against a Maccabean date which also do justice to the evidence. Perhaps the most convincing of these arguments stems from the words of I Maccabees just quoted: ἕως τοῦ ἀναστῆναι προφήτην πιστόν, a passage often cited to show the belief in the Maccabean period that prophecy had ceased in Israel.[4] On the other hand, we

[1] *Psalms* (ICC), p. 374; see also the remarks of Kraus, *Psalmen*, II, 755.

[2] That is, without any special arrangement. See, for instance the 11QPsᵃ scroll.

[3] For the evidence for Simon's date cf. Emil Schürer, *The Jewish People in the Time of Jesus*, Nahum N. Glatzer, ed., trans. John Macpherson (Schocken Paperbacks, No. 8; New York: Schocken Books, 1961), pp. 58–9. For the position that the priest-kingship of the Maccabees arose out of the functions of the high priest as head of a 'temple state' cf. M. A. Beek, 'Hasidic Conceptions of Kingship in the Maccabean Period', *The Sacral Kingship* (Studies in the History of Religions, Supplements to *Numen*, vol. IV; Leiden: E. J. Brill, 1959), pp. 349–55, especially in this regard pp. 351–2.

[4] George Foot Moore, *Judaism in the First Centuries of the Christian Era*, vol. I (Cambridge, Mass.: Harvard University Press, 1927), 240, and cf.

have seen that the prophetic element is unusually strong in Ps. cx as is shown in the part played by the introductory formula 'says the LORD'. According to 1 Macc. xiv. 41 the Hasmonean dynasty is to remain in power during the time of the absence of prophecy. It is impossible to think that Simon, or any other Maccabee, could be enthroned at the words of a prophet. We may also agree with Briggs and Briggs[1] that the crowning of Joshua the son of Jehozadok in Zech. vi. 9ff. is not meant. Probably 'Joshua' is a gloss for 'Zerubbabel',[2] especially since in Zech. vi. 13 there are two independent figures, priest and king. Hence, we are able to exclude the two most likely periods in the time of the Second Temple from which such a psalm as Ps. cx might originate, and we may with confidence look to a date during the period of the monarchy, a result almost universally accepted on the part of Old Testament scholars.

Is it, however, possible to go further and assign a more definite date to Ps. cx? Within the context of our concern with Melchizedek we must use special care to avoid circular argument. Hence we must, so far as possible, exclude reference to the priesthood of Melchizedek as we attempt to pin down the date for the psalm more exactly. I have already mentioned that Ps. cx. 1 suggests the picture of the king's exercising authority in the midst of enemies. This could point to several different historical periods and is not in itself of much help in dating. The statement in vs. 3, however, 'your people are a freewill offering in the day of your might' is possibly more promising. Artur Weiser[3] refers to the sacred duty of the tribes to wage the wars of Yahweh (cf. Judges v. 23). This is a rather apt comparison since it suggests the unity of the people under the charismatic leadership of a single ruler, a ruler in Zion (cx. 2). Only one period in history can conform to this picture, the early reign of David in Jerusalem. The willingness of the people to engage in war on behalf of the king ceases to be a decisive factor during

W. D. Davies, *The Setting of the Sermon on the Mount* (Cambridge: Cambridge University Press, 1964), pp. 143f.

[1] *Psalms* (ICC), p. 375.

[2] Cf. Martin Noth, *The History of Israel*, p. 312 n. 2, and John Bright, *A History of Israel* (Philadelphia: The Westminster Press, 1959), pp. 353 and 353 n. 68.

[3] *The Psalms: A Commentary*, trans. Herbert Hartwell (The Old Testament Library; Philadelphia: The Westminster Press, 1962), p. 95.

most of the reign of David since David relied most heavily on his personal troops. Only in the war against the Syrian–Ammonite coalition does David make use of troops from 'Israel', perhaps due to the tenacity of the border fortresses held by Ammon at that time.[1] After that time David's relationship with the Northern tribes steadily deteriorated to the point that these same tribes were twice involved in revolt against him. That the references to victory over enemies in vss. 5–6 cannot apply to Solomon is shown by the fact that Solomon, so far as we know, participated in no war or battle during his reign.[2] The only other period which would fit as well would be the reign of Josiah who briefly revived the territorial fortunes of the Judaean state to a small extent, but during this period it is unlikely that a reference to Melchizedek's priesthood, applying to the king, would have been formulated since the purpose of the Reform of Josiah included securing the prerogatives of the Zadokite priesthood.

Results

If the early period of David's reign in Jerusalem were the historical setting for the psalmist, then this would pave the way for understanding one of the most difficult parts of the psalm, vs. 6b, which reads: מחץ ראש על ארץ רבה.[3] The translation 'He has crushed a head [leader?, prince?, chief?] upon a great land...'[4] makes very little sense. Note, however, that without even so much as a change in pointing we may read the same text as, 'He has crushed a prince upon the land of Rabbah.'[5] The words 'land of Rabbah' might well be an apt description of the small

---

[1] Cf. George M. Landes, 'The Material Civilization of the Ammonites', *The Biblical Archaeologist Reader*, II (Anchor Books, No. 250b; Garden City, N.Y.: Doubleday & Company, Inc., 1964), 72. David does not even have to use tribal levies in his defeat of the Philistines at Baal-Perazim or again in the valley of Rephaim. Cf. 2 Sam. v. 20ff.

[2] Cf. Noth, *History*, p. 205.

[3] The suggestion of Briggs and Briggs, *Psalms* (ICC), p. 381, that an original עלה has been lost here through haplography from an original עלה על ארץ רבה is perhaps possible, but there is no direct evidence for it.

[4] ארץ רבה in Codex א is rendered as ἐπὶ τὴν πολλήν.

[5] Cf. Josh. xi. 3 where 'land of Mizpah' refers to the immediate region around Mizpah. Although this would be an unusual usage in Hebrew, it is not impossible.

amount of territory left to the Ammonites by the time David finally entered the battle in order to receive credit for the victory.[1] The reference to 'kings' in vs. 5 might then be taken to refer to the kings of Moacah, Hodadezer, and Hanun, whereas the reference to ראש in vs. 7 would refer to Hanun alone (cf. 2 Sam. x). Following through along this line, vs. 7a becomes intelligible as a possible reference to the 'city of waters', as Ammon was known to the Hebrews (cf. 2 Sam. xii. 27), and vs. 7b as a reference to David's taking the crown of Ammon (2 Sam. xii. 26ff.). With this victory, David completed a chain of victories which insulated his kingdom within an envelope of conquered states (with the exception of the already friendly Tyre), conforming rather closely to the meaning which we found for 'footstool for your feet' in vs. 1. I suggest, then, the possibility that Ps. cx represents a song of victory sung upon David's return to Jerusalem.[2]

To what extent the possibility I have suggested is a probability is another question. There is something inherently risky in attempting to place a psalm, written in such general terms, in a concrete historical setting. With some changes the psalm might be applied to other historical periods. Ps. cx, however, has been related by several scholars to the time of David, though always with reference to and speculation on the priesthood of Melchizedek.[3] I have tried to show on other grounds that the psalm could come from the time of David's reign.

MELCHIZEDEK IN THE OLD TESTAMENT

Melchizedek and the sacral kingship

Having dealt at some length with the main passages, we must now say something about Melchizedek himself. In recent years the identity of Melchizedek has come to be important for those who would see the Davidic kingship in Jerusalem as an out-

---

[1] Cf. 2 Sam. x; xii. 26–31.   [2] Cf. 2 Sam. xii. 31.

[3] For instance Hugo Gressmann, *Der Messias* (Forschungen zur Religion und Literatur des Alten und Neuen Testaments, New Series, vol. xxvi; Göttingen: Vandenhoeck & Ruprecht, 1929), p. 25, suggests that the psalm deals with David's takeover of an ancient Amorite priest-kingship in Jerusalem, perhaps even as a reappearance of Melchizedek! Rowley, 'Melchizedek and Zadok', p. 469, following Bentzen, considers the psalm

growth of an earlier Jebusite priest-kingship.[1] The use to which Melchizedek has been put by the so-called 'Ritual Pattern School' is interesting and important, 'weil hier offenbar ein konkreter historisch greifbar Entlehnungsvorgang nachgewiesen werden kann'.[2] Indeed, even among those who are not adherents of that school the assumption that Melchizedek was, in fact, a pre-Israelite, Canaanite king of Jerusalem has become widely accepted. For instance, John Bright, certainly no friend of his school,[3] says, without discussion, about the time of Abraham, 'Nor is the fawning 'Abdu-Hepa king in Jerusalem, but Melchizedek',[4] as though this were a firmly established result. For this reason, and not out of any desire to add to the mountain of literature on the sacral kingship, we must at least deal with the subject so far as it touches on Melchizedek in the Old Testament.

In general, those who discuss the sacral kingship with reference to the ritual patterns of other oriental peoples are trying to take seriously the position of Palestine as a bridge between Mesopotamian and Egyptian culture. However unique may have been the religion and culture of ancient Israel, it still shared certain fundamental patterns with its neighbors.[5] As a pre-

to come from the time of David as his enthronement psalm, but he goes beyond Bentzen in thinking of it as a legitimization of David's kingship and Zadok's priesthood. Schmid, 'Melchisedech und Abraham', p. 149, considers David and Zadok to be contained within the figures of Abram and Melchizedek, David having taken over a local Hebron tradition from the time of his reign there.

[1] For a complete bibliography on this subject until 1961 cf. Bernhardt, *Das Problem*, pp. 307–24. Works of interest since that date might include Josef Schreiner, *Sion-Jerusalem Jahwes Königssitz* (Studien zum Alten und Neuen Testament, vol. VII; Munich: Kösel-Verlag, 1963); and Nick Poulssen, *König und Tempel im Glaubenszeugnis des Alten Testaments* (Stuttgarter biblische Monographien, No. 3; Stuttgart: Katholisches Bibelwerk, 1967). See now John G. Gammie, 'Loci of the Melchizedek Tradition of Genesis 14: 18–20', *JBL*, xc (December 1971), 385–96.

[2] Bernhardt, *Das Problem*, p. 81.

[3] In reference to this school he says, *A History of Israel*, p. 205, 'This view is emphatically to be rejected. There is no real evidence for the existence of any such single ritual pattern throughout the ancient world, and much to the contrary.'

[4] *Ibid.* p. 77.

[5] The words of S. H. Hooke from the introduction to the work *The Labyrinth: Further Studies in the Relation between Myth and Ritual in the Ancient*

viously nomadic people, these patterns were vouchsafed to the Israelites as they conquered the settled population of Palestine, and as the nomadic beliefs and practices of the Israelites were gradually adapted to fit the patterns imposed by native Palestinian culture. In reference to the kingship, the ceremonies surrounding the ascension of the king to the throne, and the theological understandings which lie behind these ceremonies share common ground with those of the peoples of Egypt and Mesopotamia. The ritual of enthronement in Jerusalem simply represents a version of the western form of the common Near Eastern enthronement rite,[1] which involves the understanding of the king as being divine, and partaking of the world of the gods as much as of the world of men.[2] According to this theory, then, we should find that the king was thought of as being divine. To support this certain passages from the Psalms may be brought forward:

> I will recount concerning Yahweh's decree:
> He said to me, 'You are my son,
>   today I have begotten you.' (Ps. ii. 7)

> Your throne, O God,[3] is for ever and ever.
> The staff of uprightness is the scepter
>   of your kingdom. (Ps. xlv. 7)

World (London: SPCK, 1935), p. v, are informative as to just what is meant by 'pattern' here and deserve quotation: 'This pattern consisted of a dramatic ritual representing the death and resurrection of the king, who was also the god, performed by priests and members of the royal family. It comprised a sacred combat, in which was enacted the victory of the god over his enemies, a triumphal procession in which the neighboring gods took part, an enthronement, a ceremony by which the destinies of the state for the coming year were determined, and a sacred marriage.' On what Hooke sees to be the Canaanite form of this pattern cf. his 'Traces of the Myth and Ritual Pattern in Canaan', *Myth and Ritual*, ed. S. H. Hooke (London: Oxford University Press, 1933), pp. 68–86. See A. R. Johnson's later work, *Sacral Kingship in Ancient Israel* (Cardiff: University of Wales Press, 1955).

[1] Bernhardt, *Das Problem*, pp. 295ff., gives the essential elements of the enthronement ritual as conceived by Oesterley, Widengren, Johnson and Leslie. For more discussion cf. Sigmund Mowinckel, *He that Cometh*, trans. G. W. Anderson (New York and Nashville: Abingdon Press, 1954), pp. 23–4.

[2] Or as Gressmann, *Der Messias*, p. 21, would have it, both god and king are of the same family.

[3] Taken here to refer not to Yahweh but the king. Cf. Oesterley, *The Psalms*, p. 463.

A word of Yahweh to my Lord: 'Sit on my
    right hand until I shall have set
        your enemies as a footstool for your feet.

. . .

    Upon holy mountains, from the womb of the
        dawn, as dew[1] have I begotten you.' (Ps. cx. 1–2a, 3a)

The king, upon his enthronement, becomes a son of the deity
(Ps. ii. 7; cx. 3). His true origins are in the mountains of the
North, the mythical land of Eden where God dwells (Ps. cx. 3).[2]
In the hands of such writers as Mowinckel, Schmidt, and A. R.
Johnson the theory began to change its emphasis from emphasis
on an overall pattern to the emphasis on the unique functions
of the king.[3] Interest began to center around Israel's particular
assumption of the pattern[4] which has led to study of the pecu-
liarly Israelite features of the kingship ideology together with a
recognition that Egyptian and Mesopotamian kingships were
of radically different orders.[5] Indeed, Mowinckel set up a

---

[1] Or *Tal*, a Near Eastern god? According to Mowinckel, *The Psalms in
Israel's Worship*, I, trans. D. R. Ap-Thomas (Oxford: Basil Blackwell, 1962),
64, *Tal* is a Canaanite fertility god, supposedly representing here the youth
of the king. This translation follows Kraus' rendering of vs. 3a about which
I have raised questions above (pp. 25f.).

[2] Cf. Mowinckel, *He that Cometh*, p. 62; Gunkel, *Genesis*, pp. 33ff., but the
essay of Gressmann, *Der Messias*, pp. 164–70, on the divine mountain is
perhaps still the best in terms of collecting the evidence. Kraus, *Psalmen*,
p. 760, on the other hand, takes the phrase נאם יהוה as a polemic against the
belief in the origin of the kingship in the world of the gods.

[3] Perhaps out of reaction to the excesses of the 'pan-Babylonian' school
which say everything in terms of an original Babylonian myth. See on this
Mowinckel, *He that Cometh*, p. 24.

[4] On the change in method which was introduced by Mowinckel,
Schmidt, and Johnson, cf. A. R. Johnson, 'The Psalms', *The Old Testament
and Modern Study*, ed. H. H. Rowley (Oxford Paperbacks, No. 18; Oxford:
The Clarendon Press, 1961), pp. 196–7. For Johnson's own views cf. his
article, 'The Role of the King in the Jerusalem Cultus', *The Labyrinth:
Further Studies in the Relation between Myth and Ritual in the Ancient World*, ed.
S. H. Hooke (London: SPCK, 1935), pp. 71–111.

[5] See, for instance, the very balanced article of Mowinckel, 'General
Oriental and Specific Israelite Elements in the Israelite Conception of the
Sacral Kingdom', *The Sacral Kingship* (Studies in the History of Religions,
Supplements to *Numen*, vol. IV; Leiden: E. J. Brill, 1959), pp. 283–93.
Bernhardt, *Das Problem*, underplays the difference between Hooke and
Mowinckel.

dichotomy between Egypt and Mesopotamia: in Egypt the king is begotten by the god and is therefore divine, whereas in Mesopotamia the king is not god except in a 'cultic-mystical way'.[1] The kingship ideology mediated to the Israelites through the ancient Jebusites represents a composite of these very different views of the kingship which is further merged with the native Israelite conception of the king as a nomadic chieftain.[2] The king as Elohim is an Israelite view, for although in Egypt or Mesopotamia such an ascription would suggest the equality of the king with the high god, in Israel this was a way of associating the king with the host of lesser attending deities.[3] Therefore, the very assertion that the king is Elohim emphasizes, rather than submerges, the difference between Yahweh and the king.

In all of this Melchizedek is a rather important figure. Melchizedek is the priest-king of Salem, which city is to be identified with pre-Israelite Jerusalem on the basis of Ps. lxxvi. 3.[4] He is the priest of the Canaanite deity El Elyon (Gen. xiv. 18), not the priest of Yahweh. Ps. cx, an enthronement psalm, represents the taking over of this priest-kingship by the Israelite king.[5] This is made plain by the words of the psalm (vs. 4): 'You are a priest forever according to the order of Melchizedek.' By the word 'priest' we should understand priest-king,[6] and 'forever' refers to the perpetual holding of this priest-kingship by the Davidic dynasty.[7] There is some division of opinion as to

[1] 'Oriental and Israelite Elements', p. 285. Another way of stating this is that the king is the son of the god by adoption, as in Mowinckel, *He that Cometh*, p. 37. Cf. also Kraus, *Psalmen*, II, 759.

[2] Mowinckel, 'Oriental and Israelite Elements', pp. 288–9. Cf. also his *Psalms in Israel's Worship*, I, 114.

[3] 'Oriental and Israelite Elements', p. 285. On the king as Elohim cf. Kraus, *Psalmen*, II, 759. One wonders what might now be done with the 11Q Melchizedek document which speaks of Melchizedek as Elohim. Does this conception go back to pre-Israelite times? For a discussion of this problem see the next chapter.

[4] Presumably on the basis of synonymous parallelism; but are Israel and Judah synonymous in vs. 2, or do they represent the two parts of the divided monarchy?

[5] Cf., for example, Gressmann, *Der Messias*, p. 24.   [6] *Ibid.* p. 23.

[7] On the meaning of לְעוֹלָם cf. E. Jenni, 'Das Wort 'ōlām im Alten Testament', *ZAW*, LXIV (1952), 237; Kraus, *Psalmen*, II, 760; Bernhardt, *Das Problem*, p. 95. Cf. also James Barr, *Biblical Words for Time* (Studies in Biblical Theology, No. 33; Naperville, Ill.: Alec R. Allenson, Inc., 1962), p. 117.

whether Melchizedek was an actual person. Rowley[1] and Schmid[2] see no necessity for Melchizedek's having to be a historical figure, those of the 'Myth and Ritual' School, on the other hand, as well as many other scholars treat Melchizedek as a historical personage.[3] Can we with any certainty say who Melchizedek was? We turn now to examine the main evidence which must be taken into account if an answer is to be given to this question.

The El-Amarna tablets

First of all we turn to the extra-Biblical evidence for the pre-Israelite kingship in Jerusalem. This evidence is chiefly limited to certain letters written by one 'Abdi-Ḫiba, the ruler of the city of *Urusalim*,[4] to kings of the Eighteenth Dynasty in Egypt

[1] 'Melchizedek and Zadok', p. 469.

[2] 'Melchisedech und Abraham', p. 149. On the kind of approach used by Rowley and Schmid the remarks of Bernhardt, *Das Problem*, p. 96 are right to the point: 'Ausserdem ist es misslich, einerseits dem Text einen hohen historischen Wert zuzusprechen, anderseits ihn aber zugleich aus seiner überlieferungsmässigen eindeutigen Geschichtsbezogenheit auf Abraham als nicht geschichtsmöglich zu lösen und auf Davids Jerusalemer Königtum anzuwenden.'

[3] As we have already seen in relation to John Bright. Martin Noth, 'Jerusalem und die israelitische Tradition', *Gesammelte Studien zum Alten Testament* (Munich: Chr. Kaiser Verlag, 1957), p. 173, recognizes the historical problem, but in another essay, 'Gott, König, Volk im Alten Testament', *Gesammelte Studien zum Alten Testament* (Munich: Chr. Kaiser Verlag, 1957), p. 219, does not let this historical insight inform his otherwise excellent critique of the theory of divine kingship in Israel. For a similar dualism of thought one may see von Rad's rejection of the idea that the king took over some of the powers of the high priest (*Old Testament Theology*, 1, 44) and compare this with his acceptance of El Elyon's being the deity worshipped in Jerusalem. See the more balanced statement of R. Kittel, *Die Psalmen*, p. 358. It has not yet become obvious to scholars that there are many assumptions involved in making Melchizedek the king of pre-Israelite Jerusalem. One must assume, first of all, the literary unity of Gen. xiv and assign that chapter to an early date. Secondly, one must accept the equation Salem = Jerusalem which is not completely certain. Thirdly, one must give great historical value to Gen. xiv. All three of these conditions must at least hold true before one may speak of Melchizedek's pre-Davidic priest-kingship in Jerusalem. Even if true, such assumptions deserve more study and attention than they are usually given.

[4] Written variously ᵃˡÚ-ru-sa-lim, 287: 25, ᵃˡÚ-ru-sa-limᵏⁱ, 287: 46. 63, Ú-ru-sa-limᵏⁱ, 287: 61, 290: 15. For the texts and translations of the majority of the tablets cf. J. A. Knudtzon, *Die El-Amarna Tafeln*, 2 vols. (Vorderasia-

during the first half of the fourteenth century B.C.[1] These letters are rather revealing as to the situation in Palestine as Egyptian control there broke down in the wake of the so-called Amarna Revolution. 'Abdi-Ḫiba writes to the king, swearing his fealty and asking for as few as 50 soldiers to help him repel the on-slaughts of the *'Apiru*. From the evidence of the letters it appears that the Egyptian king simply ignored these requests, and it is quite possible that 'Abdi-Ḫiba succumbed to the *'Apiru* pres-sure.[2] These letters are interesting to us in that they furnish us with knowledge of the rule of a prince in Jerusalem before David.

'Abdi-Ḫiba acknowledges that he owes his position to the good pleasure of the Egyptian king:

Behold, as for me, (it was) not my father, and not my mother (who) set me in this place; the arm of the mighty king brought me into the house of my father! Why should I commit transgression against the king, my lord? (286: 9–15)[3]

'Abdi-Ḫiba is but a low-ranking officer in the administration of the king (285: 5f., 14; 288: 9f.; 287: 69).[4] He pays tribute to the Pharaoh (288: 12ff.). The Pharaoh should send relief to 'Abdi-Ḫiba because the king has 'set his name in the land of *Urusalim* forever' (289: 6of.). We note first of all the disclaimer of dynastic succession. Such a succession is integral to the theory

tische Bibliothek, Part 2; Leipzig: J. C. Hinricks, 1908–15). Also of interest though of limited usefulness, is Samuel A. B. Mercer, *The Tell El-Amarna Tablets*, 2 vols. (Toronto: The MacMillan Company of Canada, Limited, 1939). See the remarks of Albright and Mendenhall on this latter work, *ANET²*, p. 483. For uniformity the spellings used in Knudtzon's work will be used here.

[1] That is, during the reigns of Amen-hotep III, Amen-hotep IV (= Akh-en-Aton), and possibly the early years of the reign of Smenkh-ka-Re.

[2] A rather different picture of 'Abdi-Ḫiba is to be found in the letters of Suwardata (cf. 280: 17. 22. 23) which suggests that 'Abdi-Ḫiba may have himself indulged in a bit of adventuring, and it is possible that the Egyptian king had good reason to withhold support.

[3] *ANET²*, p. 487. This formula is repeated several times, e.g. at 287: 25–8, 288: 13–15. Skinner, *Genesis*, p. 270, compares this to the ἀπάτωρ, ἀμήτωρ, ἀγενεαλόγητος of Heb. vii. 3 but thinks of this, as do I, as accidental.

[4] The word here is *u-i-u* which is not an Akkadian word but an Egyptian word, *wʿw*. Ivan Engnell, *Studies in Divine Kingship in the Ancient Near East* (Uppsala: Almqvist & Wiksell, 1943), p. 86, took this to indicate a priestly function, but Noth, 'Gott, König, Volk', p. 219 n. 35, corrected him and substituted the word 'officer'. This writer on further checking holds that

that the line of 'Zadokite' rulers continued from Melchizedek, through Adonizedek down to Zadok from whom David receives the kingship. In *Urusalim* in the early fourteenth century, the ruler of the city is placed in his position by the Egyptian king, and we may presume that this was the state of affairs from the time of Thut-mose III (1490–1436 B.C.). The only sacral kingship affecting Jerusalem was that of the Pharaoh. Mowinckel's statement[1] that the practice of anointing the ruler of Jerusalem as priest-king is presumed in the El-Amarna tablets simply does not fit the evidence of the tablets themselves which, if anything, try to play down any personal claims of 'Abdi-Ḫiba. Two other facts are to be noted: (1) *Urusalim* can, in fact, be none other than Jerusalem,[2] and (2) 'Abdi-Ḫiba is partially a Semitic name,[3] suggesting that the prince is a native ruler and not a frontier official of some sort.[4] There is simply no evidence here for a 'Zadokite' priest-kingship in Jerusalem during the Amarna period, and we have every reason to think that the situation reflected in the letters as to the complete subjugation of the Jerusalemite ruler to the Pharaoh obtained from the earliest stages of the Egyptian Empire.[5] It could be argued that there

even a lower rank of common soldier is indicated. Compare the word *iwꜥyt* 'garrison', 'soldiery'. The intention behind the word *u-i-ú* is obviously to place emphasis on 'Abdi-Ḫiba's low position *vis-à-vis* the Egyptian Pharoah. Cf. Knudtzon, *Die El-Amarna Tafeln*, II, 1541 under the word *we(i)ꜥu*.   [1] *He that Cometh*, p. 5.

[2] The first mention of Jerusalem outside of the Bible is in the Execration Texts of the Middle Kingdom in Egypt, texts which mention the rulers of Jerusalem, but tell us nothing about them; cf. *ANET*[2], p. 329. Certainly the name 'Jerusalem' predates Israelite occupation and opposes the picture painted by Joshua and Chronicles that the original name of the city was 'Jebus' and its inhabitants known as 'Jebusites'. Perhaps this was a native Israelite designation. Cf. Noth, *The History of Israel*, p. 190.

[3] The first element of the name is obviously Semitic (compare עֶבֶד). The second element appears to be Hittite (compare names such as Giluhepa, Taduhepa, Puduhepa which are purely Hittite). Cf. Knudtzon, *Die El-Amarna Tafeln*, II, 1333. There was a definite Hittite influence in Jerusalem (cf. Mercer, *The Tell El-Amarna Tablets*, II, 704–5) as is shown by passages such as Ez. xvi. 3. One remembers too that Uriah in 2 Sam. xi is a Hittite.

[4] Indeed, from what has been said we have no reason to regard 'Abdi-Ḫiba as either an Egyptian frontier official or a royal personage. He is more like a local, appointed native official.

[5] Cf. John A. Wilson, *The Culture of Ancient Egypt* (Phoenix Books, No. 11; Chicago and London: The University of Chicago Press, 1956), pp. 180ff.

would be no occasion for the Zadokite priest-kingship to emerge in the letters. Certainly we must agree with this. The Amarna letters do not disprove the theory, but they do offer evidence against it. If such a sacral kingship existed in Jerusalem at the time of 'Abdi-Ḫiba, then it must have been all but powerless as control of the city was completely in the hands of 'Abdi-Ḫiba. One questions if there was room in *Urusalim* for 'Abdi-Ḫiba and a priest-king of Melchizedek's order. Further, if we may question this, we may even more cogently question any thought of 'Abdi-Ḫiba himself being such a prince, since he disclaims any royal or priestly genealogy.

Biblical evidence

Jerusalem is never mentioned in the Pentateuch.[1] It is mentioned several times in the narratives of Joshua and Judges, sometimes as 'Jebus' in Joshua, but usually as 'Jerusalem'. The Canaanite inhabitants of the city are known as Jebusites, but whether or not this is their own designation for themselves we cannot tell. What interests us most is the name of the ruler of Jerusalem mentioned in Josh. x. 1, 3, Adonizedek. Structurally this name is the same as Melchizedek, consisting of two elements, the second being *-zedek* in both cases, and the first having the ending *-î*. Here it might be instructive to list some other names of the same morphology for reference:[2]

Table 2.2

1.	מלכי צדק	– Gen. xiv. 18; Ps. cx. 4
2.	אדני צדק	– Josh. x. 1, 3
3.	אדניהו	– 1 Kings i. 8, etc.
4.	אדניבזק	– Judg. i. 5, 6, 7
5.	מלכיהו	– Jer. xxi. 1; xxxviii. 1, 6, etc.
6.	גבריאל	– Gen. xlvi. 17; Num. xxvi. 45
7.	מלכיאל	– Deut. viii. 16; ix. 21
8.	חניאל	– Num. xxxiv. 23; 1 Chron. vii. 39
9.	צדקיהו	– 2 Kings xxiv. 17, 18, 20, etc.

We notice that in 3, 5, 6, 7, 8, 9 the second element is a known divine name. In 4 the second element is the name of a town. The

---

[1] Unless, of course, Gen. xiv. 18 is an exception. Cf. Noth, 'Jerusalem und die israelitische Tradition', p. 173.

[2] Cf. Noth, *Die Israelitischen Personennamen.*

יִ ending is the *hiriq compaginis* in 7 and 8 expressing a genitival relationship.[1] We may question whether 4 is actually a proper name at all. This seems to have puzzled the Masoretes also who placed a *Maqqeph* between the two elements only in Josh. i. 7 and not in the other two places where he is mentioned. On the analogy of the other names in the list, we may conclude with some certainty that *zedek* represented originally a proper name and that the elements *malchi* and *adoni* stand in a genitival relationship to that name. This would yield the following meaning for the two names:

> Melchizedek – Zedek's king
> Adonizedek – Zedek's prince

On the analogy of the other names it is most likely that Zedek here is a divine name.[2] The first elements refer to the office, and demonstrate that these names are, as it were, throne names. The first elements do not give other divine names such as Moloch or Adonis.[3] It has often been pointed out that the word *zedek* in one form or another is frequently associated with the city of Jerusalem, as for instance, at Isa. i. 21, 26; Jer. xxxi. 23.[4] I can, however, think of nothing more natural than to associate the word *zedek* with the capital city. Certainly the evidence does not allow us to follow Mowinckel and reconstruct the pre-Israelite theology of Jerusalem whereby Melech (the king), Shalem (the

---

[1] G.-K. §90l. The name Melchizedek is translated here as 'king of righteousness'.

[2] On Zedek as a god cf. Mowinckel, *The Psalms in Israel's Worship*, II, 132 n. 85. A god by that name is also known to have been worshipped in Phoenicia and South Arabia. Cf. Skinner, *Genesis*, pp. 267–8. Against this view, Noth, *Die Israelitischen Personennamen*, p. 161 n. 4, says: 'Dagegen fasse ich gegen v. Gall (Wellhausenfestschrift, Beih. z. ZAW 27, S. 155ff) u. a. in den Namen מלכיצדק und אדניצדק wegen der Wortstellung, zumal es sich um alte Namen handelt, das zweite Element prädikativ, kann also die gewiss interessante Annahme, dass der Name des (vorisraelitischen) Stadtgottes von Jerusalem gewesen sei, nicht richtig finden.' Of course I have not viewed the second element as being the predicate, and I still reach the conclusion that Zedek is the name of a deity. Noth offers no historical proof against my position.

[3] For the opposite view cf. A. R. Johnson, 'The Role of the King', pp. 84f., and Mowinckel, *The Psalms in Israel's Worship*, II, 132, but see also p. 114.

[4] Cf. A. R. Johnson, 'The Role of the King', pp. 75–7.

covenant),[1] and Sedeq (justice) are all seen as personifications of El Elyon.[2]

The evidence to be found in Josh. x cannot be dismissed. The king of Jerusalem at the time of the Conquest is remembered to be Adonizedek, a name with the same morphology and essential meaning as Melchizedek. There is something compelling about the association

Melchizedek

Adoni zedek

Zadok

which is so often used to establish Melchizedek as a priest-king of Jebusite Jerusalem. We cannot, however, make a firm historical judgement simply on the basis of a similarity in names no matter how striking that similarity may be. We have seen that the god Zedek was worshipped in several places in Palestine, and there are other 'Zadokite' names attested in Palestine apart from Jerusalem.[3] I simply am not able to exclude the possibility of coincidence.

This rather brief summary of the Biblical and extra-Biblical evidence for pre-Davidic Jerusalem leaves us without a definite conclusion. The priest-kingship of Melchizedek envisaged by the several scholars we have studied is not completely

[1] We note with interest Mowinckel's apparently independent agreement with Albright, 'Abram the Hebrew', pp. 51–2, on the meaning 'covenant' in this passage. There may have been a god, Shalem, worshipped in the region. The evidence for this comes from the El-Amarna literature in which Ahimiliki ·of Tyre styles himself as 'servant of šal-ma-ia-a-ti' (rendered by Knudtzon as Salmaiatis) in 155: 8. 22. Even if this is a title applied to the Egyptian Pharaoh (Knudtzon, *Die El-Amarna Tafeln*, II, 1254–6), it is still a divine name. On this Professor Weber says: 'Es wäre dann also anzunehmen, dass sowohl Tyrus als Jerusalem einen Gott Salim verehrten, der aus guten Gründen mit Ninib gleichzusetzen ist' (*ibid.* p. 1255). This is going too far, perhaps, but it represents a possibility which cannot be lightly dismissed. Again this raises the possibility suggested by Winckler that מלך שלם should actually be read as a doublet of מלכי צדק. Mowinckel, *The Psalms in Israel's Worship*, II, 132, thinks that the שלם of ירושלם comes from the name of this deity and compares ירואל in 2 Chron. xx. 16.

[2] *Ibid.*

[3] For instance, we find the name *Irab-zi-id-ke* in EA 170: 37. Cf. Knudtzon, *Die El-Amarna Tafeln*, II, 1274 and 1567.

44

excluded, but there are certain major difficulties which I would list as follows.

(1) In neither of the extra-Biblical sources is there evidence of any ruling dynasty in pre-Israelite Jerusalem, and the evidence of the El-Amarna tablets is against such a view.

(2) In the Biblical records there is no evidence of a ruling dynasty in Jerusalem of a sacral variety or otherwise.

(3) Melchizedek in the Old Testament is never unequivocally identified as king of Jerusalem.

This leaves us but two areas in which convincing proof may be found, and we now turn to these.

The priesthood

At this point we stand on firmer ground because of the agreement of our sources that Melchizedek was a כהן. Not only so, but Melchizedek as a priest is brought into relationship with Jerusalem (i.e., Zion) in Ps. cx. The nature of this priesthood, however, is rather difficult to define. It is usual in commentaries on Ps. cx to mention the priestly functions of the king.[1] The king wears priestly garments (2 Sam. vi. 14); he performs sacrifice (1 Sam. xiii. 7; 2 Sam. vi. 13, 17), approaching the mercy-seat like a high priest (Jer. xxx. 21). He is even assigned a role in the Temple envisioned by Ezekiel (Ez. xliv. 3; xlv. 16f., 22ff.; xlvi. 2ff.). We note, however, that nowhere in the Old Testament, apart from Ps. cx. 4, is the king described as a כהן. Now we should reasonably expect that the king would have cultic duties. The anthropologist or historian would find that society stranger in which the king had no such duties. To show that the king, usually David,[2] had cultic functions in the Jerusalem Temple is not very significant, and certainly does not show that the term כהן was applicable to the king. Certainly the king is not a priest in the same way as are the Levites or the Zadokites. The Davidic king is eternally deprived by genealogy from functioning

---

[1] In this case I have followed the list of Kraus, *Psalmen*, II, 760, but this list does not differ significantly from other lists in other commentaries.

[2] This is in itself important. David was the first of the Israelite kings in Jerusalem, a bridge, as it were, between the old tribal confederation under a charismatic leader and a royal state under a sovereign king. We cannot assume that every function of David was carried on by later monarchs.

as a priest in the normal sense of the word.[1] Could there be other meanings for the word כהן which make more sense when used in reference to the king?

Besides Gen. xiv. 18 and Ps. cx. 4 there are other places in the Old Testament in which the word 'priest' is used of someone other than a Levitical or Zadokite priest. The best-known of these, perhaps, are in the references to Moses' father-in-law, the 'priest of Midian' (cf. Ex. ii. 16; iii. 1; xviii. 1). We see that only in Ex. xviii. 10–12 does Jethro have any cultic function; otherwise he appears as a local chieftain, though called a priest. Another occurrence is to be found in Gen. xli. 45, 50 (E) and xlvi. 20 (P) where Potipherah, Joseph's father-in-law, is called 'the priest of On'.[2] He is described as the priest of the city On rather than the priest of a god, in this case probably Re. This suggests not only a cultic but an administrative position as well, and it is known that the high priest of Heliopolis from the late Eighteenth Dynasty on held just such a position.[3] Our third group of passages come from the administrative lists in 2 Sam.

[1] Which is exactly the argument of Heb. vii. 14: πρόδηλον γὰρ ὅτε ἐξ Ἰούδα ἀνατέταλκεν ὁ κύριος ἡμῶν, εἰς ἣν φυλὴν περὶ ἱερέων οὐδὲν Μωϋσῆς ἐλάλησεν. R. Kittel, Die Psalmen, p. 357, says: 'Es kann danach keinem Zweifel unterliegen, dass die Könige Israels und Judas bis gegen das Ende des 8. Jahrhunderts, wahrscheinlich aber bis gegen das Ende der vorexilischen Zeit, sich tatsächlich als Priester betrachten. Sie sind nicht Berufspriester, aber sie haben als oberste Leister des Staates und als besalbte Jahwes auch in besonderen Fällen das selbstverständliche Recht an den Kultus.'

[2] The city On is none other than iwnw, 'Heliopolis'. Cf. Skinner, Genesis, p. 470.

[3] Cf. Hermann Kees, Das Priestertum im Ägyptischen Staat vom Neuen Reich bis zur Spätzeit (Probleme der Ägyptologie, vol. 1; Leiden: E. J. Brill, 1953), pp. 62–9. Even though this is after the Hyksos period when presumably Joseph would have been vizier in Egypt, it does reflect political reality in the late Eighteenth Dynasty. This meets, to some extent, Skinner's objection, Genesis, p. 471, that the names found in this section are not attested before the Twenty-Second Dynasty. The position of the priests in the last part of the Eighteenth Dynasty was a reaction to the damage caused by Akh-en-Aton's heresy and was inaugurated by Tut-ankh-Amon (1352–1344 B.C.) and made secure by the decree of Har-em-hab (1342–1303 B.C.). On the history cf. Wilson, The Culture of Ancient Egypt, pp. 233f., 237f. Although as applied to Joseph this function of the priesthood may or may not be an anachronism, these passages do suggest that the Joseph stories, which on other grounds have many connections with Egypt, again demonstrate accurate knowledge of Egypt in this regard. Cf. Skinner, Genesis, p. 442.

viii. 16–18; ii. 23–6; and 1 Kings iv. 2–5. These are especially interesting and deserve quotation (emphasis mine).

And Joab the son of Zeruiah was over the army; and Jehoshaphat the son of Ahilud was recorder; *and Zadok the son of Ahitub and Ahimelech the son of Abiathar were priests*; and Seraiah was secretary; and Benaiah the son of Jehoiada was over the Cherethites and the Pelethites; *and David's sons were priests.* (2 Sam. viii. 16–18 RSV)	Now Joab was in command of all the army of Israel; and Benaiah the son of Jehoida was in command of the Cherethites and the Pelethites; and Adoram was in charge of the forced labor; and Jehoshaphat the son of Ahilud was the recorder; and Sheva was secretary; *and Zadok and Abiathar were priests and Ira the Jairite was also David's priest.* (2 Sam. xx. 23–6 RSV)	*Azariah the son of Zadok was the priest*; Elihoreph and Ahijah the sons of Shisha were secretaries; Jehoshaphat the son of Ahilud was recorder; Benaiah the son of Jehoiada was in command of the army; *Zadok and Abiathar were priests*; Azariah the son of Nathan was over the officers; *Zabud, the son of Nathan, was priest and king's friend.* (1 Kings iv. 2–5 RSV)

From this we may see that Zadok, Abiathar, Ahimelech, and Azariah are official priests with the proper genealogical qualifications. David's sons are certainly not of priestly stock. Ira, the Jairite, is almost certainly not of a priestly family, and we notice that Zabud's brother is a military officer. What the 'priest to David' is in 2 Sam. xx. 26 is difficult to say. We should not think of him as a chaplain, as this role would more naturally belong to Zadok or Abiathar. Ira and Zabud appear to hold the same position from the similarity of their status in the texts. Some order may come out of this if we are to look for a class of courtly officials called כהנים unrelated by genealogy or function to the Aaronic or Zadokite priesthoods. The evidence for this is not strong, but some support is to be found in the translation of 2 Sam. viii. 17–18 in the LXX:

καὶ Σαδδουκ υἱὸς Αχιτωβ καὶ Αχιμελεχ υἱὸς Αβιαθαρ ἱερεῖς καὶ Ασα ὁ γραμματεύς, καὶ Βαναιας υἱὸς Ιωδαε σύμβουλος καὶ ὁ Χελεθθε καὶ ὁ Θελεττι· καὶ υἱοὶ Δαυιδ αὐλάρχαι ἦσαν

The word αὐλάρχης is not well attested, but it seems to mean something like the mayor of the palace or chief of the court.[1] I suggest the possibility that כהן in these places may indicate a secular official who may or may not have any cultic duties. The

---

[1] Cf. L.–S., p. 276a, and compare αὐλαρχία at 3 Kings iii. 1.

word 'minister' to an American always means a cultic official but to a Canadian, say, it can mean either a cultic or a secular official. Perhaps the word כהן at one time had such a variety of meanings.

I have attempted to enlarge our idea of the meaning of כהן in the Old Testament so as to understand its use in Ps. cx. 4, for the 'priesthood' of the king must be something other than the 'priesthood' of such persons as Zadok and Abiathar. Nor do we have any reason to think that Ps. cx. 4 is addressed to anyone other than the king. Rowley's theory[1] that the words of Ps. cx. 4 are addressed to Zadok by David is rather weak since if Zadok were, indeed, the last of the Jebusite priest-kings[2] he would already possess the priesthood. Further, we have seen that the king's functions in the cultus nowhere earn him the title כהן. We must conclude that the 'priesthood' of Melchizedek assumed by the Davidic kings cannot be the cultic office of priest in the temple and that some other, extended meaning of the word כהן must apply here.

Salem

The last approach is the possible identification of the Salem of Gen. xiv. 18 with Jerusalem. Throughout this chapter we have had occasion to mention several theories about Salem, and it would be well to list them briefly here.

(1) Salem is identical with pre-Israelite Jerusalem (Mowinckel, Bright, Noth, *et al.*).

(2) Salem represents the name of a god; and מלכי צדק and מלך שלם are doublets (Winckler).

(3) The words מלך שלם הוציא should be read מלך שלמה הוציא 'a king allied to him' (Albright).

---

[1] 'Melchizedek and Zadok.'

[2] As we have seen, only a certain similarity in names impels us to the notion that Zadok was the last of the Jebusite priest-kings. One would be rather hard-pressed to find any warrant for this in the places in which Zadok is actually mentioned in the Old Testament. One wonders why David would keep the leader of the Jebusites in power after his complete defeat of the city, even though the leader were stripped of his ruling power. It is even more incredible to think that Solomon, who is known for his ruthless consolidation of power, would have retained a potentially hostile official in a position of authority.

A very early understanding was that Salem was a city in the region of Shechem, an understanding based on Gen. xxxiii. 18:

ויבא יעקב שלם עיר שכם אשר בארץ כנען בבאו מפדן ארם...

which is translated by the LXX as:

καὶ ἦλθεν Ιακωβ εἰς Σαλημ πόλιν Σικιμων ἥ ἐστιν εν γῇ Χανααν, ὅτε ἦλθεν ἐκ τῆς Μεσοποταμίας Συρίας,...

This is also the understanding of the Book of Jubilees, the Vulgate, and the Syriac versions. Indeed, there is a village of *Salim* about four miles east of Nablus (= Neapolis = Shechem), a city known to Epiphanius[1] in the late fourth century A.D. Interestingly enough the Samaritan version which might have seen this as an opportunity to refute Melchizedekian claims for Jerusalem (if, in fact, there were any), render שלם as בשלום which corresponds rather exactly to the usual modern understanding of the text.[2] Another possible location is suggested by a passage in the Fourth Gospel:

ἦν δὲ καὶ ὁ ᾿Ιωάνης βαπτίζων ἐν Αἰνὼν ἐγγὺς Σαλείμ.   (John iii. 23)

Salim and Aenon were in the region of the Decapolis south of Scythopolis and across the Jordan from Pella. We have, however, no evidence at all that such a place existed during the Old Testament period. The 'Salem' of Gen. xxxiii. 18 has a greater probability and would fit the narrative of Gen. xiv. Although שלם עיר שכם is not the usual way of locating a small town,[3] there is some precedent for this form at Gen. xii. 6. On the other hand, it is easy to see how the LXX could take שלם as a place-name in this context when the Hebrew intended something like 'safely', but this meaning is anything but firmly established.[4] Finally, we note that the equation, Salem = Jerusalem, which is made

___

[1] *Panarion* LV. 2. 2. Here Epiphanius sums up the discussion of this site rather well:

Σαλὴμ δὲ ἡ πόλις ἐκαλεῖτο, περὶ ἧς ἄλλος ἄλλως ἐξέδωκε καὶ ἄλλος ἄλλως. οἱ μὲν γάρ φασιν αὐτὴν εἶναι τὴν νῦν ῾Ιερουσαλὴμ καλουμένην, τοτὲ δὲ ᾿Ιεβους λεγομένην, ἄλλοι δέ φασιν ἄλλην τινὰ Σαλὴμ εἶναι ἐν τῷ πεδίῳ Σικίμων κατάντικρὺ τῆς νυνὶ Νεαπόλεως οὕτω καλουμένης.

It is difficult to see that the discussion has advanced very far since Epiphanius' day.

[2] Cf. Skinner, *Genesis*, pp. 415–16.
[3] *Ibid.* p. 415.   [4] *Ibid.*

on the basis of Ps. lxxvi. 3 is not completely sure. In fact, the same passage might be used to show that Salem was a northern city:

נודע ביהודה אלהים בישראל גדול שמו
ויהי בשלם ומעונתו בציון

The chiasmus brings out another possible parallel:

Judah – Zion
Israel – Salem.

If 'Israel' in this psalm refers to the northern state, then 'Salem' should also be identified as a northern city. We do not consider that this provides firm proof for a northern location, but at least it may be seen that the facile Salem = Jerusalem equation which is often posited on the basis of this text is also not proven.[1]

CONCLUSIONS

It should be obvious that there are very few positive conclusions which one may draw from the Old Testament evidence concerning Melchizedek, and several negative ones. In particular, I have been concerned with the theory of Melchizedek's supposed reign as a priest-king in the city of Jerusalem before the Israelite conquest. This theory I have found to be weak on many sides, but the same lack of positive evidence which makes the theory questionable also prevents me from disproving it. I can say, however, that the reconstructions of a priest-kingship and of a Jebusite royal theology which have sometimes been associated with this theory have no support, and, as Noth points out, to accept the idea of Melchizedek's reign as a priest-king in pre-Israelite Jerusalem is not necessarily to accept the notion of its being a divine kingship.[2] Whatever value the idea of the

---

[1] John G. Gammie, 'Loci of the Melchizedek Tradition', has given a thorough discussion of the Salem = Jerusalem equation which gives excellent reasons for holding this equation not yet to be established. M. Delcor, 'Melchizedek from Genesis to the Qumran Texts and the Epistle to the Hebrews', *JSJ*, II (December 1971), 115–35, simply repeats the arguments already considered here for adoption of the equation.

[2] 'Jerusalem und die israelitische Tradition', p. 173.

sacral kingship may have for the description of the royal theology of the Davidic dynasty, it has no historical antecedents that I can find in the person of Melchizedek. Can we, however, make any positive statements? I shall end this chapter with a few statements which I think have some support in the evidence.

The major difficulty with the Biblical sources for Melchizedek is their relative chronology. We saw the almost total impossibility of finding a satisfactory date for Gen. xiv. 18–20 since this passage could be assigned to almost any date in the Old Testament period. With regard to Ps. cx, on the other hand, we found some reason to assign it to the time of the Monarchy, and some arguments were brought forward to suggest its coming from the time of David's reign. Although this is far from firmly established, it is a possibility. Were Ps. cx to date from the time of David, it would stem from a time in which the features of the Monarchy were just beginning to take shape and as such may well contain ideas which were not developed in later years. In fact, this is almost certainly the case with the priesthood of Melchizedek. Since the death of the *midrash* theory of Gen. xiv. 18–20, it is impossible to point to any development, any structure, in the Jerusalem Monarchy which we can say unequivocally is built upon the idea of Melchizedek's priesthood. The references to the cultic acts of David, such as his dancing before the ark upon its entry into Jerusalem, and his offering of a sacrifice, are not repeated in relation to other Jerusalemite kings, and it is most reasonable to view these acts as representing an intermediate period between a charismatic kingship such as Saul's and a dynastic kingship which David began. The various expanded meanings of the word כהן which we found, such as chieftain or administrative officer, might well be applied to David during the early years of his reign. Perhaps the former meaning 'chieftain', would be best, as the role of chieftain always involves some cultic functions.[1] I suggest the possibility that Melchizedek was remembered as a local chieftain, a position which could be described variously as כהן or מלך depending upon emphasis. One is reminded of the Canaanite rulers of the Amarna letters who ruled in certain small localities, sallying forth from time to time against their neighbors not unlike the

---

[1] Cf. Davies, *The Setting of the Sermon on the Mount*, p. 121 n. 5, for reference to the cultic functions of David.

'*Apiru*. This would fit the picture of Melchizedek in Gen. xiv. 18–20 rather well. A warrior-prince of a town fits the rugged conditions of central Palestine rather better than some variation of the Egyptian god-king or the semi-divine kings of Mesopotamia or some mixture of both, and better than the kingships of Tyre and Byblos which are often discussed in this regard. Thus David would be called a כהן 'like' or 'in the manner of' Melchizedek,[1] a warrior-hero of popular tradition who appears independently in Gen. xiv. Both passages would represent passing references to a relatively unimportant traditional Canaanite hero. That Melchizedek was an actual person is very possible, since traditional heroes are often based on historical characters,[2] but there is little that can be said of him otherwise. As we shall see, there is no attestation of a belief in Melchizedek's kingship in Jerusalem before the first century B.C., and even in the first century agreement on the point was not unanimous. He may indeed have been king of Jerusalem, but he may just as well have been king of a 'Salem' no longer known to us. He would have lived before the Philistine domination of central Palestine, but one must trust the unity and historicity of Gen. xiv to trace him back to the patriarchal period. The evidence of the Amarna tablets further suggests that we should perhaps look before the fourteenth century B.C. for the time in which Melchizedek would have lived.

If this particular reconstruction does not appeal to the reader, it should be pointed out that it rests upon no more conjecture, and possibly less, than the theory of Melchizedek's kingship in Jerusalem in the time of Abraham. Further, the two reconstructions are not totally foreign to each other since, if Melchizedek was king of Jerusalem in the patriarchal period, he would still probably be a warrior-hero such as we have suggested. We have no evidence, apart from the single name 'Adonizedek', to suggest that there was a dynastic kingship founded by Melchizedek, and much evidence against such a view.

---

[1] The meaning of על דברתי is difficult. In Ecc. iii. 18; vii. 14; viii. 2 the expression על דברת means 'because of', 'for the sake of'. The י– ending is the old genitive often used in poetry (cf. G.–K. §90 (3) a). The expression can only be translated in terms of the translator's understanding of Melchizedek's priesthood and not *vice versa*. For more on the expression cf. BDB, *sub voce*. The Targumic understanding 'in the image of' will be discussed later.

[2] Eissfeldt, *The Old Testament*, pp. 38ff.

The figure of Melchizedek as a divine redeemer which emerges in the 11Q Melchizedek, the doctrine of the Melchizedekians, the doctrine of Hierakas, and the Pistis Sophia has no grounding that we can find in the Old Testament sources themselves, and we must turn to other sources to find the origins of that figure.

CHAPTER 3

THE BACKGROUND SOURCES II:
PHILO, QUMRAN, AND JOSEPHUS

INTRODUCTION

The sparsity of information about Melchizedek in the Old Testament is matched in later texts by a relative wealth of information. In this chapter we shall examine all of the sources for Melchizedek up to the end of the first century A.D. (apart from Hebrews) with a two-fold outlook. First, we shall be concerned with the exegesis of the Old Testament passages about Melchizedek in the later sources, an investigation which has been carried out before.[1] Secondly, we shall try to be alert to the presence of any Melchizedek tradition in our sources which does not stem directly from the individual author's own exegesis of the Old Testament sources, an investigation prompted especially by recent discoveries from Qumran.[2] We shall conclude this chapter with a statement of conclusions for all of the background sources.

PHILO

The texts

Melchizedek is mentioned by Philo in three different passages in as many different writtings: *Legum Allegoriae* III §§ 79–82, *De Congressu* § 99, and *De Abrahamo* § 235.[3] The section which would

---

[1] The most important study of this type is Gottfried Wuttke, *Melchisedech der Priesterkönig von Salem: Eine Studie zur Geschichte der Exegese* (BZNW, No. v; Giessen: Alfred Töpelmann, 1927) which traces the history of exegesis on Melchizedek from the first century through to the modern period.

[2] I refer here to the fragmentary document from Cave 11 which deals with Melchizedek. Although discovered in 1956, it was not made available to scholars until 1965. For a more complete discussion see below.

[3] E. R. Goodenough, *By Light, Light: The Mystic Gospel of Hellenistic Judaism* (New Haven: Yale University Press, 1935), p. 151, is incorrect when he says that Melchizedek is not mentioned in *De Abrahamo*; rather, Melchizedek is not called by name. The reference here to Melchizedek, however, cannot be questioned as a quick check of the Greek text will assure the reader.

have dealt with Melchizedek in the *Quaestiones* is missing with the exception of a small fragment.[1] I shall deal with these three passages inversely according to length.

In *De Cong.* §99, primary interest does not center on Melchizedek. Instead, the story to be found in Gen. xiv. 18–20 is taken as a proof-text in support of the practice of tithing. The central figure is Jacob who in Gen. xxviii. 22 promises God at Bethel that he would return a tenth of all that had been given him. It is interesting that the mention of giving a tenth in Gen. xiv. 20 is here called an 'oracle' (χρησμός) and is understood as requiring the payment of the tithe in the Temple. The passing reference to Melchizedek is important since Philo ascribes to him a 'self-taught' (αὐτομαθῆ) and 'instinctive' (αὐτοδίδακτον)[2] priesthood. The commandment to tithe is taken by Philo to refer not only to things sensible (κατ' αἴσθησιν), but also to refer to objects of reason (κατὰ λόγον) and of mind (κατὰ νοῦν).

The discussion of Melchizedek in *De Abr.* §235 is much fuller. In this passage Melchizedek is the 'great priest' (μέγας ἱερεύς, high priest?) of the 'greatest God' (μεγίστου θεοῦ), the latter no doubt being a reflection of the Hebrew El Elyon.[3] Philo adds certain things to the account of Gen. xiv. Abraham returns safely from the battle with the coalition, having lost none from his retinue. Seeing this, Melchizedek is awe-struck, reckoning that this could have come about only through God's wisdom (ἐπιφροσύνη) and alliance (συμμαχία). Melchizedek raises his

[1] *Ibid.*

[2] For the meaning 'instinctive' cf. L.–S., p. 280a. The two words αὐτομαθής and αὐτοδίδακτος are important in Philo's thought, at least where they refer to σοφία. The meaning of αὐτομαθὴς καὶ αὐτοδίδακτος σοφός is explained as follows: 'He has not been improved by investigation, drill and labor, but from his birth he has discovered ready prepared Sophia from above showered down from heaven...' (as cited in Goodenough, *By Light, Light*, p. 156). The difference, of course, is that we are dealing here with priesthood, not wisdom.

[3] No doubt as a paraphrase of the LXX θεὸς ὕψιστος. On Philo's knowledge of Hebrew itself see Harry A. Wolfson, *Philo: Foundations of Religious Philosophy in Judaism, Christianity, and Islam*, 1 (Structure and Growth of Philosophical Systems from Plato to Spinoza, No. 11, part 1; Cambridge, Mass.: Harvard University Press, 1947), 1, 88–90. Cf. also Joseph Klausner, *From Jesus to Paul*, trans. W. F. Stinespring (Beacon Paperbacks, No. 115; Boston: Beacon Press, 1961), pp. 179f. and 200f., who would tend to give the reader the idea that Philo was quite fluent in Hebrew.

hands towards heaven in prayer, offering victory sacrifices (ἐπινίκια) for all those who participated in the battle. Melchizedek rejoices in Abraham's victory as though it were his own which, in fact, it was, since 'the affairs of friends are held in common' (κοινὰ...τὰ φίλων), especially the affairs of good men whose common objective is to please God. The following items, then, are added to the Genesis account.

(1) Abraham lost no men in the campaign.

(2) Melchizedek 'lifts his hands to heaven' in prayer.

(3) Melchizedek offers victory sacrifices.

(4) Melchizedek and Abraham are fast friends so that Abraham's victory is enjoyed vicariously by Melchizedek.

Unlike the other two passages which are allegorical, this passage provides us with a non-allegorical account of Abraham's meeting with Melchizedek. We have here something more like haggadic midrash. The Biblical narrative has been elaborated without obvious halakic or philosophical intent *per se*.

The third passage, *Leg. All.* III, §§ 79–82 is the fullest treatment of Melchizedek which we have from Philo. God has made Melchizedek 'king of peace' (βασιλεὺς τῆς εἰρήνης), a reference to Gen. xiv. 18, and 'his own priest', perhaps a reference to Ps. cx. 4; but if so, this would be the only time that Philo makes any allusion to this psalm in reference to Melchizedek.[1] Melchizedek is a 'righteous king' (βασιλεὺς δίκαιος), a translation of the Hebrew name. God has not prefigured any of his deeds, but from the very first (πρῶτον) has made him to be a peaceable (εἰρηναῖον) king and one worthy of the priesthood. Philo begins his allegorical interpretation of Gen. xiv. 18–20 by contrasting the king with the despot, the former being one who introduces laws, and the latter one who introduces lawlessness (ὁ μὲν νόμων ὁ δὲ ἀνομίας ἐστὶν εἰσηγητής). The despot is mind (νοῦς) which, through its decrees, effects free play for the passions. The king uses persuasion and issues only those directions which are necessary to allow one to sail life's voyage, piloted by right reason (ὁ ὀρθὸς λόγος) alone. In the one case life is ruled by the arbitrary dictates of the senses as delivered by mind, whereas in

---

[1] One might take the wording here ἱερέα ἑαυτοῦ πεποίηκεν ὁ θεός, as more readily stemming from Ps. cx. 4 than from the passage in Genesis. Philo makes a point of God's having made Melchizedek his own priest. However, this interpretation is not to be insisted upon.

the other case life is ruled by reason alone. The despot is the prince of war (ἄρχων πολέμου), the king, the ruler of peace, i.e. of Salem (ἡγεμὼν εἰρήνης, Σαλήμ). The king offers the soul food full of merriment and joy (εὐφροσύνης καὶ χαρᾶς πλήρεις), interpreting Melchizedek's offering of bread and wine to Abraham. This action of Melchizedek is opposed to the refusal of the Ammonites and Moabites to supply the wandering Israel with bread and water, a refusal which entails their eternal banishment from the congregation (Deut. xxiii. 3ff.). The Ammonites take their nature from their mother, sense-perception (αἴσθησις), and the Moabites take theirs from their father, mind (νοῦς). Together they represent those who hold that the coherence of all experience resides in the cooperation of sense-perception and mind.[1] Instead of the water required of the Moabites and Ammonites, Melchizedek gives souls wine in order to intoxicate them with a divine intoxication (θείᾳ μέθῃ) which, at the same time, is a sobriety of the highest order. Melchizedek has as his portion the one who is (τὸν ὄντα), since he is, in fact, the Logos itself. The difficulty of the words θεὸς ὕψιστος is dealt with as Philo closes the section. He explains that the meaning of ὕψιστος in reference to God does not have to do with a plurality of gods which are not 'most high', but rather it deals with the lofty predicates appropriate to God. To think of God ὑπερμεγέθως καὶ ὑπεραύλως καὶ ὑψηλῶς creates a reflection (ἔμφασιν) of God.

Discussion

It is obvious that Philo has no interest in satisfying our modern curiosity about Melchizedek. In the first two passages cited, Philo discusses Melchizedek as though he were a historical character; in the last, Melchizedek is a representation of the Logos. Besides the agreements among the three passages which stem from the Biblical records, there is one point of agreement which is very important. In *De Abr.* §235, Melchizedek possesses a unique, self-taught priesthood, and in *Leg. All.* iii §79 we find that God did not prefigure any work of Melchizedek (οὐδὲν ἔργον αὐτοῦ προδιατυπώσας), but set him out from the very first as priest and king. Even allowing for the fact that the choice

[1] Here either the Stoics or the Epicureans may be meant. On Philo's tendency not to identify his opponents by name see Wolfson, *Philo*, I, 101ff.

in language and emphasis is Philonic,[1] there is the possibility that Philo is here borrowing on a tradition about Melchizedek not to be found in the Old Testament sources. This raises the question whether Philo takes Melchizedek to be the Logos because of the Old Testament sources or because of later interpretation or midrash on these sources. The former question about the existence of an independent tradition about Melchizedek cannot be treated adequately at this point, but we may say something at least about the latter question.

There is nothing strange in the fact that Philo in one place (*De Abrahamo*) deals with Melchizedek in a purely literal manner and in another place (*Legum Allegoriae*) deals with him allegorically. In principle, everything in scripture admits of allegorical interpretation, whereas not everything in scripture admits of literal interpretation.[2] To find Melchizedek dealt with literally means that Philo considered the story of Melchizedek's meeting with Abraham to be one of historical truth and in accord with reason. This should allay any suspicion that in *De Abrahamo* Philo allows his imagination free play in his description of the meeting of Melchizedek and Abraham. To reconstruct the steps which lead to Melchizedek as being the Logos is a difficult problem,[3] and any such reconstruction is attended by dangers. We shall find some help in observing more closely how Philo handles the Old Testament sources.

In *Legum Allegoriae* Philo has no interest in supplying us with any more information on the historical event itself. Interest centers not on the man Melchizedek, but on Melchizedek, the representation of the Logos.[4] To this end Philo has only to refer

[1] See above, p. 55 n. 2.

[2] Cf. Jean Daniélou, *Philon d'Alexandrie* (Les Temps et les Destins, Paris: Libraire Artheme Fayard, 1958), pp. 130ff., and Wolfson, *Philo*, I, 124f.

[3] On Philo's tendency to hide the steps which lead him to a certain interpretation cf. *ibid.* I, 100f.

[4] Wuttke, *Melchisedech*, p. 14, goes too far when he says in reference to the citation in *Legum Allegoriae* that 'Melchisedech ist hier keine personhafte, geschichtliche Wirklichkeit, die wir von unserer Gegenwart als Vergangenheit empfinden, die wir in einem zeitlichen Ablauf von Ereignissen betrachten.' That Philo considers Melchizedek to have been an actual historical character cannot be doubted from his literal treatment of Melchizedek in *De Abr.* §235. Further, in *Leg. All.* III §§ 79–82, some connections are made at least between Melchizedek the historical man and Melchizedek the representation of the Logos.

to the name and offices of Melchizedek. He dissects and interprets these items in a manner which will facilitate his later discussion. The name 'Melchizedek' means 'righteous king'. As
king, Melchizedek is something opposed to a tyrant, giving the
soul the food of joy. Melchizedek was king of Salem. He is
thereby 'king of peace', 'ruler of peace', and 'peaceable king'.
As priest, on the other hand, Melchizedek gives the soul strong
drink inducing a divine intoxication. This priesthood is unique
and without antecedents. As priest, Melchizedek is the Logos.

If one will glance at the list of additions which are made in
De Abr. §235 to the account of Gen. xiv. 18–20 which I presented above,[1] it should be obvious that none of these plays a
part in Philo's representation of Melchizedek as the Logos.
True to form, Philo has down-played the historical references to
such an extent that *Leg. All.* III §§79–82 is almost entirely an
allegorical interpretation of the name and offices of Melchizedek. Any additional tradition of the type found in *De Abrahamo*
has provided no background for the process of allegorization.
On the other hand, the theme of the uniqueness of the offices of
Melchizedek which is shared between *Legum Allegoriae* and *De
Congressu* is absolutely essential to the process. Only as these
offices are spontaneous, unlearned, and instinctive can a representative of the divine Logos be brought to light. The Logos is
the mind of God in which the pattern of all the visible world is
conceived.[2] As such, the Logos has no visible or sensible antecedents. It is the 'eldest' (πρεσβύτατος) and 'most generic'
(γενικώτατος) of all things.[3] Indeed, the Logos is the 'first-born'
(πρωτόγονος),[4] the 'shadow of God' (σκιὰ θεοῦ) and the
'pattern of the image' (παράδειγμα τῆς εἰκόνος) of God in
which image God made man.[5] Melchizedek's lack of antecedents in the priest-kingship, i.e. the fact that his priesthood is
self-tutored, lends itself to Philo's interpretation of Melchizedek

---

[1] See above, p. 56.

[2] *De Opif. Mund.* §§19–20. Cf. especially §20:
τὸν αὐτὸν τρόπον οὐδ' ὁ ἐκ τῶν ἰδεῶν κόσμος ἄλλον ἂν ἔχοι τόπον ἢ τὸν
θεῖον λόγον τὸν ταῦτα διακοσμήσαντα.

[3] *Leg. All.* III §175.

[4] A very common designation of the Logos in Philo. See, for instance,
De Agr. §51, *De Conf. Ling.* §146. Cf. Goodenough, *By Light, Light*, p. 341 and
Daniélou, *Philon d'Alexandrie*, p. 155.

[5] *Leg. All.* III §96.

as the Logos. This leads us to considerations of cause and effect. Does Philo conceive of Melchizedek in this way in the interests of his allegorical interpretation, or does the allegorical interpretation stem from a tradition of Melchizedek's unique priest-kingship? The answer to this question will depend upon other factors to be brought out in this chapter, but we may point out that the theme is found twice in Philo and that in *De Cong.* §99 no obviously allegorical purpose is achieved by describing Melchizedek's priesthood as unlearned and instinctive.

QUMRAN

As late as 1964 Herbert Braun could conclude about interest in Melchizedek at Qumran that

Melchisedek ist für die Qumrangemeinde offenbar völlig uninteressant gewesen. Seine Erwähnung in dem Qumran-Targum, dem Genesis Apocryphon, das den Text aus Gen. xiv paraphrasiert, spricht nicht dagegen. Denn nicht einer der sonstigen Qumrantexte nennt Melchisedek. Hätte Qumran sich mit Melchisedek beschäftigt, so wäre der Priesterkönig höchstwahrscheinlich genau so dem levitischen Priestertum *unter*geordnet worden, wie dies bei den Rabbinen geschah; und erst dann könnte man etwa über Hbr 7, 9f als über eine antiqumranische Polemik zu verhandeln anfangen.[1]

A recently published text has rendered this view out-of-date and has focused attention upon the figure of Melchizedek at Qumran.[2] Here I shall describe the two Qumran texts in which Melchizedek is mentioned in the order of their apparent chronology,[3] paying special attention to the 11Q Melchizedek document.

[1] 'Qumran und das Neue Testament: Ein Bericht über 10 Jahre Forschung (1950–1959) – Hebräer', *Theologische Rundschau*, xxx (June 1964), 20.

[2] I refer to the document called 11Q Melchizedek which, though discovered in 1956, was not made available to scholars until 1965, a year after Braun's article.

[3] The problem of chronology is rather difficult in the case of the Genesis Apocryphon, but it is probably to be dated in the first century B.C. We shall show later that our copy of the 11Q Melchizedek dates ca. A.D. 50, but the time of composition might certainly be earlier. For convenience we are here arranging the two texts in order of their respective palaeographical dates and hence the use of the words 'apparent chronology'.

The Genesis Apocryphon

Melchizedek is mentioned in the Genesis Apocryphon at xxii.
14ff. in a section which amounts to a translation of Gen. xiv.
18–20 with certain additions. The date of the Genesis Apocryphon is difficult to determine, and one must distinguish
between the date of the scroll and the time of its composition.
The original editors, Avigad and Yadin, considered the hand-
writing of the scroll to be more or less like that of the War
Scroll.[1] This view was later repeated by Avigad with the
qualification that the short strike above the top bar of the final
mem might suggest a later date.[2] F. M. Cross[3] considers this last
feature of the script to reflect the period of transition between
the older mode of writing final *mem* as represented in the War
Scroll and the newer Herodian method. Otherwise he holds the
War Scroll and the Genesis Apocryphon to represent typologi-
cally similar scripts.[4] This evidence favors a date in the latter
part of the first century B.C. or early part of the first century A.D.
The date of composition for the document, however, is more
difficult to determine. Some attempts have been made to date
the scroll in terms of the Aramaic in which it is written. In two
important articles E. Y. Kutscher[5] held that the Aramaic in the
Genesis Apocryphon is later than that of the book of Daniel but
earlier than that of the Palestinian Targums. He favors a date
towards the end of the first century B.C. or the beginning of the

---

[1] Nahman Avigad and Yigael Yadin, *A Genesis Apocryphon: A Scroll from
the Wilderness of Judaea* (Jerusalem: The Magnus Press of the Hebrew
University and Heikhal Ha-Sefer, 1956), p. 15.

[2] 'The Palaeography of the Dead Sea Scrolls and Related Documents',
Scripta Hierosolymitana, IV (1958), 71.

[3] 'The Development of Jewish Scripts', *The Bible and The Ancient Near
East: Studies in Honor of William Foxwell Albright*, ed. G. Ernest Wright
(Anchor Books, No. 431; Garden City, N.Y.: Doubleday & Company,
Inc., 1965), p. 230. Also cf. J. T. Milik, *Ten Years of Discovery in the Wilderness
of Judaea*, trans. J. Strugnell (Studies in Biblical Theology, No. 26; London:
SCM Press, 1959), p. 135.

[4] *Loc. cit.* Here, however, he is following the analysis of Avigad and Yadin,
A Genesis Apocryphon, p. 15.

[5] 'Dating the Language of the Genesis Apocryphon', *JBL*, LXXVI (1957),
288–92, and 'The Language of the Genesis Apocryphon: A Preliminary
Study', *Scripta Hierosolymitana*, IV (1958), 1–35.

first century A.D.[1] Fitzmyer calls this 'Middle Aramaic' and supports Kutscher in his conclusions.[2] Fitzmyer further holds that the identification of historical figures proposed for figures in the Apocryphon is anything but sure, and we are left only with linguistic criteria for a determination of the date of composition.[3] Following Kutscher, Fitzmyer argues for a date in the middle to late first century B.C. and allows that the scroll which we possess may, in fact, be the autograph.[4] I am not comfortable with dating by means of language over the short space of time from Daniel to the conjectured date for the Genesis Apocryphon, a space of time which amounts to about 100 years. No one will deny the difference between the language of the Genesis Apocryphon and that of Daniel on the one hand, and the Palestinian Targums on the other hand; but the student of linguistics knows that language change is seldom abrupt, and features of the later form of a language are usually prefigured in dialects of the earlier form. For instance, the prefixed relative, שׁ, of Qoheleth and Mishnaic Hebrew is to be found in parts of the Old Testament assignable to much earlier dates (e.g. Gen. vi. 3; Judges v. 7) where there is northern influence. This is a 'late' feature known in some dialects of Hebrew at a much earlier time. Our only solid clue to the date of the Genesis Apocryphon is the palaeography of the scroll which points us towards the beginning of the first century A.D. The time of composition might well have been earlier, especially since the scroll shows no obviously sectarian tendencies. The name חרקנוש in xx. 8 can hardly be translated other than by 'Hyrcanus', though it is impossible to say which Hyrcanus might be meant.[5] This would seem to put a lower limit on the composition of the work in the last part of the second century B.C.

The Genesis Apocryphon translates Gen. xiv. 18–20 into Aramaic in a rather literal fashion with the exception of two

[1] For a different method but the same results cf. Paul Kahle, 'Das palästinische Pentateuchtargum und das zur Zeit Jesu gesprochene Aramäisch', *ZNW*, XLIX (1958), 100–16.

[2] *The Genesis Apocryphon: A Commentary* (Biblica et Orientalia, No. 18; Rome: Pontifical Institute, 1966), p. 18 *et pass.*

[3] *Ibid.*   [4] *Ibid.*

[5] Fitzmyer (*ibid.*) rejects this but without giving any evidence for his view. Certainly I agree with him that it is impossible to identify Hyrcanus II with any assurance.

additions. In xxii. 15 it is said that Melchizedek brings out food and drink 'to Abram and to all the men who were with him', a point not found in the Hebrew text. In line 17 the problem as to who gave the tithe[1] is resolved by noting that the tithe was made from the flocks of the king of Elam and his allies. Other than these additions the translation is literal. I say this in spite of the fact that the translator has failed to carry over certain Hebrew words. 'Bread and wine' in the Hebrew text appears as 'food and drink' in the Genesis Apocryphon. Secondly, the translation 'lord' for קנה in the original is quite reasonable and supports my assertion[2] that too much should not be made of the use of the root *qnh* in Gen. xiv. 19b. The Aramaic translator has simply taken a more conventional meaning for the word. Much of the Hebrew of Gen. xiv. 18–20 has been preserved. Melchizedek is called 'king of Salem' even though in line 13 Salem is equated with Jerusalem. He is called 'priest of El Elyon', to which might be compared Onkelos' rendering 'priest before El Most High'. Even the ambiguity of the Hebrew 'and he gave him' is retained in the Aramaic translation, requiring the addition mentioned above.

The identification of Salem with Jerusalem which is to be found in line 13 is a gloss. This fact is obvious from the grammar involved. The addition of the words היא ירושלם cannot be translated as they stand and require subordination to the rest of the sentence as though preceded by די.[3] It is easy to understand how such a gloss written above the word 'Salem' in an earlier copy[4] would be brought down into the text by a later scribe. Paul Winter[5] has suggested that the purpose of the gloss is to make sure that the reader does not think of the town Salim near Shechem which would suggest that Abraham stopped to worship there or that Melchizedek was priest in that region. That is to say that the gloss represented an anti-Samaritan polemic.

---

[1] See my discussion of this problem above in Chapter 2.

[2] Cf. above, Chapter 2.

[3] Cf., for example, the translation of A. Dupont-Sommer, *The Essene Writings from Qumran*, trans. G. Vermes (Meridian Books, No. 44; Cleveland and New York: The World Publishing Company, 1961), p. 292.

[4] This view, if correct, makes Fitzmyer's suggestion, *The Genesis Apocryphon*, p. 18, that the present document is the autograph copy impossible, but the gloss could come later from the author himself.

[5] 'Note on Salem-Jerusalem', *Novum Testamentum*, II (April 1957), 151–2.

This is an interesting theory, but hardly convincing. It is more likely that whoever made the correction did so as an explanatory measure, either conjecturing the meaning or borrowing from current tradition, a question we are not yet ready to decide.[1] There is some evidence in the text that the Salem = Jerusalem equation was also intended by the original author. This evidence is to be found in xxii. 14 where the author explains that Shaveh is the King's Plain, the valley of Beth Karma'. The latter name is Aramaic for the Hebrew Beth-haccherem, a town known in the Old Testament (Jer. vi. 1; Neh. iii. 14; Josh. xv. 59 LXX) and in the Mishnah (m. Middoth 3: 4 and m. Niddah 2: 7). This town lies in the vicinity of Jerusalem, not far from Bethlehem, strongly suggesting that the author thought of Melchizedek as being a king of that region. This interpretation is reinforced by Fitzmyer's observation that the author brings the king of Sodom to Salem in an effort to smooth out the transition between vss. 17 and 18 in Gen. xiv.[2]

The Genesis Apocryphon, in addition to relating the story of Melchizedek's meeting with Abraham in Aramaic, has also given us a picture of how the story was understood by the author of the text. This should give us some idea of the understandings and associations attached to the story at Qumran toward the beginning of the first century A.D., and perhaps also some idea of how the story of Melchizedek was treated beyond the confines of the Dead Sea sect, since the translation of Gen. xiv in the Apocryphon, unlike the rest of the document, is very literal and free of sectarian tendencies.

The 11Q Melchizedek

In 1965 A. S. Van der Woude[3] published a fragmentary text from Qumran Cave 11 which dealt with Melchizedek as an eschatological figure. Since that time the Hebrew text has been

---

[1] Fitzmyer, The Genesis Apocryphon, p. 11, dismisses Winter's suggestion on the basis of the parallelism in Ps. lxxvi. 3 (incorrectly cited by him as lxxvi. 1). To cast doubt upon its being an anti-Samaritan gloss, however, is not necessarily to throw doubt upon its being a gloss at all, as Fitzmyer seems to assume. [2] Ibid. pp. 154–5.

[3] 'Melchisedek als himmlische Erlösergestalt in den neugefundenen eschatologischen Midraschim aus Qumran Höhle XI', Oudtestamentische Studiën, XIV (1965), 354–73.

published twice, once by De Jonge and Van der Woude[1] and once by Fitzmyer.[2] With the exception of some brief notices[3] very little was written about this text in the years immediately following its publication although interest in it began reviving toward the end of the decade.[4] In more recent years several attempts have been made to improve the text of the 11Q Melchizedek. Some of these attempts have been devoted to small divisions of the text,[5] while the important articles of Carmignac[6] and Milik[7] have attempted thoroughgoing revision of the text.

It cannot be my purpose to publish yet another critical text of the 11Q Melchizedek. The most obvious reason for my reluctance is that I am limited to the photographs of the 11Q Melchizedek supplied by Van der Woude in his first publication of the text.[8] Secondly, the basic content of the 11Q Melchizedek is now clear, and the recent revisions of the text have only served

[1] '11Q Melchizedek and the New Testament', *NTS*, XII (1965–6), 301–26.

[2] 'Further Light on Melchizedek from Qumran Cave 11', *JBL*, LXXXVI (March 1967), 25–41.

[3] Y. Yadin, 'A Note on Melchizedek and Qumran', *Israel Exploration Journal*, XV (1965), 152–4; D. Flusser, 'Melchizedek and the Son of Man', *Christian News from Israel* (April 1966), pp. 23–9; J. A. Emerton, 'Melchizedek and the Gods: Fresh Evidence for the Jewish Background of John x. 34–6', *JTS*, n.s.x VII (April 1966), 399–401. Friedrich Schröger, *Der Verfasser des Hebräerbriefs als Schriftausleger* (Biblische Untersuchungen, No. 4; Regensburg: Friedrich Pustet Verlag, 1968), pp. 139ff., gives the text of the 11Q Melchizedek in German translation, but does little else with it despite the potential which this text has for the study of Hebrews.

[4] Especially in the work of J. A. Sanders. Cf. his 'Outside the Camp', *USOR*, XXIV (Spring, 1969), 240 n. 1, and 'Dissenting Deities and Phil. 2_{11-1}', *JBL*, LXXXVIII (September 1969), 283 n. 19, *et pass*. This interest on the part of Sanders is carried on by his student, Merrill P. Miller, who contributed an article, 'The Function of Isa. 61_{1-2} in 11Q Melchizedek', *JBL*, LXXXVIII (December 1969), 467–9. For a discussion of some of the tendencies of Sanders' study see above, Chapter 1.

[5] Cf. D. F. Miner, 'A Suggested Reading for 11Q Melch 17', *JSJ*, II (December 1971), 114–18; and F. du Toit Laubscher, 'God's Angel of Truth and Melchizedek', *JSJ*, III (October 1972), 46–51.

[6] J. Carmignac, 'Le Document de Qumrân sur Melkisédeq', *Révue de Qumrân*, VII/3 (December 1970), 343–78.

[7] J. T. Milik, '*Milkî-Sedeq* et *Milkî-Reša'* dans les anciens écrits juifs et chrétiens (I)', *JJS*, XXIII (Autumn, 1972), 95–144.

[8] *Art. cit.*

to refine our understanding of that content. For our purposes, therefore, we require a good text of the document and very little more. Accordingly, from enlargements of the photographs of the 11Q Melchizedek supplied by Van der Woude I have attempted to put together a reasonable text which I have translated below (p. 67). Before moving to that translation, however, it might be appropriate to note what relationship the translation bears to the extant texts of the 11Q Melchizedek.

It is my belief that the revised text of De Jonge and Van der Woude[1] is still the best text of the 11Q Melchizedek. J. T. Milik,[2] however, has made an important contribution by showing that fragment 3 belongs under fragment 1, and lines 23–6 of the text of De Jonge and Van der Woude become lines 22–5 of Milik's text. Further, Milik also shows how fragment 13 joins to the left of fragment 12 and to the right of fragment 6 by finding the ע of בעדת in line 10 split between fragments 12 and 13.[3] He further believes that fragment 4 joins the left of fragment 1 at lines 12–14.[4] My own reading of the 11Q Melchizedek is less complete than that of Milik especially as regards the extensive lacunae which occur in the text.

Milik believes that the 11Q Melchizedek is only part of a larger work which he calls a 'Pesher sur les Periodes'. This work he also believes to be attested in the 4Q180 and the 4Q181.[5] Into this scheme he is also able to fit fragments 5 and 11 of the 11Q Melchizedek. He considers fragment 5 to stem from the first column of the extant 11Q Melchizedek and fragment 11 to stem from the second column.[6] The material which is denoted 11Q Melchizedek in this book is denoted by Milik as 11Q Melchizedek iii.[7] As further evidence of a column before the text translated below, Milik points to the words written vertically around line 10 which are usually read במושה כיא. Milik considers the ב in reality to be the letters יו from the word עליו and points to the marks around lines 18–20 as vestiges of words which follow those written vertically above.[8] The entire sequence

---

[1] *Art. cit.*

[2] '*Milkî-Sedeq* et *Milkî-Reša'*.'

[3] *Ibid.*

[4] For a diagram showing the complete reconstruction of the relationship of the fragments see Figure 1 of Milik's article, *ibid.* p. 111.

[5] *Ibid.* pp. 109ff.   [6] *Ibid.* pp. 96–7.

[7] *Ibid.* p. 97 *et pass.*   [8] *Ibid.* p. 101.

of words he believes to be a long insertion at line 12 of the previous column which reads

[...אשר אמר ע]ליו מושה כיא [יובל הוא]ה קודש [תהיה לכמה]

I have not believed it necessary to enter into detailed discussion of Milik's reconstructions since that would lead me far astray from my subject. My interest is in the Melchizedek material of the document, and most of the reconstructions of Milik do not affect that material. Also I have not seen fit to fill out the lacunae of the text as completely as Milik has because again such an attempt would of necessity lead me far from my main subject. It is inevitable that except for Biblical quotations the extensive filling of lacunae involves one in a process of conjecture which renders the likelihood of the entire text being correct as very small. In short, I have been content with more holes and more certainty. My own conjectured readings have been, I hope, restrained. In any case I have tried to base nothing of central importance upon my reconstructions. Following my translation I have made a few notes on the text which justify in part some of my readings.

I present below a translation of the 11Q Melchizedek.

11Q MELCHIZEDEK

1. [saying to Zion] 'your *Elohim* reigns.' ... [
2. [   ]...and where it says, 'In [this] year of jubilee you shall return, each man to his possession.'
3. [and where it says, 'Let] every holder of a debt [let drop] what he loans [to his neighbor. Let him not exact payment from his neighbor nor from his brother, for there is proclaimed a] remission
4. [of *El*.' Its interpretation concerns the e]nd of days as regards 'those taken captive' who [where] it says (?)
5. ....MH....Y H.... and from the possession of Melchizedek p[riest of *El* (?)] their B... [Melchized]ek who
6. will bring them back to them and will 'proclaim release' to them [to atone (?)] for their iniquities, and .... [   ]... [   ]
7. In the year (?) of the last jubilee he has sai[d t]ha[t...] Beli[al], and he will [   ] RYM h[e] . [   ] .... the [t]enth [ju]bilee

8. to atone in it for all the sons [of light and] the men [of the lo]t of
Mel[ch]izedek [ ]M upon the[m] HT[ ] LG[ ] their
[ ] for

9. this is the time of the year of good favor for Melchize[dek, and]
he by his strength will ju[d]ge the holy ones of *El* in the interests
of a rei[g]n of justice, as it is written

10. about him in the songs of David where it says, '*Elohim* [has ta]ken
his stand in the assembly [of *El*]; in the midst of the *elohim* he
gives judgement.' And concerning him it sa[ys] 'Above it

11. take your throne on high. *El* will judge peoples.' *vac* And it
sa[ys, 'How long will you] judge unjustly and lift [up] the face
of the evil ones? [*Se*]*lah*.'

12. Its interpretation concerns Belial and the spirits of his lot wh[o
]..in their turning away from the decrees of *El* to [do
evil. (?)]

13. And Melchizedek will exact the ven[gean]ce of the judgements
of *E*[*l* among men (?)] and he will snatch (?) [them away from
the hand] of Belial and from the hand of all the sp[irits of] his
[lot]

14. And for his aid are all the '*ēlîm* of [ ]he ' [ ] Belial. And 'on
high' [its interpretation has to do with] all the sons of mi[gh]t
and HP[

15. this. That is the day of the [slaughter (?) wh]ere it is said [as
regards the end of days by the hand of Isa]iah the prophet who
said, ['How] beautiful

16. upon mountains are the fee[t] of the heral[d pro]claiming
peace, the her[ald of good proclaiming salvatio]n, saying to
Zion, "your *Elohim* [reigns]".'

17. Its interpretation: 'the mountains' – [these are] the prophet[s],
those who [ ]TP[ ] for all . [ ]

18. and 'the herald' – th[at] is the one Anointed of the Spiri[t], as
Dan[iel] said ['herald]

19. of good proclaim[ing salvation'] this is what is written about
him where [it says,

20. to comfor[t] ..... [ ]L [he will] instruct them about all the
periods of [wrath (?)

21. [ ] truth to . [ ] . [ ] .H.. [

22. ....[ ].H she turned from Belial WT . [ ].. [

23. [ ] in the judgement[s] of *El* just as it is written concerning
him, ['saying to Zi]on your *Elohim* reigns.' [(Now) Zi]on i[s

24. [the congregation of all the sons of light (?)] who uphol[d] the
covenant, who turn from walking [in the w]ay of the people.
And 'your Elohim' – this is [

25. [   ].........D Belial, and where it says, 'And you shall send abroad the hor[n of alarm] in the seventh [m]onth[.'

Line 1

The restoration of the end of Isa. lii. 7 here is possible even though the only certain reading is יך. These two letters occur in the same combination again in lines 16, 24, 25, and in each case they belong to the word אלוהיך from Isa. lii. 7.

Line 2

The introductory formula אשר אמר is especially difficult to translate since it has no antecedent. Van der Woude very reasonably suggests that there is an understood 'God' for a subject just as the same formula in CD vi. 8 has Isaiah for an antecedent, Jeremiah in CD viii. 20 and God in CD viii. 9.[1] The author of the 11Q Melchizedek uses several variations of a typical introductory formula, and none of the introductory formulas in the 11Q Melchizedek are unrelated to it.

Line 3

Van der Woude[2] holds that the sense of יובל, שמטה, and דרור in later Judaism was that of ἄφεσις, the single translation of all three terms in the LXX at Lev. xxv. 13 and Deut. xv. 2. He considers the word ἄφεσις to have an eschatological meaning which accounts for the association of these two passages in the 11Q Melchizedek. Actually the two passages would be associated together by an author simply on the basis of content.

Line 4

The reconstruction לאל for ליהוה is almost certainly correct. Note the substitution אל of יהוה for in the quotation from Ps. vii. 9 in line 11. The word אל is the exclusive word for 'God' in the 11Q Melchizedek.

Line 5

The name מלכי צדק is read with certainty at the beginning of the line and may perhaps be read at the end of the line, but only

---

[1] 'Melchisedech', pp. 360–1. For the full evidence from which Van der Woude has taken his material cf. Karl Georg Kuhn, *Konkordanz zu den Qumrantexten* (Göttingen: Vandenhoeck und Ruprecht, 1960), pp. 17–18. Now see my article, 'Formulas of Citation in the Qumran Documents', *Révue de Qumrân*, xxvi (1971), pp. 505–13.   [2] *Ibid.* pp. 361–2.

the letter ק may be read with certainty. The reconstruction
כ]והן לאל is made on the basis of Gen. xiv. 18, but its correctness
cannot be insisted upon.

Line 6

The longer, heavier suffixes ‑ֶמָה, and ‑ֵהֶמָּה are a feature not
to be found in the major scrolls except for the War Scroll and
the second half of 1Q Isaᵃ.[1] Goshen-Gottstein points out that
texts which have these heavier endings also show the pronoun
forms הואה and היאה (cf. lines 7, 14, 15, 18, 19, 25).[2] He suggests
that two alternate paradigms came into existence through
analogy patterned on the types -C and -$C(C)a$.[3] The reading
[לכפר] is very possible,[4] but not certain. It is found below in
line 8.

Line 7

The reconstruction וי]ום הכפו]רים ה]וא[ה which Fitzmyer[5] gives
is possible but only if one does not restore בלי]על in this
line which seems equally reasonable. There is too little left of
the line for anything like a certain transcription.

Line 8

It is possible that צדק [כי]ורל מל]ג could be read as ג]ורל אל
ה]צרק,[6] a possibility which Van der Woude doubts because
there is no trace of a ה before צדק.[7] The script of the 11Q Melchizedek, however, involves heavy shading in the right upper arm
of the צ which would obscure any ligature from a preceding ה.

Line 9

In the earlier version of this work I read line 9 as הואה חקק שנת
הרצון למלכי צ]דק ו]לאנש]י גורל]ו קדשי אל לממ]ש]לת משפט כאשר כתוב.
Milik[8] on the basis of better photographs reads the same line as

[1] M. H. Goshen-Gottstein, 'Linguistic Structure and Tradition in the
Qumran Documents', *Scripta Hierosolymitana*, IV (1958), 121.
[2] *Ibid.*   [3] *Ibid.* p. 118.
[4] Fitzmyer, 'Further Light on Melchizedek', p. 35.
[5] *Ibid.* Cf. Van der Woude, 'Melchisedech', p. 363 and De Jonge and
Van der Woude, '11Q Melchisedek','p. 302.
[6] Van der Woude, 'Melchisedech', p. 364. For '1QM xviii. 18' on this
page one should read '1QM xviii. 8'.
[7] *Ibid.*
[8] Milik, '*Milkî-Sedeq et Milkî-Reša'*.'

הואה הקץ לשנת הרצון הרצון למלכי צדק [והו]אה בחזקו יד[י]ך קדשי אל למפעל[ו]ת
משפט כאשר כתוב. This includes the possibly better reading
הואה הקץ of Yadin which gets rid of the unusual חקק. It is
obvious that by adopting Milik's readings we in fact have a
slightly more difficult text. Further, I find it impossible to
accept למפעל[ו]ת for what seems to be a rather obvious
למם[ש]לת. The words [והו]אה בחזקו יד[י]ך cannot be seen at all
in the photographs of the Van der Woude article. Hence I
submit my translation of this line with some reservation.

Line 10

The עליו refers to Melchizedek who is mentioned above in line 9.
This means that אלוהים followed by the singular verb נצב also
refers to Melchizedek, whereas the second אלוהים should be taken
as a plural which refers to angelic beings in the court of God.[1]
The verb נצב, though often used of God, can also be used to
refer to beings other than God.[2] We shall discuss this understanding at greater length below.

Line 12

Here we may reasonably read בספ[רי] חוקי אל,[3] which is
parallel to מש[פ]טי אל in line 13 and line 24. The reference here
is to the Pentateuch.

Line 14

The reconstruction אלי [עולמים] of Van der Woude is not
especially satisfactory, but אלוהים does not seem quite long
enough to fill the lacuna. The word מרום taken from fragment 4
seems correctly placed here and forms a reference to Ps. vii. 8
which is cited in line 11 (Milik). I cannot follow Milik in his

---

[1] All three editions of the text agree on this point. Cf. *ibid.*; De Jonge and
Van der Woude, '11Q Melchisedek', p. 304; and Fitzmyer, 'Further Light
on Melchizedek', p. 37.

[2] E.g. Gen. xxiv. 13; Ex. v. 20; Ps. xxxix. 6 and many other places in the
Old Testament. Kuhn, *Konkordanz zu den Qumrantexten*, p. 145, lists no
example of נצב in the niphal, and Jastrow, *Dictionary*, p. 927, gives only one
example of the verb in the niphal, but this does not have God for a subject.

[3] This is a common expression at Qumran. Cf. 1QpHab. ii. 15; 1QS i. 7,
12; iii. 8.

very difficult reconstruction [הואה כל]כול בני אל והפ[ליא העצ]ה and have preferred [פשרו על]כול בני ח[י]ל והפ]. In reconstructions it seems to me that the interpreter must favor usual expressions over unusual expressions except where unusual expressions are absolutely called for in some way.

Line 15

For the introductory formula see the extended comments in my article 'Formulas of Citation', in *Révue de Qumrân*, XXVI (1971), 512f.

Line 16

The article is lost by haplography before the word הרים, but is restored in line 17.

Although many other points might be made about the text of the 11Q Melchizedek, I have tried to cover some of the main ones. The language of the document is not that of the majority of the scrolls, but shows, rather, dialectic features which are limited to a smaller number of Qumran documents.[1] These features are (a) the heavier suffixes -מה and -המה, (b) the pronoun forms הואה and היאה, and (c) an example of the so-called 'pseudo-pausal', ת[שפוטו in line 11.[2] None of these features can be due simply to a different orthography, and they point to a dialect of Hebrew different from that of the majority of scrolls.[3]

---

[1] See above, p. 70.

[2] Goshen-Gottstein, 'Linguistic Structure and Tradition in the Qumran Documents', pp. 124ff., uses the term 'pseudo-pausal' to refer to imperfects with a *waw* between the second and third radicals. This *waw* he vocalizes as /o/ as in the pausal. The problem here is that there is no occasion for a regressive accent, hence the name 'pseudo-pausal'. In the MT, however, there are occasions where instead of *shewa* or וֹ, we find וּ between the second and third radicals in an imperfect. Cf. Ruth ii. 8 לֹא־תַעֲבוּרִי and Ex. xviii. 26 יִשְׁפּוּטוּ. See also the remarks of G.-K. §47f. Perhaps this orthography reflects a tendency in some dialects of Hebrew to return to the original *yaqtūlu* form.

[3] The use of the term 'dialect' is not too strong here. It is not surprising to find that there were different dialects of Hebrew in this historical period. Since the pioneering work of J. A. Schmeller, Georg Wenker, and Jules Gillieron in dialect geography every scholar concerned with language has had to give up the model of a 'standard' language at any one historical point. What is surprising is to find dialectic differences reflected so well in the orthography which often does tend to become standard to the point of obscuring dialect differences. Milik, *Ten Years of Discovery*, pp. 130–1, has

The date of the fragments can be determined rather well palaeographically. Van der Woude[1] gives the document a date in the first half of the first century A.D. Certain letters such as the ל come closer to late Hasmonean forms, but the letters כ, ס, ק, ת come closer to the forms found in 4Q Deut^j (ca. A.D. 50), whereas פ and ש show features which only appear in documents later than A.D. 50.[2] The evidence tends to converge on a date around the middle of the first century A.D., or, we might say, ca. A.D. 50. The date of composition is a matter to which we shall not turn until later.

We move at this point to a brief discussion of Melchizedek in the 11Q Melchizedek. We must preface our remarks, however, with a word of caution. The 11Q Melchizedek is, unfortunately, a badly preserved, fragmentary text. Of the extant portions of the text there is not a single line which can be read in its entirety without reconstruction. Although some of the fragments have been pieced together with certainty on the basis of a common scripture, others have been placed together only in the most tentative way,[3] and some have not been placed at all.[4] There were originally at least two columns, and perhaps more, in the 11Q Melchizedek, but all of my references have been to Column i, since nothing but a few letters remains of Column

distinguished 'Mishnaic Hebrew' and 'Classical Hebrew' from the language of the scrolls which he calls 'Neoclassical Hebrew'. As examples of 'Mishnaic Hebrew' he includes such documents as the letter of Simon ben Kosebah. In this latter document the only criterion for 'Mishnaic Hebrew' is the relative pronoun –ש, since other features of the Hebrew of the Mishnah such as the ין– masculine plural ending, anticipation by suffix, etc., are missing. We have already discussed above (p. 62) how inaccurate it is to call this relative pronoun form 'late', and with this criterion lost to us on what basis one might call the language of the letter 'late' is not at all obvious. The use of descriptive terms such as 'dialect', rather than chronological terms such as 'late' or 'early' or grossly oversimplified terms such as 'Mishnaic' or 'classical' would turn us in the right direction as we attempt to assess the linguistic evidence from Qumran.

[1] 'Melchisedech', p. 357.

[2] Cf. F. M. Cross, 'The Development of Jewish Scripts', pp. 214ff. and Figure 2, pp. 176–7.

[3] Van der Woude, 'Melchisedech', p. 355, discusses these difficulties quite frankly. Fragments 3 and 9 which include most of what is included in lines 21–6 cannot be placed where they are with any great certainty.

[4] *Ibid.* Fragments 5 and 11 cannot be placed at all.

ii.[1] Even the name given to the document, '11Q Melchizedek', may be a misnomer, and we cannot in the absence of other supporting evidence conclude that this document is a treatise on Melchizedek. With these reservations before us we may fruitfully proceed to the discussion of Melchizedek in the document.

The most important lines for our consideration are lines 9–11.

9. This is the time of the year of good favor for Melchize[dek and] he by his strength will ju[d]ge the holy ones of El, in the interests of a rei[g]n of justice, just as it is written 10. about him in the songs of David where it says, 'Elohim has [ta]ken his stand in the as[sembly of El.] In the midst of the Elohim he will give judgement...', and where it sa[ys, 11. 'Ab]ove it on high return to it. El will judge the peoples...', and where it sa[ys, 'How long will you] judge unjustly and lift [up] the faces of the evil ones? [Se]lah.'[2]

The antecedent of the masculine singular suffix on the word עליו at the beginning of line 10 is difficult to determine due to the lacunae of line 9. Van der Woude,[3] De Jonge and Van der Woude,[4] and J. A. Sanders[5] all take the antecedent to be the Melchizedek of line 9. Fitzmyer thinks that the suffix may refer either to Melchizedek or to משפט in line 9.[6] In support of משפט as the antecedent Professor Orval Wintermute has suggested to me that we find ישפוט in line 10b and תשפוטו in line 11. Certainly this shows a thematic unity, but it does not show that the antecedent of עליו is משפט. The case against this view is strong. Although it is not totally impossible, it is extremely unusual for the *nomen rectum* of a construct chain to serve as the antecedent of a following pronominal suffix. Here, however, this is impossible considering the type of genitive involved in the expression ממשלת משפט. The word משפט in this construction serves as a virtual adjective and has no independent sense. We could translate the words ממשלת משפט either as 'a reign of justice' or as 'a

---

[1] Cf. *ibid.* plates 1 and 2. Before Milik no attempt had been made to transcribe Column ii in the published literature since such a small amount may be read.
[2] For the full text in translation see p. 68.
[3] 'Melchisedech', p. 364.   [4] '11Q Melchizedek', p. 304.
[5] 'Dissenting Deities', p. 286.
[6] 'Further Light on Melchizedek', p. 36.

just reign'.[1] Were משפט a subjective or objective genitive, a case
might be made for Fitzmyer's suggestion, but since משפט is an
attributive genitive, his view must be rejected. We get some
evidence in favor of Melchizedek's being the antecedent by
noticing that the second עליו in line 10 has the closest preceding
masculine singular noun which is not in a construct relationship
as its antecedent,[2] and this is also true in line 19 where מבשר] טוב
is the antecedent of עליו. One thing is certain: whoever is indicated by the suffix on the first עליו in line 10 is also indicated by
the word אלוהים at the beginning of the quotation of Ps. lxxxii.
1. A weakness of Fitzmyer's suggestion about this line is that he
takes the suffix to refer to משפט and אלוהים to refer to Melchizedek.[3] This is impossible, removing any and all necessity for
taking אלוהים to refer to Melchizedek. If עליו refers to משפט,
then אלוהים should be translated 'God' and should be regarded
as a synonym of אל. The last piece of evidence which I offer in
support of my view that Melchizedek is the antecedent of עליו
and hence the same as אלוהים in line 10 comes from line 24
where we read אל.[ו]היך הואה[4] The author evidently thinks that
the אלוהיך of Isa. 52: 7 needs to be explained, something which
would be unnecessary if אלוהיך were understood as 'God' (אל).
The preponderance of the evidence supports the view that עליו
refers to the Melchizedek mentioned in line 9 and that this
figure is also called אלוהים in line 10.

If I am correct in my view that Melchizedek is the אלוהים of
the 11Q Melchizedek, then I must show how this fits in with the
rest of the document. It is known that in the Old Testament the
word אלהים, used as a virtual singular, may be employed to
refer to beings other than Yahweh. It may be used of other
deities as in 1 Sam. v. 7; Judges xi. 24; 1 Kings xviii. 24, etc.
An interesting usage is to be found in 1 Sam. xxviii. 13 where
the witch of Endor describes the ghost of Samuel as an אלהים:

ותאמר האשה אל שאול אלהים ראיתי עלים מן הארץ . . .

---

[1] Cf. G.–K. §128p.

[2] That is to say that the word Elohim is a plural used as a virtual singular
masculine noun.   [3] 'Further Light on Melchizedek', p. 37.

[4] Our judgement here must be tempered by the fact that this reading
occurs at the juncture of fragments 9 and 10, a juncture considered not
completely certain by Van der Woude, 'Melchisedech', p. 355.

This word is also the antecedent of a masculine plural participle
and hence this passage is not exactly parallel. We also have
passages in Exodus where Moses is said to be an Elohim. In the
first, Ex. iv. 16 (J), Aaron is to speak for Moses to the people and
Moses is to be 'as a god' to Aaron (ואתה תהיה לו לאלהים). The
same relationship is expressed again in Ex. vii. 1 (P):

ואלר יהוה אל משה ראה נתתיך אלהים לפרעה ואהרן אחיך יהיה נביאך

And Yahweh said to Moses, 'See I have given you to be a god to
Pharaoh, and Aaron your brother will be your prophet.'[1]

We may neglect Ps. xlv. 7 here since it does not materially effect
our conclusions.[2] We shall also not consider the many places in
which Elohim, used as an actual plural, is describing beings
other than Yahweh, both human and superhuman.[3] The wide
range of concepts surrounding the word Elohim in the Old
Testament is beyond my scope in this book, but at Qumran the
word is used rather infrequently, as opposed to El, as a title for
God.[4] There is rather good evidence that at Qumran the word
El was not only a replacement for Elohim, but also came to be
the standard replacement for the tetragrammaton. We sometimes find the word אל written 𐤋𐤀 in the archaic script,[5] an
orthography usually reserved for the name Yahweh.[6] The

---

[1] Martin Buber, *Moses: The Revelation and the Covenant* (Harper Torch-
books, The Temple Library, No. 837H; New York: Harper & Row,
Publishers, 1958), p. 59, takes the word אלהים to mean 'an inspiring power'.
Walther Eichrodt, *Theology of the Old Testament*, trans. J. A. Baker (The Old
Testament Library; Philadelphia: The Westminster Press, 1967), II, 290
and 293, takes these passages to refer to Moses' special position as mediator.
Our concern here is not for the meaning of the passages in the Old Testament but with their existence and potential meaning for our understanding
of אלהים in the 11Q Melchizedek.

[2] Cf. Chapter 2 above for a brief discussion of this passage.

[3] On this cf. Eichrodt, *Theology of the Old Testament*, I, 194 ff., for an excellent discussion of the angelic figures and their many titles.

[4] Kuhn, *Konkordanz zu den Quamrantexten*, p. 16, gives only seven references
for אלוהים as compared to three pages (*ibid.* pp. 12–14) for the word אל.
Although this does not exhaust the evidence, it does give us a good idea of
the relative frequency of usage.   [5] E.g. in 4Q 180. 1.

[6] This orthography is always used for the tetragrammaton in the 11Q
Ps[a]. Cf. James A. Sanders, *The Psalms Scroll of Qumran Cave II* (Discoveries in
the Judaean Desert of Jordan, No. 4; Oxford: The Clarendon Press, 1965).

tendency to prefer El in reference to God by the Qumranites and the precedents brought forward from the Old Testament go together to suggest that use of the word Elohim to refer to Melchizedek might not have been so unusual, and that it indicates that he was regarded as some sort of super-human figure.

This conclusion squares with what we find otherwise about Melchizedek in the 11Q Melchizedek. Melchizedek will appear at the end of days (line 9) to make atonement for all the sons of light (lines 6?, 8). He is to execute the judgements against the 'lot' of Belial (line 13), assisted by the angels (line 14). Melchizedek is more than a mere human figure, and on the basis of the rest of the text apart from lines 9–11 it would be correct to view him as a heavenly being. When we include lines 9–11 in our consideration, the text takes on more coherence. Melchizedek as Elohim has a place in the divine assembly where he gives judgement (line 10). This judgement is synonymous with the judgement of אל (line 11). This brings to an end the period of evil judgements (line 11), given, perhaps, by Belial.[1] The use of Ps. vii. 8–9 in lines 10–11 is confusing. The translation of these verses even in their Old Testament setting is difficult, the word שובה seeming to indicate that God should take his throne in the heavens. In the 11Q Melchizedek the antecedent of the feminine singular suffix on שובה is perhaps ממשלת in line 9, and the person addressed seems to be Melchizedek. If correct, this agrees with the constant repetition of the phrase מלך אלוהיך in the document, which has become the *Leitmotiv* of, at least, the extant portions of the text of the 11Q Melchizedek.[2] Melchizedek

---

[1] Note that the following line begins פשרו על בליעל. Certainly the period of evil judgements cannot refer to the judgements of Melchizedek or God.

[2] The influence of Isa. lxi. 1–2 is also to be detected within the document. Merrill Miller, 'The Function of Isa. 61₁₋₂', has claimed that Isa. lxi. 1–2 has provided certain *Stichwörter* throughout the 11Q Melchizedek. The improved reading of Yadin, *art. cit.* at line 18 והמבשר הואה משיח הרוח is taken to reflect the words of Isa. lxi. 1 רוח אדני יהוה עלי יען משח יהוה אתי. The phrase ויום נקם אלהינו from Isa. lxi. 2b he finds reflected in line 13 of the 11Q Melchizedek ומלכי צדק יקום נקמת משפטי אל (but note my reading יקים). The word השבויים in line 4 is also to be found in Isa. lxi. 1. Thus suggestion by Miller that Isa. lxi. 1–2 is the thematic passage around which the extant portions of the 11Q Melchizedek are formed must, however, be weighed against the obviously strong position of Isa. lii. 7. In my view J. T. Milik, '*Milkî-Ṣedeq* et *Milkî-Reša'*', has probably gone too far in adapting the text of the 11Q Melchizedek to Isa. lxi. 1–2.

appears in this document as the adversary of Belial. Both
Melchizedek and Belial have a 'lot'.[1] This usage is slightly different from what is usual at Qumran. References to the 'lot of
Belial', and 'the spirits of Belial's lot' are quite common at
Qumran, especially in the War Scroll. See, for instance, 1QM i.
5; iv. 2; xiii. 4. The equivalent expressions for those not of the
lot of Belial speak of a 'lot of El'; cf. 1QM i. 5; xiii. 5, etc. In
11Q Melch. i. 8, however, we find צדק [כי] מל[ורל ג]י אנש[י, and
in i. 5 we find מנחלת מלכי צדק. The 11Q Melchizedek is unusual,
then, in speaking of a 'lot of Melchizedek' where we would
expect a 'lot of El'.

Besides the figures already discussed, another eschatological
figure emerges in the 11Q Melchizedek, the מבשר. Almost certainly this is a figure other than Melchizedek, as Van der
Woude[2] and De Jonge and Van der Woude[3] agree. Fitzmyer
incorrectly holds that Melchizedek might be the מבשר.[4] There is
no direct link between the מבשר and Melchizedek except for the
words מלך אלוהיך which the מבשר declares, making the identity
of the two figures impossible. Considerable argument has arisen
over the reading of line 18 in the 11Q Melchizedek. In the first
edition of the text Van der Woude[5] read the beginning of the
line as והמבשר הו[אה מ[אה הוא]ה] אשר אמר. This is the reading
of Fitzmyer as well.[6] In the second edition of the text, however,
this reading was changed by De Jonge and Van der Woude to

המבשר הו[אה מ[שיח הרו[ח] אשר אמר.[7] We would do well to quote
them here: 'Contrary to the conjecture suggested in the editio
princeps it is now proposed to read והמבשר הו[אה מ[שיח הרו[ח] אשר
אמר. This agrees with Isa. lxi. 1 רוח אדני יהוה עלי יען משח יהוה
אתי לבשר and provides a remarkable parallel to CD ii. 12
which speaks of משיחי רוח קדשו, indicating the prophets
anointed with (God's) Holy Spirit.'[8] Of course there is nothing
at all remarkable in this since one always moves from the known
to the unknown. De Jonge and Van der Woude, following
Yadin,[9] found that the change reflected the wording of Isa. lxi. 1

---

[1] Cf. lines 5, 8, 9, 12, 13.

[2] 'Melchisedech', p. 367.

[3] '11Q Melchisedek', pp. 306ff.

[4] 'Further Light on Melchizedek', p. 40.

[5] 'Melchisedech', p. 358.

[6] 'Further Light on Melchizedek', p. 27.

[7] '11Q Melchisedek', pp. 306ff.   [8] *Ibid.*

[9] 'A Note on Melchizedek and Qumran', *IEJ* xv (1965), 152–4.

as well as the thought of CD ii. 12. If we follow De Jonge and Van der Woude we have an *A*-form[1] introductory formula, which is rather uncommon, whereas if we follow Fitzmyer and Van der Woude, we have the very usual *cA*-form הואה אשר אמר.[2] Even so, the revised text in this case is probably right. The only function ascribed to this anointed figure is that of proclaiming the message of Isa. lii. 7, which is to say that the anointed one is the eschatological prophet who announces the coming reign of Melchizedek. There is a similarity between the relationship of this anointed one to Melchizedek in the 11Q Melchizedek and that of Aaron to Moses in Ex. iv; 16; vii. 1 in that both serve as a prophet to a figure described as an Elohim.

There can be no doubt that the 11Q Melchizedek is a Qumranite document. Throughout the document we find typical expressions which expose its origins among the sectarians of the Dead Sea. The format of the 11Q Melchizedek is that of a *pēšer* (lines 12, 17). The evil being of the work is Belial (lines 7, 12, 13, 23, 26), a being who stands at the head of a 'lot' of men (lines 12, 13?). Against these stand 'the holy ones of El' (line 9), the 'sons of light' (line 8?) on earth, and the angels (line 14) on high. Quotations from the Torah (lines 2, 3, 6, 25), the Prophets (lines 1?, 15, 24), and the Writings (lines 10–11, 18?) are to be found in the document and applied to the sect and events concerning the sect. At the same time the 11Q Melchizedek is atypical of the Qumranite literature owing to its use of the figure of Melchizedek.

We have just enough of the original document to tell that the author considered Melchizedek to be a superior being of some sort who will appear at the end of days to bring atonement for the sons of light and who is the direct opponent of Belial. We do not have enough of the document left to satisfy our curiosity about how the Melchizedek of Gen. xiv and Ps. cx could become such a figure or even to say (apart from the conjectured reading of line 5) that the Melchizedek of the 11Q Melchizedek and the

---

[1] For the abbreviations see Horton, 'Formulas of Citation'.

[2] We have no other example in the 11Q Melchizedek of such a form and few examples in the other Qumran literature (cf. CD iv. 20; xvi. 10) of a pure אשר אמר form. The general rule seems to be that one must use a connective such as הוא or ו or resort to the *LA*-form in which connection is made by the object of the preposition. For more details see Horton, *ibid*.

Melchizedek of Gen. xiv and Ps. cx were considered by the author to be one and the same.[1]

Another strange factor is the scheme of events of the end time. Melchizedek as Elohim expresses the judgements of El in the heavenly assembly, but he is also the one who will exact the penalties associated with these judgements, aided by the angels. He does not accomplish this through one or more 'anointed ones', as the Spirit of Truth directs the course of the last war through the agency of two anointed figures in the War Scroll. Rather, the anointed one is a prophet who announces the reign of Melchizedek. This reign is a heavenly reign to be sure (cf. line 11), but it is presumably also an earthly reign. Do we have here a *deus descendens* myth? We cannot answer in the affirmative without qualification, but the text does suggest the possibility of Melchizedek's representing such a figure in part. Yet even if there is the suggestion that Melchizedek will descend from the heavens, there is nothing in the text to suggest anything like a reascent.[2]

As to the date of the composition of the 11Q Melchizedek we can have no certainty. We have seen that the palaeography of the fragments places them ca. A.D. 50, and there is some reason to think of this as close to the time of composition. We have no reflection of the figure of Melchizedek as a heavenly redeemer in any of the other Qumran documents. In fact, he is mentioned in only one other place, in the Genesis Apocryphon, where there is no hint of such a role. If Herbert Braun was incorrect in saying that Melchizedek was 'völlig uninteressant' for the community[3] (a position not totally defensible from the material available to him at the time), he was still correct to call our attention to the fact that Melchizedek is completely missing from the major documents of Qumran other than the Apocry-

---

[1] J. A. Sanders, 'Dissenting Deities', p. 290, says, 'In 11Q Melch the great high priest of Gen. 14 and Ps. 110 is made not only a deity...in the heavenly court, but is set over all other *elohim* as king, judge, and redeemer, in the final great eschatological drama.' This position agrees exactly with the interpretation given in this chapter, but one must recognize that except for the conjectured reading in line 5 made by this writer, there is no connection at all with either Gen. xiv or Ps. cx.

[2] See now Irvin W. Batdorf, 'Hebrews and Qumran: Old Methods and New Directions', *Festschrift to Honor F. Wilbur Gingrich* (Leiden: E. J. Brill, 1972), pp. 16–35.   [3] 'Qumran und das Neue Testament.'

phon. This is not simply an argument from silence since the functions assigned to Melchizedek in the 11Q Melchizedek are elsewhere either assigned to God or to other figures such as Michael. Nor does Melchizedek fit into speculation about heavenly beings usually associated with Qumran. He is not found in the cycles of tradition about angels known from the Ethiopian Enoch or in any of the Enochian material found at Qumran. Only in one recension of the Slavonic Enoch does material about Melchizedek merge with Enochian tradition, and this text falls far beyond the chronological bounds of this present study.[1] There is no hint in the extant portions of the 11Q Melchizedek of a revolt of heavenly beings against the heavenly council, and the only dissenting spirit is the traditional Belial. In the article by Van der Woude,[2] and in the article by De Jonge and Van der Woude,[3] it was suggested that Melchizedek shows similarity here to Michael in the War Scroll, and mention is made of an explicit identification of Melchizedek with Michael in two medieval Rabbinic texts.[4] I have noted independently some similarity in wording between the 11Q Melchizedek and the War Scroll as regards the use of the word גורל. In the War Scroll Michael is the Prince of Light (1QM xiii. 9f.), the angel through whom God has sent help to the sons of light for the final war (xvii. 5–9). He is the direct opponent of Belial, and mankind is divided between his lot, the 'lot of Belial', and the 'lot of El' headed by Michael. We note that the 11Q Melchizedek differs from this in some details. In 11Q Melchizedek mankind is divided between the 'lot of Belial' and the 'lot of Melchizedek'. Melchizedek will reign in the last days, and this is never posited of Michael in the War Scroll. The 11Q Melchizedek goes beyond the War Scroll's description of Michael. The medieval evidence for the equation of Michael and Melchizedek cannot be taken seriously in the form in which De Jonge and Van der Woude present it. Christian scholars certainly need to take more note of medieval Rabbinic exegesis

[1] For the text and translation cf. A. Vaillant, *Le Livre des Secrets d'Hénoch* (Textes Publiés par l'Institut des Études Slaves, No. 4; Paris: Institut des Études Slaves, 1952). Whatever the age of the oldest strands of this material, the story of Melchizedek's priesthood is very late though not necessarily entirely Christian.

[2] 'Melchisedech', pp. 367ff.   [3] '11Q Melchizedek', p. 305.

[4] *Ibid*. See also Milik, '*Milkî-Sedeq* et *Milkî-Reša*''.

and interpretation, but there is no more justification for quoting short texts out of context from such writers than there is for similar quotations from Christian writers.

It is probable that the writer of the 11Q Melchizedek knew the War Scroll, but the only evidence which we have for a date of composition directs our attention to a period later than the War Scroll and the other major documents from Qumran. Without further evidence there is no reason to think that our copy is anything other than the autograph and datable in the middle of the first century A.D.[1]

JOSEPHUS

Josephus mentions Melchizedek in his *War* vi. §438 and *Antiquities* i. §§179–81. The reference to Melchizedek in *War* §438 occurs at the end of Josephus' narration of the capture of Jerusalem and the destruction of the Temple by Titus. He reports that the founder of the city was a 'Canaanite chieftain' (Χαναναίων δύναστης) whose name in the mother tongue means 'righteous king'.[2] He was the first to build the Temple (τὸ ἱερόν) and for this reason the city, known at first as Solyma (Σολυμᾶ), was renamed Jerusalem (ἱερο-σόλυμα).[3] This impossible etymology is abandoned by Josephus in the *Antiquities* i. §180. Here it is reported that Melchizedek was king of Solyma, a town later (ὕστερον) called Jerusalem. The passage in the *Antiquities* represents a paraphrase of Gen. xiv. 18–20.[4] Josephus solves the difficulty of the transition between Gen. xiv. 17 and xiv. 18 by having Melchizedek receive Abraham in the 'Plain

---

[1] Frank Moore Cross, *The Ancient Library of Qumran*, rev. ed. (Anchor Books, No. A272; Garden City, N.Y.: Doubleday & Company, Inc., 1961), pp. 119f., notes that the major sectarian scrolls such as the Rule, the Damascus Document, etc., date palaeographically from the first half of the first century B.C. With all of the material from Qumran, it stretches the imagination to think that if the 11Q Melchizedek were as old as these documents, a period of some 150 years could pass (during which time a great number of the documents which we have from Qumran were composed) without there being some indication of such a tradition.

[2] On Josephus' use of Hebrew names cf. D. A. Schlatter, *Die hebräischen Namen bei Josephus* (Beiträge zur Förderung christlicher Theologie, vol. xvii, 3; Gütersloh: C. Bertelsmann, 1913).   [3] *War*, vi. §438.

[4] We do not mean by this that we think Josephus is being fanciful, but this is what Wuttke, *Melchisedech*, p. 18, means when he says that this is a paraphrase.

of Kings'.[1] In i. §181 Josephus makes much of the gifts and provisions which Melchizedek gave not only to Abraham but also to the men with Abraham. In the course of the festivities (παρὰ τὴν εὐωχίαν) Melchizedek delivered a blessing to God who had delivered Abraham's enemies into his hand. Although both passages have their own functions, there is a literary relationship between the two which is important for our purposes. This relationship may best be shown by putting parts of the two passages together for examination.

...κληθεὶς βασιλεὺς δίκαιος· ἦν γὰρ δὴ τοιοῦτος. διὰ τοῦτο ἱεράσατό τε τῷ θεῷ πρῶτος...	σεμαίνει δὲ τοῦτο βασιλεὺς δίκαιος· καὶ ἦν τοιοῦτος ὁμολογουμένως ὡς διὰ ταύτην αὐτὸν αἰτίαν καὶ ἱερέα γενέσθαι τοῦ θεοῦ.
(*War* vi. §438)	(*Antiquities* i. §180)

The literary similarities, of course, may be explained as coming from a single author, but the use of the word ὁμολογουμένως in *Antiquities* i. §180 suggests the possibility that Josephus is here delivering a tradition or popular saying about Melchizedek. It is also interesting to note that in *War*. vi §438 Melchizedek is described as the first one to do priestly service before God. Does Josephus mean the first ever, or the first to do such service in Jerusalem? Melchizedek in both passages becomes a priest because he is a righteous king. No attempt is made to relate the Aaronic or Zadokite priesthood to Melchizedek. In fact, in the section immediately following the passage quoted from the *War*, Josephus says that David drove all of the Canaanites out of Jerusalem and settled his own people there. The idea that the first temple was built by Melchizedek is dropped in the *Antiquities*, but one wonders if this idea might not represent a ἱερὸς λόγος about the Temple in Jerusalem. Unfortunately we do not have enough supporting information on this last point to justify our taking a positive position.

CONCLUSIONS

We have now come to the end of our discussion of the sources which may be viewed as background to the use of Melchizedek by the author of the Epistle to the Hebrews. It will be remembered that in Chapter 2 we found no support for the idea that

[1] πεδίον βασιλικόν, LXX: πεδίον βασιλέως.

Melchizedek possessed a divine priest-kingship of the pre-Israelite city of Jerusalem. We found that there was some support, though not unequivocal support, for the idea that Melchizedek had been a Canaanite chieftain of pre-Israelite Jerusalem, and I further suggested that this function might conceivably be designated by the title כהן. The materials discussed in this present chapter which stem from the first century B.C. and the first century A.D. leave me with the same doubts about the historical person Melchizedek which I had in Chapter 2, but we do see the seeds of the traditions about Melchizedek forming which will blossom forth in the later literature, to be discussed in the next chapter. Before we proceed to the later material, however, we should take stock of what we have already found about Melchizedek from the background sources.

As an aid to this part of the discussion, certain elements of the various traditions about Melchizedek have been arranged in a chart against the sources which we have examined. Although the exact configurations of the data depend upon the wording used, certain common features emerge in rather clear fashion (see below, Table 3.1, p. 86). Notice first of all that Philo, Josephus, and the Genesis Apocryphon show several points of agreement. Some of these agreements, of course, are due to their common source in Genesis. Others are not, especially items 15 and 16. It was mentioned in Chapter 2 that Gen. xiv. 20 does not make clear who gave the tithe, and I gave some reasons for thinking that the author may have meant to say that Melchizedek gave a tithe to Abram. Philo, Josephus, and the Genesis Apocryphon all agree that Abram gave the tithe to Melchizedek. This could be inferred from the text of Gen. xiv, but it is not necessarily to be inferred. All three likewise agree that Melchizedek entertained not only Abram but also the warriors who were with him. Again, it would be possible to infer this from Gen. xiv, but not necessary. In addition to the places where Philo, Josephus, and the Genesis Apocryphon all three agree, there are places where two of these agree and the third is silent.[1] Josephus and the Genesis Apocryphon both agree that Salem is Jerusalem. Josephus and Philo both agree that מלכי צדק should be understood as βασιλεὺς δίκαιος. Philo and the Genesis Apo-

---

[1] Never do we find that one of these sources offers information in direct contradiction to information found in the other two.

cryphon both mention that Melchizedek was priest of El Elyon. Interestingly enough, we see that the Genesis Apocryphon offers no unique information about Melchizedek. Josephus gives three items of information not found in the other sources, and Philo four. One wonders, however, whether Philo and Josephus might not be closer together on one point than is indicated by this analysis. This point is that of Melchizedek's priesthood. Josephus claims that Melchizedek was the founder of the first temple in Jerusalem and was also the first priest before God. This certainly does not contradict what Philo says and could actually be taken as offering a rationale for Philo's position that Melchizedek's priesthood was untutored and unique. Were Philo to find a tradition such as is handed on by Josephus, he might naturally mold the tradition into conformity with his idea of the αὐτομαθής καὶ αὐτοδίδακτος σοφός which we found to be thematic in Philo.[1] The Table further emphasizes what we had already found, that the 11Q Melchizedek offers thoroughly unique information about Melchizedek. The emphasis on Melchizedek as an angelic, eschatological figure is something on a different plane from Philo, Josephus, and the Genesis Apocryphon. Even Philo's making of Melchizedek into a representation of the Logos has nothing to do with what we find in the 11Q Melchizedek, since Philo, as we saw above, is practising allegorical exegesis on a figure which he believed to be thoroughly human and historical. We have here the suggestion of two separate streams of tradition, the one represented by Philo, Josephus, and the Genesis Apocryphon, and the other represented in the fragments of the 11Q Melchizedek. The only objection to a two-fold division might be the fact that Josephus and the Genesis Apocryphon agree that Salem is Jerusalem, whereas Philo shows no knowledge of this. It is true that we might reasonably expect Philo to mention that Salem is Jerusalem if he had received this information, even though strictly this is an argument from silence. However, it is not unreasonable to suggest that Philo did not know of this equation while at the same time he shared other pieces of information common to the interpretation of Gen. xiv by Josephus and the Genesis Apocryphon. We note that a source roughly contemporaneous with Philo, the Genesis Apocryphon, has the Salem = Jeru-

---

[1] Cf. above, pp. 55 and 55 n. 2.

salem equation. Perhaps this identification reflects a special Palestinian or Jerusalemite tradition unimportant to, or unknown to, those outside of Palestine.

We now move to consider those sources which are later than the Epistle to the Hebrews with a view to finding any connections with the earlier sources. We should be especially mindful of the suggested division of tradition hinted at in the 11Q Melchizedek to see whether this hypothesis can be maintained.

Table 3.1

	Gen. xiv	Ps. cx	Philo	Josephus	Gen. Ap.	11Q Melch.
1. King of Salem	×	.	×	×	×	.
2. Priest	×	×	×	×	×	× ?
3. Salem = Jerusalem	.	.	.	×	×	.
4. Priest of El Elyon	×	.	×	.	×	.
5. Founder of Temple	.	.	.	× ×	.	.
6. Founder of Jerusalem	.	.	.	× ×	.	.
7. Heavenly figure	.	.	.	.	.	× ×
8. First priest to God	.	.	.	× ×	.	.
9. Unlearned priesthood	.	.	× ×	.	.	.
10. βασιλεὺς δίκαιος	.	.	×	×	.	.
11. King of peace	.	.	× ×	.	.	.
12. Logos	.	.	× ×	.	.	.
13. Eschatological figure	.	.	.	.	.	× ×
14. Friend of Abraham	.	.	× ×	.	.	.
15. Receives tithe	× ?	.	×	×	×	.
16. Entertains army	.	.	×	×	×	.
17. Elohim	.	.	.	.	.	× ×

NOTES × – information given by source. × × – unique information given by source. × ? – information perhaps given by source.

CHAPTER 4

THE LATER SOURCES I:
THE EARLY CHURCH AND THE RABBIS

INTRODUCTION

It is surprising that the figure of Melchizedek in Hebrews received little notice in the earlier writings of the fathers of the church, but the evidence of the written records tends to indicate that Christian interest in Melchizedek began to develop seriously only towards the end of the second century A.D. and the beginning of the third century A.D. By way of contrast, interest in Melchizedek among the Rabbis is already to be noted in the early part of the second century A.D. This chapter is devoted to the development of the tradition about Melchizedek in the early church and among the Rabbis within the first five centuries of our era. The Gnostic sources are too extensive to be dealt with in this chapter and I have therefore given over a separate chapter to their discussion (see Chapter 5). Since we are dealing with literary documents later than Hebrews, we shall have to be especially conscious of its influence on the sources described in these next two chapters. I shall leave for the last chapter consideration of the meaning of the figure of Melchizedek in Hebrews.

THE EARLY CHURCH

Epiphanius of Salamis, writing in the last quarter of the fourth century A.D.,[1] suggests that there may indeed have been a wide latitude allowed for speculation about Melchizedek as a divine or angelic being in the early church.[2] Usually we are informed

---

[1] For a discussion of the date of composition for his *Panarion* see Johannes Quasten, *Patrology*, III: *The Golden Age of Greek Patristic Literature from the Council of Nicaea to the Council of Chalcedon* (Westminster, Maryland: The Newman Press, 1960), 388, who assigns it to the year A.D. 377.

[2] *Panarion* LV. 7. 3:
'Εν δὲ τῇ ἐκκλησίᾳ φύσει τινὲς διαφόρως τοῦτον τὸν Μελχισεδὲκ ὁρίζονται. οἱ μὲν γὰρ αὐτὸν νομίζουσι φύσει τὸν υἱὸν τοῦ θεοῦ, ἐν ἰδέᾳ δὲ ἀνθρώπου τότε τῷ 'Αβραὰμ πεφηνέναι. *(cont.)*

of this speculation only as it arose within heretical movements and was countered by the church fathers. The only break in this picture is the report of Jerome at the beginning of the fifth century A.D.[1] that Origen considered Melchizedek to be an angel or supernatural power of some kind, an opinion also held by his secretary Didymus.[2] In searching the fathers, Jerome found that, except for Origen, those who dealt with Melchizedek all considered him to be a man, a Canaanite, and the king of Jerusalem.[3] In general the function of Melchizedek for the

This resembles closely the heresy condemned later by Mark the Hermit (see below), but the important point to be made here is that even though Epiphanius disagrees with this view (LV. 7. 4), he does not seem free to condemn it as a heresy as he does the thought of the Melchizedekians. I am using the text of Karl Holl, *Die Griechischen Christlichen Schriftsteller der ersten drei Jahrhunderte: Epiphanius*, vol. II (Leipzig: J. C. Hinrichs'sche Buchhandlung, 1922). The chapter devoted to the Melchizedekians (chapter 55) is to be found on pp. 324–37. Since there is no translation of the *Panarion* into any modern language, all translations from the *Panarion* will be mine.

[1] Cf. F. Cayré, *Manual of Patrology and History of Theology*, I, trans. H. Howitt (Paris: Desclée & Co., 1936), 586–7. As we shall see below, this letter No. 73 fits the situation as we know it right at the turn of the century.

[2] 'Statimque in fronte Geneseos primam omeliarum Origenis repperi scriptam de Melchisedech, in qua multiplici sermone disputans illuc devolutus est, et eum angelum diceret, isdemque paene argumentis, quibus scriptor tuus de spiritu sancto, ille de supernis virtutibus est locutus. Transivi ad Didymum, sectatorem eius, et vidi hominem pedibus in magistri isse sententiam.' For the full text see Isidorus Hilberg, *Sancti Eusebii Hieronymi Epistulae* (Corpus Scriptorum Ecclesiasticorum Latinorum, vol. LV; Leipzig: G. Freytag, 1912), II, 13–23. I shall discuss this epistle at greater length later. W. Baehrens, *Überlieferung und Textgeschichte der lateinisch erhaltenen Origeneshomilien zum Alten Testament* (Texte und Untersuchungen zur Geschichte der altchristlichen Literatur, vol. XLII/I; Leipzig: J. C. Hinrichs'-sche Buchhandlung, 1916), pp. 6–8, thinks that the fragment of a homily given in the Catenae-MS Barber. Graec. vi. 8 (579)f. 128r is from the homily referred to here by Jerome. The relevant portion reads:
ἐπειδὴ μήτε ἀρχὴν ἡμερῶν μήτε ζωῆς τέλος ἔχειν Μελχισεδὲκ ὁ θεσπέσιος Παῦλος ἔφη ταύτῃ τοι καὶ δύναμιν λογικὴν καὶ ἱερουργὸν ὑπάρχειν αὐτὸν διαβεβαιούσθωσαν.
The suggestion made by De Jonge and Van der Woude, '11Q Melchizedek and the New Testament', p. 323 n. 2, that this passage corresponds closely to the argument of Cyril of Alexandria has little to recommend it.

[3] *Ep. ad Evangelum* LXXIII. 1. One cannot escape the impression that here Jerome is following the tradition also known to Josephus more than any of the fathers he cites. This is especially true where he says that 'Melchisedech hominem fuisse Chananaeum, regem urbis Hierosolymae, quae primum Salem, postea Iebus, ad extremum Hierusalem appellata sit'. Note the

church fathers was that of a priest of the uncircumcision, a priesthood carried on through Christ. For them the Aaronic or Levitical priesthood was subordinate to the more inclusive priesthood of Melchizedek, and the priesthood of Christ once again took up this former, greater priesthood of Melchizedek. This priesthood is understood as being continued in the priesthood of the church.[1] Interest in the bread and wine brought out by Melchizedek to Abram as prototypes of the elements of the Eucharist was first taken by Clement of Alexandria writing around the beginning of the third century A.D.[2]

The great majority of writings about Melchizedek in the early church stem from writers opposing heretics who make of Melchizedek a heavenly being. These writings are of prime interest for us and form the basis for our further discussion. I shall deal in turn with the Melchizedekians, Hierakas, and the Melchizedek heresies at the turn of the fifth century A.D.

Greek derivation of the name *Hierusalem* which we also found in Josephus, *War* vi. 438. This, however, may have been a common Palestinian tradition.

[1] Cf. for instance, Justin Martyr, *Dialogue with Trypho* §33 (ca. A.D. 155):

καὶ οὗτος τῶν ἐν ἀκροβυστίᾳ ἱερεὺς ἦν, καὶ τὸν ἐν περιτομῇ δεκάτας αὐτῷ προσενέγκαντα ᾿Αβραὰμ εὐλόγησεν, οὕτως τὸν αἰώνιον αὐτοῦ ἱερέα, καὶ κύριον ὑπὸ τοῦ ἁγίου πνεύματος καλούμενον, ὁ θεὸς τῶν ἀκροβυστίᾳ γενήσεσθαι ἐδήλου.

'And this one (Melchizedek) was priest of those who were in uncircumcision, and he blessed Abraham who was in circumcision, who offered him tithes. Thus God has shown that his eternal priest, also called "Lord" by the Holy Spirit, would become priest of those in uncircumcision.'

For a complete discussion of this point see M. Simon, 'Melchisédech dans la polémique entre juifs et chrétiens et dans la légende', *Revue d'Histoire et de Philosophie Religieuses*, XVII (1937), 64ff. Gustave Bardy, 'Melchisédech dans la tradition patristique', *RB*, XXXV (1926), 499f., gives further references and concludes that for the most part the fathers did not depart from Gen. xiv for their information about Melchizedek. Tertullian makes the same point as does Justin when he says, 'Melchisedech quoque, summi Dei sacerdos, incircumcisus et non sabbatizans ad sacerdotium Dei allectus est' (*Adv. Iud.* §2, MSL 2, 600). As I stated in Chapter 1, I shall not follow this line of discussion in the present chapter but will concentrate on the discussion which deals with Melchizedek as an angelic being. The reader is referred for more information to the articles by Bardy and Simon.

[2] Bardy, 'Melchisédech dans la tradition patristique', p. 500, notes that Tertullian who wrote about the same time as Clement of Alexandria makes no use of the bread and wine as symbols of the Eucharist when he mentions them in *Adv. Iud.* §3 (MSL 2, 602). Why the fathers were so slow to pick up what seems to us to be an obvious parallel between Gen. xiv and the

The Melchizedekians

Our single most important source for the Melchizedekians is the refutation made of them by Hippolytus, *Refutation of All Heresies* VII. 35–6, and X. 23–4. Since X. 23–4 is but a recapitulation of VII. 35–6, I shall give only the latter which has proved to be normative for later writers.

VII. 35   A certain Theodotus who was from Byzantium introduced a new heresy, holding as regards the origin of everything partly what is in accord with the teachings of the true church, and confessing that all things are brought into being by God. Yet, having branched off from the school of the Gnostics, Cerinthus and Ebion, he says that Christ appeared in just this way, i.e. that Jesus was a man who was begotten from a virgin according to the will of the Father and who lived in common with all men. Since he had been most holy, finally at his baptism at the Jordan the Christ came from above in the form of a dove. Wherefore it was not from the first that the powers operated in him, but when the Spirit which had come down was displayed in him, the Spirit who greeted him as being the Christ. They want to hold that he never did become *theos* upon the descent of the Spirit, and others say that he became *theos* only after the resurrection from the dead.

36   Different questions having arisen among them, a certain one, himself called Theodotus, a banker by trade, attempted to say that a certain Melchizedek is the great power, and this one is greater than Christ, in whose likeness, they say, the Christ happens to be. And they, like the aforementioned Theodotians, say that Jesus is a man and just like them that the Christ came down unto him.[1]

Hippolytus represents the Melchizedekians as being a splinter group among the Theodotians, differing mainly in their understanding of the heavenly position of Christ. If we take VII. 36 at face value, we perceive a three-fold scheme: (1) Melchizedek is the highest heavenly power (δύναμις); (2) the Christ is formed in the likeness of this highest power; and (3) the Christ descended upon Jesus at the latter's baptism. This simply adds another step

Eucharist is difficult to say. Note, however, that the Epistle to the Hebrews also makes nothing of this parallel for whatever reason. Perhaps the reluctance of the fathers to pick up this typology is due, at least in part, to the silence of Hebrews. Even after Cyril the typology was not extensively used by the fathers.

[1] My translation.

to the Theodotian adoptionism described in VII. 35 in which it is said only that the Christ descended upon Jesus in the form of a dove at his baptism. Although Hippolytus suggests that Theodotus of Byzantium 'branched off' (ἀποσπάσας) from the Gnostics, he admits that Theodotus' cosmological views were thoroughly orthodox and found Theodotus wanting only as regards the incarnation. I suspect that Hippolytus is indulging in name-calling at the expense of perfectly accurate detail. 'Branching off' actually implies nothing more serious than a certain affinity between Theodotus and the Gnostics on the issue of the incarnation: Jesus became the Christ through adoption.

Theodotus of Byzantium came to Rome around A.D. 190 and taught there until he was excommunicated by Pope Victor for teaching that Jesus was a mere man (ψιλὸς ἄνθρωπος).[1] The work of Theodotus of Byzantium is said by the author of the 'Little Labyrinth' to have been continued by Theodotus the banker together with one Asclepiodotus.[2] According to this account Theodotus and Asclepiodotus formed a heretical sect and appointed a certain Natalus as bishop with a monthly

---

[1] Eusebius, *HE*, v. 2. 9. Cf. Williston Walker, *A History of the Christian Church*, rev. Cyril C. Richardson, Wilhelm Pauck, and Robert T. Handy (New York: Charles Scribner's Sons, 1959), pp. 68–9. For a longer discussion see Adolph Harnack, *History of Dogma*, III, trans. Neil Buchanan (New York: Dover Publications, 1961), 20–32. Also see J. N. D. Kelly, *Early Christian Doctrines* (2nd ed.; New York: Harper & Row, Publishers, 1960), pp. 115–19. The most extensive work on the Melchizedekians is that of Hellmuth Stork, *Die sogenannten Melchizedekianer mit Untersuchungen ihrer Quellen auf Gedankengehalt und dogmengeschichtliche Entwicklung* (Forschungen zur Geschichte des neutestamentlichen Kanons und der altkirchlichen Literatur, vol. VIII/2; Leipzig: A. Deichert, 1928). This last work has, unfortunately, not been available to me.

[2] The 'Little Labyrinth' is usually ascribed to Hippolytus. Cf. Harnack, *History of Dogma* III, 20 n. 1, and Edgar J. Goodspeed, *A History of Early Christian Literature*, rev. Robert M. Grant (Chicago: The University of Chicago Press, 1966), p. 147. The latter suggests that the 'Little Labyrinth' formed something of a supplement to the *Refutation* which in X. 5 calls itself a λαβύρινθος τῶν αἱρεσέων. Whatever the value of this position, Eusebius, *HE* v. 28 does give three quotations from a polemical writing directed against Artemon, a source which cannot be much later than the date conjectured by Goodspeed for the writing by Hippolytus of his supplement. This means that whether or not Hippolytus is the author of the tradition to be found in Eusebius, we are still dealing with material from roughly the

salary of 150 denarii.[1] Further along the same writer insists that followers of the sect applied themselves to philosophy, mathematics, and natural science, and that they held Aristotle, Theophrastus, and Galen in special esteem.[2] It should be obvious that there is a certain amount of tension between this account and the account of Hippolytus quoted above, but the tension is capable of resolution. Even if the Melchizedekians[3] did arise as a splinter group out of the larger body of Theodotians, the excommunication of Theodotus of Byzantium might well have left the leadership of the movement open to be filled by Theodotus the banker in which case Melchizedekianism and Theodotianism would again be one. We may test this reconstruction by reference to other sources to which we now proceed.

In addition to the account given by Hippolytus in his *Refutation of All Heresies*, and the account of the 'Little Labyrinth', there are other accounts of the movement begun by Theodotus the banker. An extremely important account is given by Pseudo-Tertullian, *Against All Heresies* §28[4] in which it is stated

first third or first half of the third century A.D. For convenience we shall refer to this tradition cited by Eusebius as the 'Little Labyrinth' without necessarily agreeing with the position that Hippolytus was the author. The passage to which we have reference here is *HE* v. 28. 8.

[2] *HE* v. 28. 10.

[2] *HE* v. 28. 14. Kelly, *Early Christian Doctrines*, p. 117, suggests that the Theodotians might well have belonged to the circle of Galen in Rome.

[3] Hippolytus never actually uses the word 'Melchizedekian', and it is first used only by Epiphanius, *Panarion* LV. Until we are able to give more substance to the word, we shall mean by 'Melchizedekians' those who followed Theodotus the banker, reserving the name 'Theodotians' for the followers of Theodotus of Byzantium. We are not, however, excluding the possibility that they are one and the same.

[4] The full text reads: 'Accedet his Theodotus haereticus Byzantius, qui posteaquam Christi pro nomine comprehensus negavit, in Christum blasphemare non destitit. Doctrinam enim introduxit, qua Christum hominem tantummodo diceret, Deum autem illum negaret; ex spiritu quidem sancto natum ex virgine, sed hominem solitarium, atque nudum, nulla alia prae caeteris, nisi sola justitiae auctoritate. Alter post hunc Theodotus haereticus erupit, qui et ipse introduxit alteram sectam, et ipsum hominem Christum tantummodo dicit ex Spiritu Sancto, ex virgine Maria conceptum pariter et natum; sed hunc inferiorem esse quam Melchisedech, eo quod dictum sit de Christo: "Tu es sacerdos in aeternum secundum ordinem Melchisedech." Nam illum Melchisedech praecipuae gratiae coelestem esse virtutem: eo quod agat Christus pro hominibus deprecator et advocatus ipsorum factus Melchisedech facere pro coelestibus angelis atque virtutibus, nam esse illum

that Theodotus of Byzantium introduced a new doctrine which described Christ[1] as being 'merely a man' (*hominem tantummodo*). On the other hand Theodotus the banker introduced another sect (*alteram sectam*) in which it was held that Melchizedek was heavenly power (*coelestem...virtutem*). This account follows the outline set forth by Hippolytus, *Refutation* VII. 35–6, but it changes the relative weight of importance of the two men named Theodotus from what is found in the *Refutation*. Special interest falls on the sect which arose around Theodotus the banker, and a somewhat different picture of the roles of Christ and Melchizedek is presented from that presented in the *Refutation*. According to Pseudo-Tertullian Melchizedek is to act as 'intercessor and advocate' (*deprecator et advocatus*) for the heavenly beings, and Christ is to play the same role for men. Melchizedek is the greater of the two since he is without mother, father or genealogy, having neither a beginning nor an end, and is not capable of being comprehended. This, of course, is a direct reference to Heb. vii. 3, unlike the account of the *Refutation* which contained no such direct reference. Although the superiority of Melchizedek is retained here, it is important to observe that the reason for this superiority is different also from that given in the *Refutation*. Christ had a mother and hence a genealogy, and it is for this reason that he cannot be as great as Melchizedek who has no parentage.

We can see that Pseudo-Tertullian has followed the arrangement set out by Hippolytus in his *Refutation* although the relationship of Theodotus of Byzantium to the followers of Theodotus the banker is somewhat different. The *Refutation* presents the Melchizedekians as a branch of the Theodotians. Pseudo-Tertullian, on the other hand, presents Theodotus of Byzantium as simply introducing a new doctrine, whereas Theodotus the banker organized a new sect. This agrees with the 'Little Labyrinth' even though no mention is made of Natalus or Asclepiodotus. However, it diverges from the 'Little Labyrinth'

usque adeo Christo meliorem, ut apator sit, ametor sit, agenealogetos sit, cujus neque initium, neque finis comprehensus sit aut comprehendi possit.' (MSL 2, 91B–92A.)

[1] We can only assume that at this point Pseudo-Tertullian means Jesus upon whom the Christ descended, but the rhetorical effect of saying that the Theodotians held that Christ was a mere man may have led him to misrepresent them to this extent on purpose.

to the extent that the latter represents Theodotus the banker as carrying on the program of Theodotus of Byzantium. The work of Pseudo-Tertullian has the importance of showing contacts with both the *Refutation* and the 'Little Labyrinth' while at the same time offering new information.

When we add the account of Philastius[1] we have gained very little in the way of new information, though we notice that he does not mention Theodotus the banker by name and uses instead a plural subject as though speaking of a group. Our last main source is the report of Epiphanius on the Melchizedekians which is to be found in his *Panarion* LV. As we have already seen,[2] this work dates from A.D. 377 and hence is very late relative to the *Refutation* of Hippolytus. The amount of information actually available in the *Panarion* about the Melchizedekians is disappointing. Epiphanius, in his typically loose style,[3] spends more time in chapter LV on misuse of the figure of Melchizedek among other groups than he does on the doctrine or history of the Melchizedekians. The initial paragraph of chapter LV is the most important, and I quote at length in translation:

Further,[4] others call themselves Melchizedekians, perhaps having branched off from those called Theodotians. They revere the Melchizedek who is mentioned in the scriptures, believing him to be some great power and to exist above in ineffable places, and actually holding him to be not only some power, but also, by this error of theirs, they consider him a greater power than Christ. They hold that Christ simply came and was considered worthy of Melchizedek's order. They actually claim on the basis of the word of scripture which says, 'You are a priest forever according to the order of Melchizedek', that he was inferior to Melchizedek. Now concerning Melchizedek himself, they say that he was 'without father, without mother, without genealogy...' hoping to demonstrate this from the Epistle to the Hebrews of the holy Paul. Also they fabricate false books for themselves, deceiving themselves. (*Panarion* LV. 1. 1–5)

[1] Ca. A.D. 383–91. Cf. Cayré, *Manual of Patrology*, I, 604. The passage in question comes from his *Haer.* LII and we give it as quoted by Bardy, 'Melchisédech dans la tradition patristique', p. 505: 'Post istos alii recedentes ab his edixerunt similia. addunt etiam Melchisedech sacerdotem dicentes virtutem Dei magnam esse, et nomina quaedam diversa hominum adserunt a fide catholica dissonantes.'

[2] See above, p. 87 n. 1.   [3] Cf. Quasten, *Patrology*, III, 388.

[4] Chapter LV follows a chapter devoted to the Theodotians, thus recapitulating the order set down by Hippolytus.

This passage shows agreement with the sources already mentioned. The order in which Epiphanius deals with the Melchizedekians follows that of Hippolytus' *Refutation*, i.e. the Melchizedekians follow the Theodotians. Further, Epiphanius suggests that the Melchizedekians may have branched off from the Theodotians, but he does not seem to have the same assurance on this fact that Hippolytus has. There are also points of agreement with Pseudo-Tertullian and with the 'Little Labyrinth'. Epiphanius quotes from Ps. cx. 4 and Heb. vii. 3 as does Pseudo-Tertullian. Secondly, Epiphanius quotes the Melchizedekians as saying that Melchizedek is a heavenly power, whereas in the *Refutation* there is no mention of Melchizedek's existing in the heavens. The agreement with the 'Little Labyrinth' is in the fact that the followers of Theodotus the banker fabricated false books for themselves. The only other place where we can be certain that Epiphanius is speaking of the Melchizedekians is in LV. 8 where he says that the Melchizedekians make offerings in the name of Melchizedek since Melchizedek is a heavenly priest who intercedes for man eternally. The basis for this assertion is that God has made Melchizedek an 'Archon of Righteouness' which, though a rendering of the Hebrew name מלכי צדק, also has cosmological implications for Epiphanius. Here is the only other hint of 'Gnosticism' in the thought of the Melchizedekians, the first being Hippolytus' suggestion that Theodotus of Byzantium broke off from the school of the Gnostics. Nothing more is said about this cultic intercessory activity, and it is difficult to determine the worth of Epiphanius' account of this activity. We shall see later that there are Gnostic prayers in the Second Book of Ieû which invoke Melchizedek's name, and it is possible that Epiphanius has here assigned to the Melchizedekians a cultic practice known to him from a contemporary Gnostic sect.[1] If this were true, then the only discussion of the Melchizedekians proper would be found in the paragraph from the *Panarion* just quoted (LV. 1.1–5). In point of fact Epiphanius' discussion in chapter LV relates more to groups other than the Melchizedekians than to the Melchizedekians themselves.

[1] In Chapter 6 below we shall see that this sect was current in the fourth century and that the Second Book of Ieû was written in the early part of that century.

Other sources for the Melchizedekians are clearly secondary. One has only to refer the reader to the brief notations of St Augustine (first quarter of the fifth century A.D.),[1] Isidore of Spain (first third of the seventh century A.D.,[2] St John of Damascus (first half of the eighth century A.D.);[3] Theodoret,[4] writing in the first third of the fifth century A.D. uses a freer style than the others mentioned, but he offers nothing new. This leaves us with four major touchstones for the Melchizedekians: Hippolytus, *Refutation* VII. 35–6 (X. 23–4); Pseudo-Tertullian, *Against All Heresies* § 28; the 'Little Labyrinth'; and Epiphanius, *Panarion* LV. 1. 1–5. Of these four sources we note that each of the first three makes a unique contribution to our knowledge about the Melchizedekians, but the same cannot be said about Epiphanius. Leaving Epiphanius aside for the moment, we find that the first three sources provide us with our most important information about the Melchizedekians. Further, all three go together better than any two of them. Pseudo-Tertullian here plays a mediating role. As we have seen, although the 'Little Labyrinth' and the *Refutation* are in tension, Pseudo-Tertullian finds points of agreement with both. Also Pseudo-Tertullian may make clear certain problems which we have with the other two accounts.

The reason why Melchizedek is understood to be superior to Christ in the *Refutation* is because Christ is 'according to the image' of Melchizedek (so also Epiphanius). What is meant here by κατ' εἰκόνα is made clear by Pseudo-Tertullian who

---

[1] *De Haeresibus* I. 34 (MSL 42, 31): 'Melchisedeciani, Melchisedec sacerdotem Dei excelsi, non hominem fuisse, sed virtutem Dei esse arbitrantur.'

[2] *Etymologiarum* VIII. 5. 17 (MSL 82, 299C): 'Melchisedechiani vocati pro eo quod Melchisedech sacerdotem Dei, non hominem fuisse, sed virtutem Dei esse arbitrantur.' This is practically a quotation from Augustine as cited above.

[3] *De Haeresibus* II. 55 (MSG 94, 712):

Μελχισεδεκιανοί· οὗτοι τὸν Μελχισεδὲκ γεραίροντες, τινὰ δύναμιν αὐτὸν φάσκοντες, καὶ μὴ μόνον ἄνθρωπον ψιλόν, καὶ εἰς τὸ τούτου ὄνομα πάντα ἀγαγεῖν τετολμηκότες.

[4] *Haereticarum Fabularum* II, 6 (MSG 83, 392D–393A):

Περὶ Μελχισεδεκιανῶν· τοὺς δὲ Μελχισεδεκιανοὺς τμῆμα μὲν εἶναι τούτων φασὶ καθ' ἕν δὲ μόνον διαφωνεῖν τὸ τὸν Μελχισεδὲκ δύναμίν τινα καὶ θείαν καὶ μεγίστην ὑπολαμβάνειν, κατ' εἰκόνα δὲ αὐτοῦ τὸν χριστὸν γεγενῆσθαι. Ἦρξε δὲ τῆς αἱρέσεως ταύτης ἄλλος Θεόδοτος ἀργυραμοιβὸς τὴν τέχνην.

shows that the sect believed that Melchizedek had the role of intercessor and advocate for the angels whereas Christ had the same role for men. Pseudo-Tertullian also shows us how to resolve another tension between the *Refutation* and the 'Little Labyrinth'. Hippolytus informs us that the Melchizedekians arose as a splinter group out of the Theodotians, led by one Theodotus the banker. When next we see Theodotus the banker in the 'Little Labyrinth' he is the disciple of Theodotus of Byzantium, carrying on his word by organizing a sect. Pseudo-Tertullian may solve this difficulty for us by showing us that there never was a sect of Theodotians *per se* other than perhaps a circle of people who agreed with the doctrine of Theodotus of Byzantium. The only sect organized was that by Theodotus the banker who agreed with the adoptionist Christology of Theodotus of Byzantium, but who added to this Christology a theory about the heavenly role of Melchizedek. When Theodotus of Byzantium was excommunicated by Victor, the leadership of the 'dynamic monarchian' position fell to Theodotus the banker who took steps to remove the following of Theodotus of Byzantium from the control of the church in Rome, organizing a schismatic sect. This theory explains our three main sources for the Melchizedekian heresy: the *Refutation*, the 'Little Labyrinth', and Pseudo-Tertullian. According to this view it would be proper to use the words 'Theodotian' and 'Melchizedekian only as positions within the 'dynamic monarchian' movement begun by Theodotus of Byzantium. The *Refutation* reflects only the situation as it existed before the excommunication of Theodotus of Byzantium, whereas the 'Little Labyrinth' and Pseudo-Tertullian represent a later situation in which an actual sect of 'dynamic monarchians' had been organized by Theodotus the banker. Following Pseudo-Tertullian, we might hold that this sect thought of Melchizedek as a superior heavenly power whose function in the heavens was recapitulated or reflected in the work of Christ on earth. Once we have dispensed with the misleading (but up to now necessary) designation 'Melchizedekians' for this sect, we may legitimately question whether this doctrine was in any way fundamental to the sect, or the belief was made more of by those who wrote in opposition to the sect in an effort to retain the distinction made initially by Hippolytus in the *Refutation*.

Harnack has held that the Melchizedekians are a creation of Hippolytus who formulated this heresy in response to the Theodotian exegesis of Hebrews.[1] Bardy, on the other hand, more accurately points out that the term 'Melchizedekian' is an invention of Epiphanius of Salamis. His position which closely resembles my own ought to be quoted here:

Autant il est probable que parmi les disciples de Théodote de Byzance quelques-uns aient enseigné la supériorité de Melchisédech sur le Christ, autant il y a peu de chances pour qu'il ait jamais existé un groupe de Melchisedéciens. Ceux-ci sont la création de génie d'Epiphane qui ne se lasse pas d'inventer de nouvelles sectes pour grossir artificiellement son catalogue.[2]

I have not, however, accused Epiphanius of creating an artificial heresy, but rather of being so far away from the historical reality as to be totally dependent upon older sources. His contribution is solely in giving us the name 'Melchizedekians'. This name he coined on the model of the name 'Theodotians' which he had already found in Hippolytus (*Refutation* vii. 35) but neither did Hippolytus 'create' the sect of Melchizedekians or a Melchizedekian heresy. Harnack's position comes from reading Hippolytus in terms of Epiphanius whereas the opposite method should be used. The *Refutation* presents the Melchizedekian position as nothing more than one point of view within the 'dynamic monarchian' movement, certainly not as a heretical sect in and of itself. The obvious difficulty is that a single historical development, the rise of the dynamic monarchian schism in Rome, has been artificially divided into two movements because of Hippolytus' early account of a disagreement within the group before the actual schism.

It is apparent that the 'dynamic monarchian'[3] movement in Rome quickly died out after the founding of the sect. Certainly the repentance of Natalus before Pope Zephyrinus (A.D. 198–

---

[1] *History of Dogma*, iii, 26–7.

[2] 'Melchisédech dans la tradition patristique.'

[3] I have been placing this term in quotation marks as a reminder that we are here concerned with a single historical movement which culminated in the founding of a sect by Theodotus the banker. Whatever the theological connection between this sect and others designated as 'dynamic monarchians' the historical connections are not at all clear and fall beyond the scope of this study.

217) is symbolic of the end of the schism, though certainly not the end of monarchian sympathies within the Roman church.[1] The author of the 'Little Labyrinth' suggests that the heresy of Artemon (ca. A.D. 230–70)[2] was something of a revival of the position of Theodotus of Byzantium, and the author reminds his readers that Theodotus was excommunicated by Victor.[3] Harnack, however, has correctly suggested that the author of the 'Little Labyrinth' may simply have associated the views of Artemon, about which we know nothing at all, with the views of one already demonstrated to be a heretic in response to the charge that Pope Zephyrinus had misrepresented the views of the followers of Artemon, views considered ancient and apostolic by the followers of Artemon.[4] Hence, there may be no actual historical connection between Artemon and Theodotus of Byzantium at all. The chief value of Artemon's heresy is that it helps us date the 'Little Labyrinth' ca. A.D. 230–35 as a response to this heresy.[5]

It is more difficult to date Pseudo-Tertullian. Harnack attempted to show that this treatise was identical with the work *Adversum omnes haereses* attributed to Victorinus, the bishop of Poetovino (died A.D. 304).[6] Goodspeed remarks, however, that the only thing which stands in the way of this theory is the good style of Latin to be found in Pseudo-Tertullian as compared to the poor Latin of Victorinus' commentary on Revelation, the only extant work from his pen.[7] Jerome is equally uncomplimentary about Victorinus' Latin when he says: 'Victorinus,

[1] Eusebius, *HE* v. 28, 12. For the dates of Pope Zephyrinus see Walker, *A History of the Christian Church*, p. 70.
[2] *Ibid.* p. 68.   [3] Eusebius, *HE* v. 28. 3ff.
[4] *History of Dogma*, III, 31–2.
[5] Cf. Goodspeed, *A History of Early Christian Literature*, p. 147.
[6] Harnack, *History of Dogma*, III, 52 n. 1. Some slight support for this position may be found in the fact that Jerome in his work *On Illustrious Men* attributes to Victorinus a work by this name. The difficulty is that he does not indicate its length or content. It is quite certain, however, judging from the heresies opposed in this work and the theological outlook that it has nothing at all to do with Tertullian and that his name was appended to it at a much later date to increase its stature.
[7] *A History of Early Christian Literature*, p. 188. This is also the judgement of Carl Albrecht Bernoulli, *Der Schriftstellerkatalog des Hieronymus: Ein Beitrag zur Geschichte der altchristlichen Literatur* (Freiburg and Leipzig: Akademische Verlagsbuchhandlung von J. C. B. Mohr (Paul Siebeck), 1895), p. 264, from which we have taken our text of Jerome's treatise.

Pitabionensis episcopus, non aeque latine ut graece noverat. Unde opera eius grandia sensibus viliores videntur conpositione verborum.'[1] It is perhaps best simply to consider Pseudo-Tertullian's work as pseudonymous since we have little evidence to link it with any known writer. Fortunately for us, we have been able to authenticate enough of the information given by Pseudo-Tertullian as stemming from an early tradition relative to the Melchizedekians. It has been held that Pseudo-Tertullian makes use of the lost *Syntagma* of Hippolytus.[2] I have not examined enough of the treatise to make an informed judgement on this position other than to say for the material considered here that the tradition about the Melchizedekians contained in the work is consistent with a view which would assign it to the first half of the third century A.D., whatever the actual composition date of the final work itself. In summary, then, Pseudo-Tertullian is an acceptable source for the Melchizedekians because of the quality of its tradition, not its authorship.

In reality the quest for the Melchizedekians is the quest for a phantom. The historical reality is the development of a 'dynamic monarchian' sect in Rome by Theodotus the banker based on the teachings of Theodotus of Byzantium. This sect appears to have held the belief that Melchizedek is a heavenly power who intercedes for the angels. The 'Melchizedekian' party came to control the sect of 'dynamic monarchians' only because the leader of that party was the instrument by which it was formed into an actual sect. The split over the issue among the 'dynamic monarchians' was probably not severe and no doubt some adjustments were made in the theology of the party of 'dynamic monarchians' as it was organized into a sect. It is possible that the view of the 'dynamic monarchians' given by Pseudo-Tertullian represents a compromise between the two groups which gave deference to the Melchizedekian position while effectively removing Melchizedek from the arena of human life. That is to say, Melchizedek may have been 'kicked upstairs' so as to focus attention again on the role of Christ in the redemption of men. Epiphanius' suggestion that this group actually brought petitions and sacrifices before Melchizedek has

[1] *On Illustrious Men* LXXIV.

[2] Goodspeed, *A History of Early Christian Literature*, pp. 146–7, and Harnack, *History of Dogma*, III, 52 n. 1.

no support in the more contemporary descriptions of the sect. The life of the sect was quite short. It could not have been formed before the excommunication of Theodotus of Byzantium by Victor (ca. A.D. 198) and it was to all intents and purposes dead by the end of the reign of Pope Zephyrinus in A.D. 217. Thus the sect lasted less than two decades so far as our evidence gives us a basis for making a judgement. We have little evidence that the theology or the practices of the sect survived in other heretical movements.[1]

Hierakas[2] the Egyptian

Hierakas lived most probably in the last half of the third century A.D. and was a native of the Egyptian town of Leontos.[3]

---

[1] There does exist a fragment ascribed to Eustathius of Antioch, who was bishop of Antioch ca. A.D. 324 (Quasten, *Patrology*, III, 302), in which there is a refutation of the Melchizedekians. Quasten (*ibid.*) incorrectly ascribes this refutation to Eustathius along with the rest of the contents of the fragment, but this has been convincingly disproved by B. Altaner, 'Die Schrift ΠΕΡΙ ΤΟΥ ΜΕΛΧΙΣΕΔΕΚ des Eustathios von Antiocheia', *Byzantinische Zeitschrift*, XL (1940), 30–47. The portion of the fragment which refutes the Melchizedekians is to be found substantially in the same form in two sermons ascribed by tradition to John Chrysostom (cf. MSG 61, 740–2; MSG 56, 260–3). We do not need to go into the detailed textual argument brought forth by Altaner, but rather I shall state his main conclusions. Although Altaner agrees that these two sermons should not be assigned *in toto* to Chrysostom, he finds that the refutation of the Melchizedekians does go back to Chrysostom. He holds that the sermon found in MSG 61, 740–2 may be traced back to the first part of the fifth century A.D. and that it must stem from a sermon delivered by Chrysostom towards the turn of the fifth century. Chrysostom, not unlike Epiphanius, has placed together all of the heretical positions about Melchizedek of which he is aware, including the Melchizedekians, the Hierakians, the Jews, and others. It is of little use to us as a primary source for the 'Melchizedekian' heresies. The occasion for Chrysostom's refutation, however, is very real. Chrysostom is reacting to the claims of a later Melchizedekian heresy which began in the last quarter of the fourth century and continued into the fifth century, the Melchizedekian heresy represented in *Quaestiones Veteris et Novi Testamenti* CXXVII, which is opposed in more detail by Jerome and Mark the Hermit. See pp. 108–11 for a full discussion of that heresy and its refutations.

[2] Also spelled 'Hieracas'.

[3] Aside from the discussion of Hierakas in Epiphanius, we know almost nothing about the man or the sect which grew up around him. We may arrive at an approximate date for him by pointing out that he was greatly influenced by Origen who died ca. A.D. 251 and that he is mentioned by the

We are dependent upon Epiphanius, *Panarion* LV and LXVII for almost all of our information about him. In chapter LXVII Epiphanius does not wander all around his subject as he is wont to do elsewhere, and he gives us a clearer picture of Hierakas than of the Melchizedekians. According to Epiphanius,[1] Hierakas mastered not only the sciences, magic arts, and tongue of the Egyptians, but the knowledge and tongue of the Greeks as well. He became a Christian and devoted himself earnestly to the study of the scriptures even committing both Testaments to memory! He was greatly influenced by Origen, which by itself would earn him a place within Epiphanius' list of heretics, but his brilliance led him into what Epiphanius considered to be a virulent heresy which denied the flesh entirely and which thereby attracted many Egyptian ascetics. Harnack has rightly pointed out that Hierakas represents a bridge between Origen and the Coptic monks.[2] Although heretical in certain aspects of his thought, Hierakas was considered sound in his Christological doctrine.[3]

Hierakas' theology and practice stemmed from his ascetic life. He rejected marriage as being a feature only of the old covenant, pointing out that Christ (Mt. xxv. 1ff.) compared the kingdom of heaven to virgins, foolish and wise virgins to be sure, but virgins none the less.[4] He rejected the idea that children before the age of reason (πρὸ γνώσεως) can be saved at death, holding that only those who have struggled and (on the basis of 2 Tim. ii. 5) struggled according to the rules, can receive the crown.[5] He believed that paradise is not a 'sensible' locality (αἰσθητός) and that there is no resurrection of the flesh after

Arians in their letter to Alexander of Alexandria at the time of the Synod of Egypt ca. A.D. 320–3 as a recognized heretic. We therefore have a period of some seventy years during which we know that Hierakas lived. It is usual to assign him a date ca. A.D. 300 and I shall adopt that practice.

[1] All of our information about Hierakas in this brief biographical sketch is taken directly from the *Panarion*, chapter LXVII.

[2] *History of Dogma*, III, 98–9.

[3] *Ibid.* p. 98 n. 4. According to the letter of the Arians, Hierakas' Christology may be summed up on the basis of the familiar expression 'a lamp kindled from a lamp, or like a torch divided into two' (οὐδ' ὡς Ἱεράκας λύχνον ἀπὸ λύχνου, ἢ ὡς λαμπάδα εἰς δύο), an expression already used by Tatian. Cf. Edward Rochie Hardy and Cyril C. Richardson, eds., *Christology of the Later Fathers* (The Library of Christian Classics, Vol. III; Philadelphia: The Westminster Press, 1954), p. 333 n. 5.

[4] *Panarion* LXVII. 2. 6.   [5] *Panarion* LXVII. 2. 7.

death. Resurrection is something of a spiritual and mythological nature.[1] Epiphanius reports that Hierakas wrote works both in Greek and in Egyptian (Coptic). He wrote tracts on the six days of creation, spinning myths and allegories about them. Further, he wrote new psalms, presumably for the worship of his community.[2] Epiphanius informs us that Hierakas kept his discipline faithfully throughout his long life which extended over ninety years, but reports that many followers were not so observant. He continued his trade of calligraphy right up until the day he died.[3]

My interest in Hierakas stems from his unusual beliefs about the Holy Spirit which he identified with Melchizedek. As we have already seen, Hierakas seems to have been rather orthodox as regards the relationship of the Son to the Father, and Epiphanius admits that in this regard Hierakas does not follow Origen. Hierakas says that the Son really comes from the Father, and also says that the Holy Spirit comes from the Father.[4] It is possible to prove, however, that this Holy Spirit is also known as Melchizedek by means of two scriptural proofs. Paul says that the Spirit 'intercedes for us with ineffable groanings' (Rom. viii. 26). The one who remains a priest forever (Ps. cx. 4; Heb. vii. 3) is a priest because of his eternal intercession. Thus, Melchizedek and the Holy Spirit are one and the same.[5] The second scriptural proof is similar, although it involves a departure from our canon. Quoting from the Ascension of Isaiah ix. 33,[6] Hierakas makes reference to the two figures

---

[1] *Panarion* LXVII. 2. 8.   [2] The full text deserves quotation here:

συνεγράψατο δὲ Ἑλληνικῶς τε καὶ Αἰγυπτιακῶς ἐξηγησάμενος καὶ συντάξας ⟨περὶ⟩ τῆς ἑξαημέρου, μύθους τινὰς πλασάμενος καὶ κομπώδεις ἀλληγορίας, εἰς ἄλλα δὲ πόσα ἀπὸ τῆς γραφῆς συνέταξε, ψαλμούς τε πολλοὺς νεωτερικοὺς ἐπλάσατο.   [3] *Panarion* LXVII. 3. 9.

[4] *Panarion* LXVII. 3. 1.   [5] *Panarion* LXVII. 3. 2.

[6] We are led to believe here that such a work as the Ascension of Isaiah had canonical standing for Hierakas since Epiphanius lays such stress at the beginning of his refutation of Hierakas' mastery of scripture and also by the context here. The text from the Ascension of Isaiah as quoted by Epiphanius, *Panarion* LXVII. 3. 4 reads:

ἔδειξέ μοι ὁ ἄγγελος περιπατῶν ἔμπροσθέν μου, καὶ ἔδειξέ μοι καὶ εἶπε· τίς ἐστιν ὁ ἐν δεξιᾷ τοῦ θεοῦ; καὶ εἶπα· σὺ οἶδας, κύριε; λέγει· οὗτός ἐστιν ὁ ἀγαπητός, καὶ τίς ἐστιν ὁ ἄλλος ὁ ὅμοιος αὐτῷ ἐξ ἀριστερῶν ἐλθών; καὶ εἶπα· σὺ γινώσκεις. ⟨λέγει⟩· τοῦτό ἐστιν τὸ ἅγιον πνεῦμα τὸ λαλοῦν ἐν τοῖς προφήταις. καὶ ἦν, φησίν, ὅμοιον τῷ ἀγαπητῷ.

sitting to the right and left hand of God. The figure to the right is the 'beloved' (ὁ ἀγαπητός), and the figure to the left is the Holy Spirit who speaks through the prophets. The Holy Spirit is said to be 'like the beloved' (ὅμοιον τῷ ἀγαπητῷ) which proves that he is Melchizedek since Heb. vii. 3 informs us that Melchizedek is ἀφωμοιωμένος τῷ υἱῷ τοῦ θεοῦ. If Melchizedek was the Holy Spirit, how could he have met Abram in the scene depicted in Gen. xiv. 18–20? This is not difficult to explain if we return once more to Heb. vii. 3 and observe that Melchizedek's being made like unto the Son of God implies the ability to take on flesh like the Son.[1] Even so, it is correct to hold with Hebrews that Melchizedek was 'without father, without mother, without genealogy' since he had no mother at all and no father upon the earth.[2] Apparently it is correct to consider God the Father of the Holy Spirit in Hierakas' system of thought.

There is no connection in evidence between the followers of Theodotus the banker and Hierakas. Both make use of Melchizedek as a heavenly figure, but for different reasons. For the followers of Theodotus the banker, Melchizedek fits into an adoptionist Christology as the heavenly type for the earthly antitype Christ. On the other hand, Melchizedek in Hierakas' system is the same as the Holy Spirit, related on an equal footing with Christ to the Father. The only point of agreement between the two is in Melchizedek's being a heavenly figure. The acute difference between the two has to do with the view taken of Christ. Since both agree that Melchizedek is a heavenly figure, his role will be determined more or less in terms of the role given to Christ. The only possible connection between the two groups is geographical, as suggested by Epiphanius.[3] In closing his discussion of the Melchizedekians, Epiphanius compares this heresy with the venom of a desert rodent which is above all to be found in Egypt. Were it true that the 'dynamic monarchians' had come from Rome to Egypt, we might have some reason for making a historical or sociological connection between them and Hierakas. However, the balance of the evidence contradicts such a view. As we have already seen, the sect of 'dynamic monarchians' was *in extremis* within a few years of its founding in Rome. We found that our sources for the sect

---

[1] *Panarion* LXVII. 3. 3.   [2] *Panarion* LXVII. 3. 3.
[3] *Panarion* LV. 9. 18.

became highly stylized even within the third century A.D., depending mainly upon Hippolytus for information. This is consistent with the death of the sect, not its relocation. Epiphanius' suggestion might be substantiated if we were able to find similarities between the two systems of thought, but we have been able to find only one, the heavenly status of Melchizedek, hardly enough on which to base a claim for dependence. Of course, it is impossible to say that no 'dynamic monarchian' ever went to Egypt, but we can say that there is no real evidence that a significant number ever went there. Another possibility is that Epiphanius here has another group in mind. He has just finished refuting a party which says that Melchizedek is the Father,[1] and even though he seems to be returning to the Melchizedekians at the close of the chapter, it is possible that he has in mind the other heresy. This, as we shall soon see, accords well with what we know otherwise about the group with which Epiphanius is dealing, which he quotes as saying that Melchizedek is the Father.

Harnack[2] thinks that there is a connection between the 'dynamic monarchians' and Hierakas through Origen. According to this view the tendency to depreciate the historical Jesus as subordinate to the heavenly Son of God which is found in the thought of the Theodotians is carried through the school of Origen along with the same speculation about Melchizedek to Origen's disciple Hierakas. Harnack here ignores Epiphanius' comment that Hierakas departs from Origen precisely at this point.[3] Further, the only evidence which we have for speculation about Melchizedek is Jerome's comment that Origen and his secretary considered Melchizedek to be an angel.[4] Even if Jerome is correct, this does not necessarily imply that Melchizedek had any connection with Origen's Christology. The only similarity is Melchizedek's heavenly status.

The turn of the fifth century

From the beginning of the fourth century A.D. until about the time in which Epiphanius wrote his *Panarion* (A.D. 377), we

[1] *Panarion* LV. 9. 11–15. See the discussion of this, pages 106–8.
[2] *History of Dogma*, III, 28–9.   [3] *Panarion* LXVII. 3. 1.
[4] *Ep. ad Evangelum* LXXIII. 2.

have little information about the treatment which Melchizedek received in the church. Beginning with Epiphanius and continuing through the turn of the fifth century A.D., our information once again improves, and we may pick up the thread. Epiphanius, *Panarion* LV. 9. 11ff., following a general proof that Melchizedek cannot be any of the three persons of the Godhead, takes special pains to prove that Melchizedek is not the Father.

Now again it has come to our attention that some have erred even more than all of those already mentioned and have been prepared for such speculation by even greater pretension. They have dared to deal with a very difficult problem and have come to a blasphemous conclusion so as to say that Melchizedek is the Father of our Lord Jesus Christ. How careless is the reasoning of men, and the deception of their heart which also does not have the support of truth! For from the Apostle's saying that Melchizedek was without father and without mother and without genealogy, these persons have imagined a blasphemous error, having been led astray in reason by the excessiveness of language and frivolously concluding that these things said about Melchizedek fit in themselves the Father of All. For from saying that the Father of All, the Creator of All, has neither father nor mother nor beginning of days or end of life (for this is agreed to by everyone), they have fallen into a foolish blasphemy by comparing Melchizedek to the Father on the basis of what the Apostle said about him, not taking cognizance of the other things said about him.

This heresy is obviously an addendum, and the opening words of the paragraph just quoted suggest that the rest of the chapter had been penned before Epiphanius had heard of the heresy involved here. We know that the composition of the *Panarion* took at least two years,[1] which would allow ample time for rewriting and inclusion of more systems of thought. Although the actual number of heresies could not be changed (eighty in all), it is apparent from chapter LV that in fact many heresies could be grouped together under one heading when that suited the author's purpose. We cannot escape, of course, the possibility that Epiphanius may have created this heresy. He has already described heresies in which Melchizedek is thought of as Son and Holy Spirit and given a general proof that Melchizedek can be none of the persons of the Trinity. Is he simply inventing a

[1] Cf. Quasten, *Patrology*, III, 388.

heresy to represent the last position that Melchizedek is the Father? This would be an inviting solution were it not for the fact that Epiphanius' words go together with those of other writers to show us another actual heresy which was alive at the end of the fourth century.

Mark the Hermit was, according to tradition, a student of St John Chrysostom. He was an abbot of a monastery in Galatia but in his later years retired to a life of seclusion in the desert of Judaea. He must have died after A.D. 430 since he was involved with the Nestorian controversy.[1] Mark had occasion to write a treatise on Melchizedek[2] in which he challenged those who said that Melchizedek is the Logos and Son of God before entering the womb of the Virgin. This group, however, also called Melchizedek θεός, asking, 'If he was not θεός how was he without father and without mother?' Mark takes this to imply that his opponents believe Melchizedek to be the Father, to which charge the heretics themselves reply that they do not consider him to be the Father but the θεὸς Λόγος before he was incarnate or born out of Mary.[3] Mark's opponents seem to question the formula of Heb. vii. 3, 'made like unto the Son of God' as it applies to Melchizedek, claiming that there is no likeness (ἀφομοίωσις) shared by the two. Melchizedek is without genealogy; Christ has a genealogy. Melchizedek has neither beginning of life nor end of life; Christ has both.[4] Finally Mark represents his opponents as thinking that Christ was a 'mere man' (ἄνθρωπος ψιλός).[5] We may at this point legitimately inquire whether Mark is accurately reflecting the view of his opponents. We have already seen that the opponents consider Melchizedek to be the Logos who took on flesh and was born of Mary. This is not adoptionism in any form known to us, and the associations which Mark suggests with dynamic monarchianism are questionable. It seems probable to me that Mark is attempting to reject the arguments of his opponents by appealing to the already successful rejection of the 'dynamic monarchians'. How

[1] *Ibid.* pp. 504–5.
[2] The Greek text is to be found in MSG 65, 1117–40.
[3] *On Melchizedek* §2, MSG 65, 1120. Ἡμεῖς οὐ λέγομεν αὐτὸν Πατέρα ἀλλὰ τὸν θεὸν Λόγον πρὶν σαρκωθῆναι ἢ ἐκ Μαρίας γεννηθῆναι.
[4] *On Melchizedek* §4, MSG 65, 1121.
[5] *On Melchizedek* §4, MSG 65, 1121. From this point on, Mark tends to treat his opponents as though they were adoptionists.

it is possible that Christ should at one time be the incarnate Logos (= Melchizedek) from his birth and also a 'mere man' is beyond the comprehension of this writer.

Both Epiphanius and Mark are offended by the use of the word θεός to describe Melchizedek. Epiphanius gives a general proof that Melchizedek in no way can be considered to be a part of the Godhead. He especially wants to discredit a group which he thinks calls Melchizedek the Father. Mark, a half century later, also opposes a group which calls Melchizedek θεός which makes him at first think that they consider him to be the Father. Finally he comes to understand that they mean the God Logos. These similarities suggest that Mark and Epiphanius may have been opposing a single movement or belief. Obviously neither author understands the position of his opponent especially well, but that should not make us think that the opponent is imaginary. There is evidence of another Melchizedekian heresy existing at the turn of the century and thereafter which may explain the veiled references of Mark and Epiphanius, and to that evidence we now proceed.

In the last quarter of the fourth century A.D. a work in Latin appeared which in later years was assigned by tradition to St Augustine entitled *Quaestiones Veteris et Novi Testamenti CXXVII*.[1] Question 109 in this work is devoted to Melchizedek, raising once more the theory that Melchizedek is the Holy Spirit. This designation is based on an exegesis of Ps. cx. 4 whereby Christ is understood to be a priest after Melchizedek's order, implying that Melchizedek and Christ are of a single nature, though not the same person. Christ is the high priest whereas Melchizedek is simply a priest into whose order Christ came to be high priest. There is a unity of nature and a similarity of function, leaving the distinction between the two to be made only on the basis of person. Since Christ has the primary position and Melchizedek the secondary position in this scheme, Melchizedek can be none other than the Holy Spirit.[2] Bardy thinks that this is a revival of the doctrine of Hierakas which was formulated some three

---

[1] The text is to be found in Alexander Souter, ed., *Pseudo-Augustini Quaestiones Veteris et Novi Testamenti CXXVII* (Corpus Scriptorum Ecclesiasticorum Latinorum, vol. L; Leipzig: G. Freytag, 1908), pp. 257–68.

[2] Question 109: 20–1.

quarters of a century earlier.[1] It is possible that Hierakas' belief has taken on a new guise in the *Quaestiones*, but in other respects the *Quaestiones* do not seem to share the theological outlook of Hierakas. We note too that the equation of the Holy Spirit with Melchizedek is accomplished by Hierakas in a very different manner from that employed in the *Quaestiones*.

Both Souter[2] and Bardy[3] believe that Question 109 is the occasion for Jerome's *Epistle* LXIII. The opening paragraph of the *Epistle* certainly does suggest that possibility in that Jerome indicates that the anonymous author of the document sent him believes that Melchizedek who blessed Abraham

> divinioris fuisse naturae nec de hominibus aestimandum. Et ad extremum ausus est dicere Spiritum Sanctum occurrisse Abrahae et ipsum esse, qui sub homine visus sit.[4]

Bardy thinks that this is a very good argument for equating the document sent to Jerome with the *Quaestiones*, but he notes that over twenty years would have elapsed between the time of composition of the *Quaestiones* and the writing of the letter (ca. A.D. 398).[5] Actually, it is difficult to hold that the document received by Jerome was the *Quaestiones*. In the first place, the *Quaestiones* are concerned with much more than just Melchizedek, whereas Jerome's letter deals only with Melchizedek. In the second place there are no exact verbal parallels. However, there can be little doubt that the document received by Jerome was very much like Question 109 in tone and argument.[6]

---

[1] 'Melchisédech dans la tradition patristique', p. 26. Bardy, however, does not necessarily mean a direct continuation of the thought of Hierakas, but rather, a rediscovery of that thought by a later generation.

[2] *Pseudo-Augustini Quaestiones*, pp. xx–xxi.

[3] *Op. cit.*, p. 28 n. 1, but he does not hold this without some reservations as we shall see.   [4] *Ep. ad Evangelum* §1 (Hilberg, *Epistulae*, II, 13).

[5] 'Melchisédech dans la tradition patristique', p. 26.

[6] This same group is attacked by Cyril of Alexandria (bishop A.D. 412–44) in his *Glaphyrorum in Genesim* II. 7–11 (MSG 68, 97–110). This is directed especially against those who say that Melchizedek was not a man but is the Holy Spirit or some other power:

ἐνιστάμενοι δὲ μετὰ τοῦτο καὶ οὐδὲν ἧττον λέγουσιν ὡς ἄνθρωπος μὲν οὐκ ἦν Μελχισεδέκ· τὸ Πνεῦμα δὲ μᾶλλον τὸ ἅγιον· ἢ γοῦν ἑτέρα τις δύναμις τῶν ἄνωθεν καὶ ἐξ οὐρανοῦ, τὴν λειτουργικὴν ἔχουσα τάξιν. (II. 7.)

Cf. also II. 7–8 (MSG 68, 101B). This is also the theme of a work entitled *Sermo Origenis de Melchisedech: non aliud nisi hominem illum fuisse* which was first published by W. A. Baehrens, *Überlieferung und Textgeschichte*, pp. 243–52.

I suggest the possibility, therefore, that both Mark the Hermit and Epiphanius are reacting to those who argue in a manner similar to the argument found in the *Quaestiones* that Christ and Melchizedek share the same divine nature. This argument is designed to prove that Melchizedek is the Holy Spirit, but the argument that Melchizedek and Christ share the divine nature could also be misinterpreted to say that Melchizedek is the Logos (Mark) or even that Melchizedek is the Father (Epiphanius). In support of my theory I would point to the fact that the composition of the *Quaestiones* occurred somewhere around A.D. 375[1] and that the *Panarion* of Epiphanius was composed in A.D. 377.[2] This might well account for Epiphanius' speaking of this group as an afterthought without much factual information since second-hand reports about this view of Melchizedek may have preceded any primary sources.

Behind this last view of Melchizedek is again the conviction that Melchizedek was something other than a man, a conviction that he was a divine being who could be described as θεός. To that extent this view differs little from that of the Melchizedekians or Hierakians, and I repeat my observation[3] that it is the role of Christ in all these systems which determines the role of Melchizedek. In the *Quaestiones* a rather orthodox view of Christ is held, and the view as regards Melchizedek, while unusual, cannot be strictly called heretical. Only in the sense that the Holy Spirit is thought of as being capable of taking on human form is there room for condemnation by Jerome. Melchizedek's superhuman, divine role remains constant throughout all the systems here described although his exact function varies according to the Christology of each system. In no instance is there any evidence that one's view of Melchizedek determines one's view of Christ. Even the 'dynamic monar-

As Baehrens points out (p. 243), this sermon has nothing at all to do with Origen. One is led to believe that this text was actually written in response to Jerome's *Epistle* LXXIII which says that Origen considered Melchizedek an angel. Baehrens shows the dependence of the anonymous writer on Epiphanius and Mark the Hermit (pp. 244–5) which helps us date it after Jerome. Since the object of polemic may be Jerome and not any Melchizedekian heresy, it may be assigned to a later date.

[1] Bardy, 'Melchisédech dans la tradition patristique', p. 26; Souter, *Pseudo-Augustini Quaestiones*, pp. xx–xxi.

[2] See above, p. 87 n. 1.   [3] See above, p. 104.

chians' began with their adoptionist Christology, bringing Melchizedek in to make that adoptionism more explicit. In Hierakas' thought Melchizedek is made to fit into a Christology which is considered by Arius to be representative of the orthodox position which was taken by the Synod of Egypt, a position expressed in the same terms by Tatian in the last part of the second century A.D.

Before leaving the Christian sources, we should make some important observations. First of all, we have found no system which does not make use of Hebrews, especially Heb. vii. 3 and the understanding of Ps. cx. 4 to be found in Hebrews (cf. Heb. v. 6, 10; vi. 20; vii. 11, 15, 17, 21). Secondly, the only certain link among the three systems discussed is the conviction that Melchizedek is a heavenly power. Lastly, there seems actually to have been less speculation about Melchizedek in Christian circles in our period than is at first suggested by the sources. These first two points have been adequately discussed above; the last requires some further comment.

In terms of quantity there is a good deal of material devoted to a refutation of Melchizedekian heresies. One might at first be led to believe that there was no limit to speculation about Melchizedek in the early church and that Melchizedekian sects of one sort or another regularly broke off from the church. Sifting the evidence, however, reveals only three movements in which Melchizedek as a divine figure played any important role, and if Bardy is to have his way about the theory of Melchizedek represented in the *Quaestiones* being a revival of the system of Hierakas, then actually we have only two. It was perhaps the very fact that Melchizedekian heresies were so small and ineffectual that accounts for the misunderstandings of their beliefs and practices shown in the refutations we have examined. Where we encounter a clear picture of a group that believes Melchizedek to be a heavenly power, we invariably find that belief not to be central to the system of thought involved. Certainly this is true of the system of Hierakas which seems to be rather well preserved for us in Epiphanius' *Panarion*. Such is also the case with the *Quaestiones*, our one and only primary source for a Melchizedekian error, in which concern with Melchizedek is limited to one out of 127 questions. I have also held the same to be true for the 'dynamic monarchians' who, by elevating Melchizedek to the role of intercessor for the angels effectively removed him from the arena of human life.

In the next chapter we shall see what Gnostic speculation about Melchizedek was like. Wuttke[1] has greatly damaged the usefulness of his work by categorizing both the 'dynamic monarchians' and the Hierakians as Gnostics. As regards the 'dynamic monarchians' Hippolytus[2] does associate Theodotus of Byzantium with the Gnostics, but at the same time we must remember that the 'Gnostic' element is the adoptionism and not the cosmology of Theodotus. Aside from pointing to Epiphanius' use of the words τάξις, ἄρχων, μύσται, γνῶσις in reference to the Melchizedekians, quite apart from their context, Wuttke can only point to the belief that Melchizedek was a δύναμις as evidence of 'Gnosticism'.[3] It is certainly not the case that Gnosticism can be established on either basis. We have already seen that Epiphanius knows nothing more about the Melchizedekians than does Hippolytus. One cannot conclude from his choice of words, especially words of such broad meaning as these, that Epiphanius thought of this as a Gnostic sect. In attempting to put the words picked up by Wuttke back into context, I found no instance of the use of the word τάξις apart from Ps. cx. 4 and so cannot identify the passage Wuttke had in mind. The words ἄρχων, γνῶσις and μύσται all occur in *Panarion* LV. 8. In LV. 8. 1 it is said that it is necessary to bring offerings to Melchizedek because ἄρχων ἐστὶ δικαιοσύνης, which amounts to a translation of the name מלכי צדק. In LV. 8. 3 it is said that Christ was chosen and anointed in order to turn us from many paths into one γνῶσις.[4] In LV. 8. 5 it is said that the members of the sect are μύσται of Melchizedek who, as the greater of the two, blessed Abraham. One would be very hard-pressed under any of the common definitions to call any of what is described here Gnosticism. It is true that Epiphanius may assign cosmological meaning to the term ἄρχων here, but that does not demonstrate that such was the belief of the Melchize-

---

[1] *Melchisedech*, pp. 31 and 34–5. [2] See above, p. 90.

[3] *Op. cit.*, p. 31.

[4] The text reads:

καὶ χριστὸς μέν, φησιν, ἐξελέγη ἵνα ἡμᾶς καλέσῃ ἐκ πολλῶν ὁδῶν εἰς μίαν ταύτην τὴν γνῶσιν ὑπὸ θεοῦ κεχρισμένος καὶ ἐκλεκτὸς γενόμενος, ἐπειδὴ ἀπέστρεψεν ἡμᾶς ἀπὸ εἰδώλων καὶ ὑπέδειξεν ἡμῖν τὴν ὁδόν.

dekians. There is certainly no characteristically Gnostic terminology in *Panarion* LV. 8 which can be pointed to with certainty; and even if Epiphanius does have such Gnostic associations in mind, there is no proof that this represents any feature of the sect itself. Hippolytus' use of the word δύναμις to describe Melchizedek elicits from us only the comment that the Gnostics did not have a corner on belief in heavenly, angelic powers. Wuttke's reasoning in calling the system of Hierakas Gnostic is even more troublesome, and in the main his judgement seems to be influenced by Hierakas' use of the Ascension of Isaiah: 'Charakteristisch ist, dass Hierakas seine spekulativen Gedankenzüge auf eigene, geheime Offenbarung stützt. Hier wird die gnostische Melchisedech-Exegese einen breiteren Raum eingenommen haben, als der kirchliche Bericht des Epiphanius erkennen lässt.'[1] This is almost the opposite of the truth. We have no evidence that Epiphanius ever refused to discuss heretical beliefs because of his own dogmatic position. Rather, one must sometimes be careful in reading the *Panarion* since Epiphanius is likely to associate 'Gnostic' ideas with non-Gnostic sects as in the case of the Melchizedekians. What Wuttke holds true only for the group opposed by Mark the Hermit is just as true for the other two systems I have discussed. All three are 'kirchliche Melchizedech-Spekulationen'.[2] The 'dynamic monarchians' and Hierakians were definite heresies. The same should probably not be said about the Melchizedek speculation of the *Quaestiones* since in most other respects that document is not heretical.

We now leave the Christian sources and turn to the Rabbinic sources. We close this section with an outline designed to show the historical progression discussed in this section and which should be kept in mind for comparison as we deal with the Rabbis.

Table 4.1[a]

I	'Dynamic Monarchians'	A.D. 190–217
	a Theodotus of Byzantium	A.D. 190–8
	b Theodotus the banker	A.D. 198–217

[a] The reader should understand that many of these dates are only approximations and should refer for more detail back to the relevant discussion in this chapter.

[1] *Op. cit.*, p. 34. [2] *Ibid.* p. 35.

Table 4.1 (cont.)

II	Hierakas	A.D. 300
III	Belief represented in *Quaestiones*	A.D. 375–450
	a *Quaestiones*	A.D. 375
	b *Panarion* LV. 9	A.D. 377
	c *Ep. ad Evangelum*	A.D. 398
	d John Chrysostom	*ca.* A.D. 400
	e Mark the Hermit	A.D. 420

THE RABBINIC SOURCES

The Rabbinic sources, with minor exceptions which will be discussed, admit of a division into two types of material. The usual interest in Melchizedek has to do with the origins of the Levitical priesthood, Melchizedek in one way or another being seen as the precursor of the priesthood. Another interest, much less important in conception and development, has to do with Melchizedek as an eschatological figure. In this section I shall attempt to describe these two areas of speculation about Melchizedek in the Rabbinic sources and to show as clearly as possible the course of development which each underwent. We must also examine the Rabbinic material to see if there is any evidence for the view that the Rabbinic position was developed partially, at least, in response to the use made of Melchizedek by Hebrews and/or other writers in the early church.

Melchizedek and the priesthood

From an early time Melchizedek was identified by the Rabbis with Shem, the son of Noah. The reasons for this identification are not easy to determine, and so far as the Rabbis themselves were concerned there was little necessity for proving this proposition. The Melchizedek–Shem identification was a commonplace from a very early time, being found even in the Targums.[1]

---

[1] Fitzmyer, *The Genesis Apocryphon of Qumran Cave I*, pp. 31–2, has given us an exceptionally useful tabular survey of the Targumic evidence from which we discover that the identification of Melchizedek with Shem is to be found in Neofiti I and Pseudo-Jonathan, while it is missing in Onqelos. He does not mention the Fragment Targum (Jerusalem II), but in that document, which does contain Gen. xiv. 18, the identification is also made: מלכי צדק מלכא

Table 4.2

Arpachshad was the father of Shelah when he had lived	35 years
Shelah was the father of Eber when he had lived	30 years
Eber...Peleg	34 years
Peleg...Reu	30 years
Reu...Serug	32 years
Serug...Nahor	30 years
Nahor...Terah	29 years
Terah...Abram	*70 years*
Number of years since the birth of Arpachshad was	*290 years*
Number of years Shem lived after the birth of Arpachshad	*500 years*
Number of years Shem lived after the birth of Abram	*210 years*

Wuttke has suggested, not improbably, that the reason for this identification is to remove the mystery surrounding Melchizedek's single appearance in the Torah by claiming that this is only a new name, not a new figure.[1]

If one reads Gen. xi carefully, one discovers that according to the genealogy of vss. 10ff. Shem had 210 years of life left to him at the time of the birth of Abraham. This result is gained from the information that Shem lived 500 years after the birth of his son Arpachshad (Gen. xi. 10) and from the ages given for the descendants of Shem when they begat their first sons. I have arranged the data from Gen. xi in Table 4.2 above. Not only was Shem alive at the time of the birth of Abraham, he also outlived Abraham by 35 years! According to Gen. xxv. 7 the days of Abraham's life numbered 175 years, but we have seen that Shem lived 210 years after the birth of Abraham, leaving us with a difference of 35 years. We may also observe, following the same method, that every one of the descendants of Shem mentioned in Gen. xi lived until after the birth of Abraham, and

בירושלם דהוא שם רבה. By the time we meet this concept in the Talmud and Midrashim the identification is an assumption which requires no proof. I find one proof, a very late proof, in the Midrash Tehillim on Ps. lxxvi. 3, which falls outside of the period under consideration.

[1] *Melchisedech*, p. 19. He applies on p. 19 n. 1 the principle *quod non in thora non in mundo*, but it is difficult to see exactly how that applies to this problem since Melchizedek is, in fact, mentioned.

Table 4.3. *Years lived after birth of Abraham*

Arpachshad	148 years
Shelah	178 years
Eber	239 years
Peleg	48 years
Reu	78 years
Serug	91 years
Nahor	49 years
Terah	135 years

Shelah and Eber actually outlived Abraham. This may be easily seen by reference to Table 4.3.

These facts were probably not lost upon the Rabbis. In *Gen. R.* (*Lech Lecha*) XLIV. 7, in commenting on Gen. xv. 1, it is explained that the Lord told Abraham not to fear because Abraham was afraid that Shem (= Melchizedek) would be angry with him for slaying his sons. Shem, on the other hand, was afraid lest Abraham should be angry with him for giving birth to such wicked sons as those who took part in the coalition which Abraham defeated at Dan. Hence, not only is Melchizedek Shem, the four kings of the Elamite coalition were Shem's sons. The most likely candidates, since Abraham presumably did not fight against his father Terah, are Arpachshad, Shelah, Eber, and Serug, and this view is supported at least in the later tradition, as Wuttke points out.[1] It may be, however, that in the Talmudic period no actual identification of names was made.[2]

[1] *Ibid.* p. 22 n. 6.

[2] This scheme is possible only in the MT. In the Samaritan version, the LXX, and Jubilees, 940, 1070, and 567 years respectively have passed from the birth of Arpachshad to the birth of Abram. Epiphanius, *Panarion* LV. 6 uses the LXX of Gen. xi to prove that Shem could not possibly have been Melchizedek, a doctrine which he assigns to the Samaritans instead of to the Jews. Skinner, *Genesis*, p. 233, has laid out the evidence of the Versions in a very convenient chart. My reconstruction is supported by the chronology of the synagogue from a later time as is pointed out by Hermann Strack and Paul Billerbeck, 'Der 110. Psalm in der altrabbinischen Literatur', Str.-B. IV/1, 453 n. 2. This is easily the most important and most comprehensive review of the important topic of the use of the 110th Psalm by the Rabbis, and although much of it is not directly applicable to our study, it is very important for an understanding of the psalm in the New Testament. I shall hereafter simply refer to this article as 'Der 110 Psalm'.

Another factor which may underlie the identification of Melchizedek with Shem is the blessing of Shem in Gen. ix. 26:

> Blessed be Yahweh, the God of Shem,
> and may Canaan be a servant to him.

To this we might compare the blessing which Melchizedek gives to Abram which has some similarity from a form-critical standpoint:

> Blessed be Abram by El Elyon,
>   maker of the heavens and the earth;
> and blessed be El Elyon, who has
>   delivered your enemies into your hand.

What may have been more important than the form of this passage is that Yahweh in Gen. ix. 26 is called the 'God of Shem', and in Gen. xiv. 18 Melchizedek appears as priest of El Elyon, which deity the Rabbis as well as Philo and Josephus identified with the true God. Between Gen. ix. 26 and Gen. xiv. 18 there is no other passage in which Yahweh is said to be the God of anyone other than Shem. Further, the words וישכן באהלי שם, 'and let him dwell in the tents of Shem', were taken by some to refer to the Shekinah instead of Japheth.[1] It would be natural to see in the narrative of Gen. ix the blessing of Shem which is passed on directly to Abraham by Shem in Gen. xiv. The reader will recognize that this reconstruction is to a large extent a matter of speculation and borrows from materials which come from several centuries. I have been able to suggest some reasons why Melchizedek and Shem might have been identified in the Rabbinic materials. I have not isolated *the* reason since that degree of certainty lies beyond the information contained in the sources. The only certainty is that they were in fact identified from the second century A.D. on.

---

[1] *Gen. R.* (*Noah*) XXXVI. 8, which reads '*And let him dwell in the tents of Shem...* The Shekinah does not dwell except in the tents of Shem.' Since this opinion is not assigned to any single authority, we cannot date it any earlier than the fourth century A.D., the time of the compilation of *Genesis Rabbah*. On this point cf. Moore, *Judaism* I, 166. See also Hermann L. Strack, *Introduction to the Talmud and Midrash*, trans. Elaine Lustig and Bernard Cole (Harper Torchbooks, The Temple Library, No. 808L; New York: Harper & Row, Publishers, 1965), pp. 217–18. This latter work will hereafter be cited as Strack, *Introduction*.

Whatever the reasons for this identification, the identification of Melchizedek with Shem had already been made by the first third of the second century A.D. as is shown by several quotations from R. Ishmael ben Elisha, the contemporary and exegetical opponent of R. Akiba (ca. A.D. 110–35).[1]

R. Zechariah[2] said in the name of R. Ishmael, 'The Holy One, blessed be He, desired to derive the priesthood from Shem, as it is said, *And he was priest to El Elyon*. Since he prefaced the blessing of Abraham to the blessing of the Place,[3] he derived it from Abraham, as it is said, *And he blessed him and said, " Blessed be Abram by El Elyon who acquires*[4] *the heavens and earth, and blessed be El Elyon . . . "* (Gen. xiv. 19b–20a).' Abraham said to him, 'Does one[5] actually preface the blessing of the slave to the blessing of his acquirer?'[6] From the hand (of Shem) he gave it to Abraham, as it is said, *The Lord said to my Lord, 'Sit on my right hand until I shall set your enemies as a stool for your feet'* (Ps. cx. 1), and after this it is written, *The Lord has sworn and will not repent, 'You are a priest forever according to the order*[7] *of Melchizedek'* (Ps. cx. 4), i.e. 'according to the utterance[8] of Melchizedek'. This corresponds to what is written, *And he was priest to El Elyon*. He was a priest, but his seed was not a priest.

(t. b. Ned. 32b)

---

[1] Strack, *Introduction*, p. 112; Moore, *Judaism* I, 87–9. It might be remembered that R. Ishmael is the author of the thirteen *middoth* prefixed to *Sifra*, and that he is known for the famous dictum 'The Torah speaks the language of men.'

[2] This is perhaps the son-in-law of R. Levi who is a fourth-century Amora from Palestine. Cf. Wilhelm Bacher, *Die Agada der palästinenischen Amoräer*, III: *Die letzten Amoräer des heiligen Landes* (Strassburg: Karl J. Trübner, 1899), 753. This three-volume work (I, 1892; II, 1896; III, 1899), will hereafter be referred to as Bacher, *Pal. Amor.* I, II, or III.

[3] In Rabbinic texts the circumlocutions and euphemisms for the divine name are translated literally so as to avoid inventing new ones.

[4] קנה, the most usual meaning for the word as we have already seen.

[5] On this use of the masculine plural participle see David Daube, 'Participle and Imperative in I Peter', which is contained in Edward Gordon Selwyn's *The First Epistle of St. Peter* (2nd ed.; London: Macmillan & Co., Ltd, 1964), pp. 467–88; see especially pp. 474–5.

[6] קונו, obviously a play on קנה (see note 3 above). My translation is an attempt to render the play and loses thereby some of its idiomatic force.

[7] על דברתי.

[8] על דיבורו, play on על דברתי. The 'utterance' is the blessing of Gen. xiv. 19b–20a.

The parallel passage in *Lev. R.* (*Qedoshim*) xxv. 6 continues this argument of R. Ishmael in the more familiar format of an argument with R. Akiba:

R. Ishmael used to say, 'Abraham was high priest. This is what is written, *The Lord has sworn and will not repent,* "*You are a priest forever...*" (Ps. cx. 4), but it is written, *And you shall be circumcised in the flesh of your foreskins* (Gen. xvii. 11). Now where will he circumcise? If he were to circumcise the ear, he would at this point not be fit to offer sacrifice. If he were to circumcise the heart, he would at this point not be fit to offer sacrifice. If he were to circumcise the mouth, he would at this point not be fit to offer sacrifice. Where can he circumcise so that he will be fit to offer sacrifice? One would have to say that this is a regulation concerning the body.'[1] R. Akiba used to say, 'There are four "foreskins". "Foreskin" is said of the ear, *Behold, their ear is uncircumcised*[2]... (Jer. vi. 10). "Foreskin" is said of the mouth, as it is said, *But I am uncircumcised at the lips* (Ex. vi. 30). It is said in reference to the heart, as it is said, *And all the house of Israel is of an uncircumcised heart* (Jer. ix. 24). But it is written, *Walk before me and be perfect* (Gen. xvii. 1). Where shall he circumcise? If he should circumcise the ear, he would at this point not be perfect. If he should circumcise the mouth, he would at this point not be perfect. Where should he circumcise so as to be perfect? One would have to say this is the foreskin of the body.'[3]

To mutilate the flesh by the act of circumcision would immediately disqualify Abraham from the priesthood. The last passage quoted points to a tension between God's command to Abraham to circumcise himself and the males of his household and the passing of the priesthood from Melchizedek to Abraham. One must remember that the encounter with Melchizedek

---

[1] הגוף, 'body', 'substance'. Jastrow, *Dictionary, sub voce* lists only this passage for the translation '*membrum*', but this translation is unnecessary. The ear, lips, and heart are not portions of the external torso which I take to be meant here, but only the male organ is such a portion which also has a foreskin. If the ear, lips, and heart are not to be circumcised, this leaves only the 'foreskin of the body'.

[2] In Hebrew the word 'foreskin', ערלה and 'uncircumcised', ערל, both come from the same root, ערל.

[3] Practically the same text is to be found in *Gen. R.* (*Lech Lecha*) LXVI. 5. The text quoted from *t. b. Ned.* 32b is also contained in *Lev. R.* (Qedoshim) xxv. 6 preceding the portion quoted by us, but by looking at both texts one is able to give a fuller text than is to be found in either source. Hence, this combination allows us to get the entire argument of R. Ishmael.

(Gen. xiv. 18–20) occurs before the commandment to circumcise (Gen. xvii. 11ff.). This strongly implies that Melchizedek himself at this point was thought of as being uncircumcised, passing the priesthood on to the uncircumcised Abraham. Hence the disagreement between R. Ishmael and R. Akiba. Actually the difference between the two teachers on this point is very small, and is concerned with a minor item. R. Ishmael sees the tension to be between the priesthood and circumcision, whereas R. Akiba sees the tension between circumcision and the command to be 'perfect' (תמים) in Gen. xvii. 1. Akiba's understanding, however, would have the same effect as R. Ishmael's since a priest with a blemish (מום) is prevented from performing his priestly functions (Lev. xxi. 16ff.).

The interpretation of Gen. xiv. 18–20 by which the priesthood is understood to be passed from Melchizedek to Abraham is continued in later midrash, but many of the details of that tradition changed over a period of from one and a half to three centuries from the time of R. Ishmael. Our most extensive picture of that development is to be found in *Gen. R.* to Gen. xiv. 18–20 (*Lech Lecha* XLIII. 6–8) which gives the opinions of many of the important Palestinian Amoraim. Interestingly enough, in this exegesis the name מלכי צדק has lost its character as a proper name and is now regarded as a title, understanding the first element, מלכי as 'king of... ', and the second element, צדק, as the name of the city where Melchizedek was priest on the basis of the verse, '*Sedeq* lodges in her...' (Isa. i. 21) which is said there of Jerusalem. The midrash reports the belief that Jerusalem sanctified those who dwelled in her, and Rashi in commenting on this says that this meant that even the person who stood in the city was made righteous.[1]

On the title 'king of Salem', R. Isaac the Babylonian[2] observed that this meant that Melchizedek was circumcised, obviously understanding the word שלם in the sense of 'whole' or 'complete' (i.e. = תמים). The tension which I mentioned above

---

[1] *Gen. R.* (*Lech Lecha*) XLIII. 6. Since this is not assigned to any single authority, we cannot with certainty assign it to the time before the composition of the entire midrash, i.e. in the fifth century A.D.

[2] A Palestinian Amora of undetermined date and locale. He is called 'the Babylonian' because of the place of his birth, but he lived most of his life in Palestine. On this see Bacher, *Pal. Amor.*, I, 477ff., and Strack, *Introduction*, p. 124.

between the priesthood and circumcision is no longer known, and circumcision is now considered to be a requisite for 'completeness' instead of a barrier to it.

Symbolic interpretation of the bread and wine which Melchizedek brought out to Abram is also to be found here, though with no unanimity of opinion. R. Samuel bar Nahman[1] saw the bread as the bread of the presence and the wine as the wine of libations. He was countered by the Rabbis who understood these items as reference to the Torah, referring to Prov. ix. 5, 'Come, eat of my bread, and drink of the wine I have mixed.'[2] R. Levi,[3] noting that wine in the Torah always 'leaves an ugly mark', sees the wine as symbolic of the oppression in Egypt (cf. Gen. xv. 13).

The troublesome word קנה is also dealt with in this section.[4] R. Abba[5] said in the name of R. Kahana[6] that the word קנה is attributive, referring to God, but R. Isaac[7] held that it referred to Abraham since through his activity of revealing the name of God to men he is accredited as though he were associated with God at the creation of the world. Hence, the words 'who acquires the heavens and the earth', refer to Abram's acquiring a place with God at the creation of the world.

The interpretation of the second line of the blessing (Gen. xiv. 20a) is found in the hands of three fourth-generation

[1] Who lived in the last part of the third century A.D. See Bacher, *Pal. Amor.*, I, 477ff. and Strack, *Introduction*, p. 124.

[2] These are the words of personified Wisdom who was at a later time identified with the Torah. Certainly the introductory words of *Genesis Rabbah* show that at least by the time of the composition of that opening section the complete identification of personified Wisdom with the Torah obtained. For the evidence of an earlier date of this association see W. D. Davies, *Paul and Rabbinic Judaism: Some Rabbinic Elements in Pauline Theology* (2nd ed., SPCK Paperbacks; London: SPCK, 1965), pp. 169–70, and see below, p. 123 n. 1.

[3] A third-generation Amora. Bacher, *Pal. Amor.* II, 296ff., and Strack, *Introduction*, p. 124.

[4] *Gen. R.* (*Lech Lecha*) XLIII. 7.

[5] R. Abba bar Kahana, a third-generation Amora. Bacher, *Pal. Amor.*, II, 475ff., and Strack, *Introduction*, p. 126.

[6] A second-generation Amora of the third century. Bacher, *Pal. Amor.*, III, 607ff., and Strack, *Introduction*, p. 122.

[7] This suggests the possibility that R. Isaac the Babylonian and R. Abba bar Kahana were contemporaries and would tend to place R. Isaac in the fourth century with the third-generation Amoraim.

Amoraim, R. Huna,[1] R. Judan,[2] and R. Judah bar Simon.[3] In interpreting the words אשר מגן צריך בידיך R. Huna and R. Judan understand the word מגן as a reference to מגנון, a Greek word (τὸ μάγγανον) which means a magic charm.[4] Huna interprets the passage in a straightforward manner: 'He directs your charms (מגנין שלך) against your enemies', but R. Judan is more subtle in his exegesis, pointing to the fact that the war was begun among former friends, and that God had directed magic charms against them so as to incite them against one another.[5] R. Judah bar Simon directs his interpretation to the entire blessing, holding that the three patriarchs, Abraham, Isaac, and Jacob, received blessing because of the merit (בזכות) of Abram's having given Melchizedek a tithe.[6] The section ends with a discussion of where Israel received the priestly blessing which does not touch upon Melchizedek and hence falls beyond the scope of our present inquiry.

When we look for invariable elements in the two types of tradition presented here, that of R. Ishmael and that of the *Genesis Rabbah*, we find very little. R. Ishmael and R. Samuel bar Nahman, for instance, agree that through Melchizedek the priesthood was passed to Abraham, but the majority of the Rabbis disagreed with R. Samuel and held, rather, that Melchizedek revealed the Torah to Abraham, and this interpretation seems to be followed by R. Isaac the Babylonian who makes

[1] Not to be confused with Rab Huna (died A.D. 297), the successor of Rab at Sura. This is R. Huna b. Abin, a Palestinian who resided for a time in Babylon and who mediated Babylonian influence to the Palestinian scholars. See Bacher, *Pal. Amor.*, III, 272ff., and especially pp. 275–9, and Strack, *Introduction*, p. 129.

[2] Bacher, *Pal. Amor.*, III, 237ff., and Strack, *Introduction*, p. 129.

[3] Bacher, *Pal. Amor.*, III, 160ff., and Strack, *Introduction*, p. 129.

[4] Jastrow, *Dictionary*, *sub voce*. The word is translated 'weapon' quite often, but this is a derived meaning which shows a modern bias. Note that the translation 'weapon' makes no sense in reference to R. Judan's interpretation. It was through a charm or something magic that former friends who used to exchange letters and gifts suddenly became enemies.

[5] *Gen. R.* (*Lech Lecha*) XLIII. 8.

[6] *Gen. R.* (*Lech Lecha*) XLIII. 8. The syntax of this thrice-repeated formula is somewhat strange, but its meaning is clear: בזכות ויתן לו מעשר מכל, 'because of the merit of *And he gave him a tenth of everything* ... ' (Gen. xiv. 20b). Throughout the Rabbinic material it is always assumed that Abram paid the tithe to Melchizedek even though this is not the only possible reading of Gen. xiv. 20b, as we saw in Chapter 2.

Abraham the revealer of God's name to God's creatures.[1] The character of Melchizedek is also different in the two sources. For R. Ishmael, Melchizedek (= Shem) is an impious character who loses the priesthood to Abraham because he dared to bless Abraham before God. In point of fact, God had intended to derive the priesthood from Shem (= Melchizedek) but did not since Melchizedek committed such a great impropriety. The giving of the priesthood to Abraham is something of an accident and, in fact, conflicts with God's commandment to

---

[1] Here, perhaps, is a direct reference to the Torah. God gives credit to Abraham 'as though you were associated with me at the creation of the world'. R. Hosha'ya opens the *Genesis Rabbah* by identifying the Torah with the אמון of Prov. viii. 30 which was present with God at the creation of the world. Thus, God credits Abraham as though he were the Torah itself. It has often been claimed, as by Moore (*Judaism* i, 265), that the identification of the Torah with the personified wisdom of Prov. viii was a commonplace in Jewish teaching as far back as Sirach (ca. 200 B.C.). In Ecclus. xxiv, personified Wisdom is speaking and saying that God fixed her dwelling in Israel (xxiv. 3–8). Later on (vs. 23) we read

ταῦτα πάντα βίβλος διαθήκης θεοῦ ὑψίστου, νόμον ὃν ἐνετείλατο ἡμῖν Μωϋσῆς κληρονομίαν συναγωγαῖς...

The chapter goes on to say that the law (ὁ νόμος) 'fills (men) with wisdom like the Pishon...' (vs. 24). The words ταῦτα πάντα require a plural antecedent, and in this case the reference is probably to the various statements of personified Wisdom in chapter xxiv. This implies that the law is a record of the dwelling of personified Wisdom with Israel which is also the instrument whereby men became filled with wisdom (vs. 24) and understanding (vs. 26) and whereby instruction was made to 'shine forth as light' (vs. 27). This cannot be considered an identification of personified Wisdom with the Torah. On the other hand, in Baruch iii. 36–59, especially iii. 38–41 personified Wisdom is said to have appeared on earth to be the 'book of the commandments of God and the law which endures forever'. We note, however, that in this last passage Wisdom has no direct connection with creation or Prov. viii. 30. Rather, as in Job xxviii, Wisdom is 'found' by God (iii. 32). To be sure, this is the God who created the world (vss. 32ff.), but Wisdom is not here associated with the creation. We add to this the observation that Ecclus. xxiv. 1–8 assumes the prior creation of the world when Wisdom issued from the mouth of God (xxiv. 3). The result of all of this is to say that we may agree that the Torah was identified with personified Wisdom from an early date, but the further step of identifying this figure with the אמון of Prov. viii. 30 is not to be found explicitly in our sources until later, perhaps being made first by R. Hosha'ya in the third century. If I am correct, however, in my claim that R. Isaac belongs to the fourth century (see above, p. 121 n. 7), my interpretation entails no difficulty. The entire problem of the pre-existent Torah as the אמון of Prov. viii. 30 needs further study, especially as it relates to the time before the third century A.D.

Abraham that he should circumcise himself. For the third generation of Amoraim in *Gen. R.* (*Lech Lecha*) XLIII. 6, on the other hand, the words מלכי צדק are a title, not a name. Melchizedek, who here is not identified with Shem,[1] is the revealer of the priesthood (R. Samuel bar Kahana) or the Torah (the Rabbis). He has no independent personality or importance, and the only 'historicizing' or biographical speculation here comes from R. Isaac who thinks that the title מלך שלם implies that Melchizedek was circumcised which intentionally or unintentionally completely destroys the tension between circumcision and the priesthood envisaged by R. Ishmael. The major agreements are that Melchizedek for one reason or another passed on to Abraham something of central importance to Israel's life, either the priesthood or the Torah, and that Melchizedek always has secondary importance to Abraham. Another way of saying the same thing is to say that Melchizedek has importance in these sources only insofar as he is the agent through whom Abraham receives the priesthood or the Torah.

The passing nature of the reference to Melchizedek in Gen. xiv would be enough to explain why Melchizedek was considered a relatively minor figure in *Gen. R.* (*Lech Lecha*) XLIII in comparison to Abraham and might also be enough to explain why R. Ishmael thought it necessary to besmirch the character of Melchizedek. Since, however, we know that Melchizedek in other quarters was not thought of as such a minor figure we must entertain the possibility that Melchizedek was subordinated out of polemical considerations, and we must withhold judgement about the reason for this subordination until we have examined Melchizedek as an eschatological figure in the Rabbinic literature.

Melchizedek as an eschatological figure

So far we have found that the Qumranites discussed Melchizedek both as a historical figure (Genesis Apocryphon) and as a divine figure (11Q Melchizedek). In the early church too he was thought of both as a historical figure (e.g., in Justin, Jerome,

[1] Although we have no reason to doubt that these authorities knew of the identification with Shem, they did not have need of that identification in their exegesis of Gen. xiv. 18–20.

etc.) and as a heavenly figure (e.g., in Hierakas). Is the same duality to be found in the Rabbinic sources? This is not as easy to answer as one might expect, and the nature of our sources for this aspect of Melchizedek speculation among the Rabbis is such as to require great caution on our part. Of primary importance are three passages, two of which are parallel: (a) *t. b. Sukkah* 52b, (b) *Song of Songs R.* II. 13, 4, and (c) *ARN* (A) XXXIV. Passages (a) and (b) are parallel, and I render them below in translation:

(a) *And the Lord showed me four artificers...* (Zech. ii. 3). Rab Hana bar Bizna[1] said, 'R. Simon the Righteous[2] said, "(These are) the Messiah ben David and Messiah ben Joseph and Elijah and Kohen Sedeq (כהן צדק)."' (*t. b. Sukk.* 52b)

(b) R. Berechiah[3] in the name of R. Isaac:[4] 'It is written, *And the Lord showed me four artificers...* (Zech. ii. 3), and these are, Elijah and King Messiah, and Melchizedek, and the one Anointed for War.' (*Song of Songs R.* II. 13. 4)

The third quotation reads as follows:

(c) *These are the two sons of oil[5] who are standing by the Lord of the whole land* (Zech. iv. 14). This is Aaron and the Messiah, but I do not know which of them is beloved except that it says, *The Lord has sworn and will not repent, 'You are a priest forever...'* (Ps. cx. 4). One is given to know that King Messiah is more beloved than a righteous priest (כהן צדק). (*ARN* (A) xxxiv)

The parallel between quotations (a) and (b) helps us establish some points of equivalence which I present schematically in Table 4.4 below.

---

[1] Rab Hana bar Bizna is a second-generation Babylonian Amora who is the traditionary for R. Simon the Righteous. See Wilhelm Bacher, *Die Agada der babylonischen Amoräer* (2nd ed., p. 77, hereafter cited as Bacher, *Babl. Amor.*[2]).

[2] A Tanna of unknown date or locale. Rab Hana was his traditionary. See Bacher, *Babl. Amor.*[2], p. 77 n. 7.

[3] A third-generation Palestinian Amora. See Bacher, *Pal. Amor.*, III, 344ff., and Strack, *Introduction*, p. 131.

[4] This is R. Isaac II (Isaac Nappaha), a student of R. Johanan Nappaha who died in the last part of the third century A.D. (Strack, *Introduction*, p. 122). This indicates a date around the turn of the fourth century A.D. On R. Isaac II see Bacher, *Pal. Amor.*, II, 205ff., and Strack, *Introduction*, p. 124.

[5] בני היצהר is translated here literally to avoid confusion with the word משיח. This strange construction is found once in the Old Testament.

Table 4.4

(a) *t. b. Sukk.* 52b	(b) *Song of Songs R.* II. 13. 4
Messiah ben David	Elijah
Messiah ben Joseph	King Messiah
Elijah	Melchizedek
Kohen Sedeq[1]	Anointed for War

Quotation (c) helps us in our identification of Melchizedek in (b) as Kohen Sedeq although there is also a third identification with Aaron. Since the Messiah ben David (a) and King Messiah (b) must be identical and Elijah is given in both (a) and (b), we may regard the identification of Melchizedek as Kohen Sedeq as virtually certain for quotation (b).

The expectation of a priest in the end time is based ultimately on Zech. vi. 13:

And he (the Messiah) will build the temple of Yahweh and will bear the majesty and sit and rule upon his throne. And a priest will be beside his throne, and peaceful consultation will obtain between the two of them.

Even though this priest, the 'righteous priest', is identified in (b) as Melchizedek, such was not always the case, and the figure of the Kohen Sedeq in other passages was identified with Phineas, who was, in turn, sometimes identified with Elijah.[2] This, of course, cannot be the case here since Elijah is named separately in quotations (a) and (b). Strack–Billerbeck[3] further contend that the Messiah himself is sometimes this priest, and W. D. Davies[4] has pointed to the work of Mowinckel and others in grounding this 'priestly' function of the Messiah in the

[1] I am in doubt whether כהן צדק should be rendered as a name or as a title. Except for (c) where the meaning is clear, I have settled for a simple transliteration. This is certainly a title, but one may question if it has not become stereotyped enough to be translated as a proper name.

[2] The evidence for this is given in 'Der 110 Psalm', pp. 462–3. See also Moore, *Judaism*, II, 358 n. 1.

[3] 'Der 110 Psalm', p. 462. One notes, however, that no text is cited in support of this view.

[4] W. D. Davies, *The Setting of the Sermon on the Mount* (Cambridge: Cambridge University Press, 1964), pp. 121–2, hereafter cited as *SSM*.

kingship ideology of the Ancient Near East. In this regard I
have tried to show in Chapter 2 that great caution must be
exerted in dealing with the priestly aspects of the kingship
ideology. The term כהן when used in reference to the king or
others not of priestly stock may not have the connotations of
priesthood usually ascribed to that word. Further, the 'priestly'
acts of the kings in the Old Testament[1] are not described as
priestly acts in the sources, and a more appropriate term would
be 'cultic'. We are not told in (b) exactly what role the priest
Melchizedek is to play in the end time, nor are we certain what
sort of a figure he is. Is he, like Elijah, an early figure translated
into heaven? Is Kohen Sedeq in (a) Melchizedek *redivivus*? Our
sources do not admit of such speculation, and in this regard it is
especially interesting to note that quotation (c) takes pains to
subordinate the figure to the Messiah, perhaps to avoid inordinate speculation.

These three quotations require some discussion about date
and composition, especially quotations (a) and (b). Quotations
(a) and (b) are so obviously two forms of the same basic tradition that I need expend no effort in proving this. In addition, it
is quite simple to assign a relatively early date to (a) since the
tradition there is ascribed to a Tanna, and hence cannot be
much more recent than the turn of the third century A.D. The
tradition in (b) is at least a century later, if not more. Another
reason for considering (b) to be later than (a) is the reference to
the Anointed for War. This is also a priestly figure who derives
ultimately from Deut. xx. 2ff. in which a priest comes forward
to give Israel instructions before a battle. Deut. xx. 2ff. becomes
the subject of a midrash in *m. Sotah* viii, but neither there nor in
the *gemara* to that chapter does this figure assume an eschatological role. In *Song of Songs R.* ii. 13, 4, he is definitely an
eschatological figure, standing where we would expect to find
reference to the Messiah ben Joseph. Besides the reference from
R. Simon the Righteous we have an early reference to the
Messiah ben Joseph from R. Dosa, a fifth-generation Tanna[2]
who taught that the words 'they will look at the one whom they
pierced...' (Zech. xii. 10) are a reference to the death of the

[1] *SSM*, p. 121 n. 5. The kings mentioned are David, Solomon, Jeroboam,
Uzziah, and Josiah. For a more complete discussion the reader should consult
Chapter 2.   [2] Moore, *Judaism*, ii, 370.

Messiah ben Joseph, whereas the Rabbis disagreed and declared that this had reference to the evil impulse.[1] The Messiah ben Joseph, whether believed in or not by the majority of teachers, was an established eschatological figure in some circles by the end of the Tannaitic period, whereas our only evidence for the Tannaitic period in relation to the משוח מלחמה is of a non-eschatological nature, a picture broken in the time of the Amora only in the passage quoted from *Song of Songs Rabbah*. Thus at least from the evidence at hand, one can only conclude that (a) is prior in time to (b), and that (a) is the older form of the common tradition.

If what I have said about the relative dates of (a) and (b) is accepted, then we are able to glimpse the development of the tradition. Two figures remain exactly the same, the Messiah ben David (= King Messiah) and Elijah. The figure of the Anointed for War was substituted for the Messiah ben Joseph. There is no reason at all to equate these two figures. In the first place, there is no evidence at all that such an identification was ever made. In the second place the Messiah ben Joseph is an Ephraimite, whereas the Anointed for War is a priest. The development of the tradition as regards Melchizedek is even clearer. Quotation (c) shows us that the title 'Kohen Sedeq' was used of Melchizedek in Tannaitic times. This does not prove that he was always *the* Kohen Sedeq, as indeed he was not, but as the precursor of the Aaronic priesthood, he was a type of the Kohen Sedeq. At a later time the conclusion was drawn that Melchizedek is *the* Kohen Sedeq, now considered as a distinct eschatological figure. In the *ARN* he would be at best a prototype of a later eschatological figure. We must also be aware that the assonance of the two names כהן צדק and מלכי צדק may have made the substitution in (b) easier.

I offer the above only as one possible reconstruction, but even without this the evidence is clear. Melchizedek is considered to be an eschatological figure only in one single passage, and that passage represents a later form of an earlier tradition which did not mention Melchizedek. In no sense can the figure of Melchizedek be considered fundamental to any Rabbinic system of eschatological speculation known to us, although (b) might be

---

[1] *t. b. Sukkah* 52a. Note that (a) is derived from *t. b. Sukkah* 52b and is really a continuation of that discussion.

regarded as pointing to the existence of such a system otherwise unknown to us.

A basic conclusion which comes from this investigation is that there is no passage in the Rabbinic material which can be said without doubt to refer to Melchizedek as a divine or an angelic being. This is even true as regards (b) which does not take the trouble to inform us as to what kind of figure Melchizedek is. This could only be decided from a knowledge of what kind of figures the other three 'artificers' were considered to be by R. Isaac. Elijah, translated bodily into the heavens, will presumably return in the same form. The Messiah, although his name is known before the foundation of the earth, is still a human figure.[1] Of the Anointed for War in an eschatological setting we know nothing. Even if we could show that here Melchizedek was considered a divine or angelic being, this would be a case of the exception proving the rule since such a role would be singular within the Rabbinic materials of our period.

Returning momentarily to the question of polemic which I raised above (p. 114), we are now in a position to say that we can find no occasion for such polemic within the Rabbinic sources themselves. Even if in some quarters Melchizedek were considered an eschatological figure of some sort, this would not in itself be reason enough for majority opinion to subordinate Melchizedek completely to Abraham. The possibility that the Rabbis are making a polemic against Christian use of Melchizedek involves certain assumptions which we are not in a position to make. Certainly, any document which subordinates Melchizedek to Abraham in the way we find it done in the sources discussed here could be said to counter the thought of the church. This would not prove, however, that such was the intent of the Rabbis since one must show the opportunity for contact and discussion between the Rabbis and the church on this point. We have no evidence for this as regards Melchizedek.

One possible source of opposition is the application of Ps. cx to Christ. Justin[2] claims that the Jews applied Ps. cx. 4 to King Hezekiah, but there is no trace of this in the Rabbinic documents themselves.[3] The problem is the assignment of priesthood

---

[1] See Moore, *Judaism*, II, 344.
[2] *Dialogue with Trypho* §33. Cf. also §83.
[3] Strack–Billerbeck, 'Der 110. Psalm', p. 456, assume too readily that this

to one not of priestly stock. Hence we find Ps. cx. 1 applied to
David but not Ps. cx. 4. Quotation (c), further, was the only
instance found where Ps. cx. 4 was applied to the Messiah and
there the intent is not to make of the Messiah a priest but to
exalt the Messiah above the 'righteous priest'. I have been unable to find any Rabbinic text which suggests a direct polemic
against the use of Melchizedek in the Epistle to the Hebrews,
although certainly none of the texts brought forward is in harmony with the thought of Hebrews about Melchizedek.[1]

Our discussion of the Christian and Rabbinic sources is now
at an end, and we turn our attention next to the Gnostic sources
for Melchizedek to complete our picture of the later sources.

quotation from Justin tells us something about the Rabbinic application of
Ps. cx. 4 despite the lack of supporting texts within the Rabbinic materials.

[1] For the sake of completeness we may mention that in *t. b. Baba Bathra*
14b Melchizedek is named as one of the ten elders who assisted David in
writing the Psalter along with Adam, Abraham, Moses, Heman, Jeduthun,
Asaph, and the three sons of Korah. This ascription of authorship to Melchizedek has only to do with his appearance in Ps. cx. 4 and is of no real
importance for our consideration.

CHAPTER 5

THE LATER SOURCES II: GNOSTICISM

There are at present only four published sources for Melchizedek within Gnostic thought. It is my understanding that more material will be forthcoming from the Chenoboskion documents,[1] but within the documents already published from that find there is no mention at all of Melchizedek. The four sources which are available to us at present are (a) Kahle's Fragment 52, (b) the Pistis Sophia, Books I–III, (c) the Pistis Sophia, Book IV, and (d) the Second Book of Ieû. I shall discuss each of these in turn and present a short summary at the end of this chapter.

FRAGMENT 52

This fragment was among those discovered by Sir Flinders Petrie in 1907 at Deir El-Bala'izah and which became the property of the Bodleian Library shortly thereafter. It has been published twice, once by W. E. Crum[2] and once by Paul Kahle[3] who edited and published the entire collection of texts made by Sir Flinders Petrie. Kahle informs us that this text is written in uncials of the fourth century A.D. but that it shows some archaisms in grammar.[4] The text translated below is taken from a text essentially like that presented by Kahle with one or two minor changes and some conjectures as to the proper way of filling some of the lacunae.[5]

---

[1] Cf. Delcor, 'Melchizedek', pp. 134f., for a brief exerpt in English from one of those documents.

[2] *JTS*, XLIV (1943), 176–9.

[3] *Bala'izah: Coptic Texts from Deir El-Bala'izah in Upper Egypt*, II (London: Oxford University Press, 1954), 473–7.

[4] *Ibid.* p. 473.

[5] E.g. I believe the spelling *melxizedek* should be changed to the more usual *melxisedek*, and it perhaps should be spelled *meldjisedek* as in the Pistis Sophia. In some cases I have filled the lacunae with a reading suggested by Kahle in his translation, as *psō[ma*, line 2. This is true of lines 11–12 where I have read *hermēn]eue[etbe melxis]edek*. The context, however, cannot be determined. Do lines 1ff. represent an introduction to the text?

Text 52 is a translation of an originally Greek work. For many
of the Greek words used there are perfectly adequate Coptic
words. For example, for λογικός we have Coptic *rmnhēt*; for
γνῶσις, we have Coptic *cown*; for ἀγάπη, we have Coptic *me*;
and for κιβωτός we have Coptic *taibe* which is, incidentally,
cognate to the original Hebrew תבה in Gen. vi and vii. The
verb ἄρχεσθαι and the noun ἀρχή are paralleled in Coptic by
variations on the word *shōrp*. Further, we note the agreement
between σύμβολον and νοερόν as possibly pointing back to a
Greek original. The name Σιγή is retained in Greek even though
the Coptic word *karōf* is used to translate the noun σιγή. Below
is my translation of the fragment from the reconstruction given
by Kahle and my own additions as explained above.

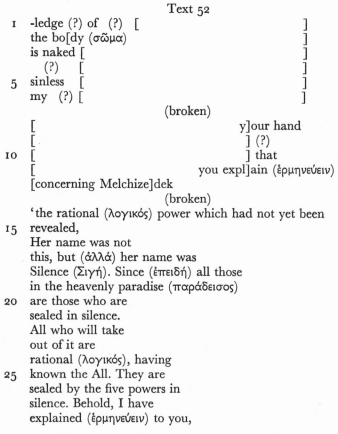

Text 52

1 -ledge (?) of (?) [   ]
   the bo[dy (σῶμα)   ]
   is naked [   ]
      (?) [   ]
5 sinless [   ]
   my (?) [   ]
                        (broken)
   [y]our hand
   [   ] (?)
10 [   ] that
   [you expl]ain (ἑρμηνεύειν)
   [concerning Melchize]dek
                        (broken)
   'the rational (λογικός) power which had not yet been
15 revealed,
   Her name was not
   this, but (ἀλλά) her name was
   Silence (Σιγή). Since (ἐπειδή) all those
   in the heavenly paradise (παράδεισος)
20 are those who are
   sealed in silence.
   All who will take
   out of it are
   rational (λογικός), having
25 known the All. They are
   sealed by the five powers in
   silence. Behold, I have
   explained (ἑρμηνεύειν) to you,

O John, concerning Adam
30 and paradise (παράδεισος)
and the five trees with an
intelligible allegory (σύμβολον νοερόν).'
When I had heard these things
                (margin)
35 I, John, said,
'I have begun (ἄρχεσθαι) with
a good beginning (ἀρχή).
    I have completed knowledge (γνῶσις)
and a mystery (μυστήριον)
40 which is hidden, and
allegories (σύμβολον) of truth.
Having been encouraged (προτρέπειν)
by your love (ἀγάπη),
now (δέ) I desire moreover to ask you
45 to explain (ἑρμηνεύειν) to me
in your love concerning
Cain and Abel. In
what manner (τύπος) did Cain
kill Abel? And (δέ)
50 not only this, but (ἀλλά) being
asked by the one (who)
spoke to him, saying,
"Where is Abel
your brother?" Cain,
55 then (δέ) denied, saying,
"Am (μή) I the keeper (...?")
                    (margin)
[....]   (?)   [   ]
[....]   (?)   [   ]
60 [...]   (?)   [   ]
[...]   (?)   [   ]
[..]   there he   [   ]
[...]   (?)   [   ]
[i]ts pl[ace s-]
65 [aying i]t
[   ] into the [pl-]
ace of the Ple[roma (πλήρωμα)]
which is completed. Be[hold]
I have explaine[d (ἑρμηνεύειν)]
70 to you, O Joh[n, c-]
oncerning Noah and h[is]
ark (κιβωτός) and [   ]

[...]   (?) [   ]
                              (broken)
75 [   ]him   (?) [   ]
    [s]ome [   ]
    [   ]   (?) [   ]
    [and (δέ) I wish,] moreover, to [ask you]
    [to] expl[ain (ἑρμηνεύειν)]
80 [to me c]oncerning Mel[chize-]
    [dek.] Is it not (μή) sa[id con-]
    [cerning him] that[1] having [no father]
    [and mo]ther, his paren[tage (γενεά)]
    not [being mentioned,]
85 he [h]as no beginn[ing (ἀρχή) of days]
    [(and) he] does not have an end of li[fe, being]
    like unto a so[n of]
    [G]od, bein[g]
    [a] priest forever? It is sai[d]
90 [a]lso concerning him that [   ].
    [   ]   (?) [   ]
                              (broken)

The text is a revelation to John and is, at least to that extent, akin to the Apocryphon of John known to us from Chenoboskion and the Berlin Codex.[2] It differs from the Apocryphon, however, in several significant features. In the first place it is an allegorical interpretation of some of the principal figures of the early chapters of Genesis: Adam, Cain and Abel, Noah, and Melchizedek, and is not similar in format to the Apocryphon of John. Secondly, it is a more abbreviated work than the Apocryphon. Thirdly, it does not have the intention of revealing completely the Gnostic cosmology lying behind it. It is, as it were, a Gnostic midrash. We note in passing the apparent placement of Melchizedek directly after Noah and suggest that the identification of Melchizedek with Shem was known to the author. On the pattern of the Apocryphon, it is reasonable to think that the text represents a dialogue between John and the Risen Christ. Less likely, but possible, is that it is a dialogue between John

---

[1] Professor Orval Wintermute has suggested to me that lines 83–4 should read w[atyōt pe mn at]maw which is an improvement that removes the awkward circumstantial and makes the expression parallel so that we should read, 'That he is fatherless and motherless...'.

[2] Kahle, Bala'izah, p. 476.

and an angel. Because of its simple style and abbreviated format, it might be suggested that it is an 'introductory' Gnostic work, designed for persons who know the Christian Bible and who have recently been 'converted' (if that is the right word) to a Gnostic form of Christianity.

Of particular note are lines 81ff. which make up a direct paraphrase of Heb. vii. 3. Even though we know nothing at all about the interpretation Melchizedek receives in this fragment, we do know that interpretation was arrived at with reference to Heb. vii. 3. Hence, this text is stamped with an unmistakably Christian character, even though the figures interpreted are all from the Old Testament.

The age of the original Greek document is impossible to determine with any accuracy. If it is, in fact, an imitation of the Apocryphon of John to the extent of its being a revelation of the Risen Christ to John, then it might well be dated anywhere from the end of the second century A.D. This relationship to the Apocryphon of John would suggest an ultimate origin for the interpretations of the text in the Barbelo-Gnostic movement which Irenaeus, *Against Heresies* I. 27 tells us was the forerunner of the Valentinian form of Gnostic speculation. On such a basis we might view this fragment as representing some of the earliest Christian Gnosticism[1] known to us, stemming ultimately from the first part of the second century A.D.[2]

THE PISTIS SOPHIA, BOOKS I–III

Only in the Pistis Sophia is there, among all the Gnostic sources, anything like a wealth of information about Melchizedek. Fortunately for us the greater part of this information is some-

[1] Since all of the sources described in this chapter are derived from 'Christian' Gnostic sects, we have no hesitation about using the term 'Gnosticism'. This author approves, as a matter of convention, of the use of the word 'Gnosticism' only in reference to Christian systems, 'Gnosis' in reference to the wider world of cosmological ideas represented in Gnosticism and 'Gnostic' as the adjective proper to either term. On this see R. McL. Wilson, *Gnosis and the New Testament* (Philadelphia: Fortress Press, 1968). I regret the parochialism which has called such terminology into play as a necessity of scholarship.

[2] For a convenient and excellent discussion of the problem of the dates of the various versions of the Apocryphon the reader is referred to Wilson, *ibid.* pp. 103ff.

what repetitive, and we shall be able to state the various views of Melchizedek in the Pistis Sophia with some economy.

The Pistis Sophia, found in Codex Askewianus, is written in two different hands of the last half of the fourth century A.D.[1] Composed of four books, it is an unwieldy, totally unsystematic collection of Gnostic speculations. Of the four books contained within the text, Books I–III are generally considered to be of a relatively late date, and Book IV of a relatively earlier date.[2] Material concerning Melchizedek is to be found in both these divisions of the work. There can be little doubt as to the correctness of the assertion that the various parts of the Pistis Sophia were originally composed in Greek, and Schmidt takes great pains to do this.[3] The location of the place of origin is without doubt Egypt, as is shown, for example, by the fact that Jesus' ascension is said to have taken place on the fifteenth of Tobe, pointing to the use of the Egyptian calendar.[4] In the fourth book specifically Egyptian deities are referred to and are identified with more traditionally Gnostic deities.[5]

The date of the fourth book of the Pistis Sophia was placed by Schmidt in the first half of the third century A.D., and the first three books were assigned to the latter part of that century.[6] The fact that Epiphanius knows a book of the 'greater and lesser questions of Mary' is taken by Schmidt to be a reference

[1] Carl Schmidt, *Koptisch-Gnostische Schriften*, I: *Die Pistis Sophia, Die beiden Bücher des Jeu, Unbekanntes Altgnostisches Werk*, Walter Till, ed. (3rd ed., Die Griechischen Schriftsteller der ersten Jahrhunderte; Berlin: Akadamie-Verlag, 1962), xvii–xviii. Walter Till's introduction to this third edition of Schmidt's classic translation should be consulted by the reader for a recent statement on introductory matters.   [2] *Ibid.* pp. xxiv–xxv.

[3] Carl Schmidt, *Pistis-Sophia* (Coptica: Consilio et Impensis Instituti Rask-Oerstediani, II; Jauniae: Gyldendalske Boghandel-Nordisk Forlag, 1925), pp. xixff. Although Schmidt's contention that the language of the Pistis Sophia is classical Sahidic has come into question, his basic contention that the work was composed originally in Greek is still accepted. One might, however, question whether the Pistis Sophia was ever found in its present form in Greek or whether the individual books might not have been translated into Coptic and composed later into a single treatise. I shall from now on refer to the Coptic text of Schmidt, the 1925 edition referred to in this note, as Schmidt, *Pistis-Sophia*, and the 1962 edition of the translation into German with Till's introduction as Schmidt–Till, *Koptisch-Gnostische Schriften*.

[4] Schmidt–Till, *Koptisch-Gnostische Schriften*, p. xxiii.

[5] *Ibid.* pp. xxiiiff.   [6] Schmidt, *Pistis-Sophia*, pp. xxxiiff.

to the format of the first three books.[1] If this were true, it would place an outside limit of A.D. 377 on the composition of the first three books. Till points out that the more recently discovered Gnostic materials, the Apocryphon of John, the Sophia of Jesus Christ, etc., which may be assigned to dates previous to A.D. 180, support Schmidt's dating of the Pistis Sophia which demonstrates a greater development of Gnostic speculation than is to be found in the earlier materials.[2]

Our discussion from here on will move chronologically backwards from the picture of Melchizedek in the first three books of the Pistis Sophia to that found in the fourth book. From there we shall move to the even earlier picture to be found in the Second Book of Ieû. All quotations below are drawn from Schmidt's Coptic text of the Pistis Sophia,[3] and all translations are mine.

We get a basic picture of the view of Melchizedek to be found in the first three books of the Pistis Sophia from the answer which Jesus gives to Mary in response to a question about the mode of purification of souls:

Before I had yet preached to all the archons of the aeons and also all the archons of Heimarmene and the Sphere (σφαῖρα), all of them were bound in their bonds and in their spheres (σφαῖρα), bound in their seals (σφραγίς), as (κατά-) Ieû, the Overseer (ἐπίσκοπος) of the Light had bound them from the beginning; and each one of them was continuing in his order (τάξις), and each one was going according (κατά) to his course (δρόμος) as (κατά-) Ieû, the Overseer (ἐπίσκοπος) of the Light had set them. Now when the time of the number (ἀριθμός) of Melchizedek, the great Receiver (παραλήμπτωρ) of Light would come, he would come into the midst of the aeons and all the archons who were bound in the Sphere (σφαῖρα) and in Heimarmene; and he would take the purity of the Light from all the

[1] *Ibid.* p. xxv.
[2] Schmidt–Till, *Koptisch-Gnostische Schriften*, p. xxv. I have doubts about setting a date in reference to 'development', but I have given this for the information of the reader.
[3] Schmidt, *Pistis-Sophia*. Since this Coptic text is the only standard Coptic text of the Pistis Sophia and is likely to remain so for a long time to come, I have cited the text according to the page and line in Schmidt's transcription, citing the line number as a superscript to the page number. This will allow the reader to locate the text cited faster than if it were cited according to the page and line number of the Coptic original, the numbering of which has become somewhat confused over the years.

archons of the aeons and from all the archons of Heimarmene and those of the Sphere (σφαῖρα).[1]

Here we are introduced to some very difficult ideas as regards Melchizedek. The title 'Receiver', παραλήμπτωρ, is a little-used Greek word, and its meaning can only be determined from the context. Here 'Receiver' indicates the function of descending into the midst of the aeons and collecting the Light contained within them, or, more exactly, the 'purity of the Light'. This activity takes place periodically as is shown by the tense and voice of the verb which is a habitude converted to the preterite by the particle *ne-*, which might be translated 'he used to be coming'. This refers to action which took place habitually before Jesus preached to the archons.

An amplification of this basic picture of the function of Melchizedek is provided in the passage immediately following the one quoted:

For (γάρ) he would take that which troubled them and would cause the transport-master (ἐπισπουδαστής) who was over them to move; and he would cause them to turn in their circles (κύκλος) forthwith; and he would take their power which was within them, and the breath of their mouth, and also the waters of their eyes and also the sweat of their bodies (σῶμα).[2]

This quotation makes explicit the manner in which the Light is taken from the archons. The receiving of the Light of the archons is associated with the removal of the vital functions of life. The breath of the archons and their tears are taken away. Indeed, their strength or power is completely sapped, leaving them inert, lifeless. Coincidental with this process is another process of confirming the archons in their preappointed orbits (κύκλος) and the appointment of the 'transport-master' over them to insure their eternal rotation. Hence, the receiving of the Light is a process of rarefaction resulting in a lifeless universe, eternally moving in the same prearranged pattern.

The removal of the Light is the occasion for the creation of

---

[1] *Ibid.* pp. 34⁷–34²³. I have observed some conventions in my translations. Greek words taken over into the Coptic text have either been transliterated (as with 'archon', 'aeon', etc.) or placed in parentheses. Important words have been capitalized such as 'Light', 'Overseer', 'Receiver', etc.

[2] *Ibid.* pp. 34²⁴–35¹.

the word (κόσμος) which we know. This process is first described in the following manner:

And Melchizedek, the Receiver (παραλήμπτωρ) of the Light would purify those powers and take their Light to the Treasury (θησαυρός) of the Light, and all the matter (ὕλη) of each of the servants (λειτουργός) of all the archons would gather together, and the servants (λειτουργός) of all the archons of Heimarmene and the servants of the Sphere (σφαῖρα) which are below the aeons would take them. These who were under the archons would make them into the soul (ψυχή) of man and of beast and of reptile and wild beast (θηρίον) and bird; and they would send them into this world (κόσμος) of mankind.[1]

Melchizedek takes the strength or power which he has received from the archons and purifies it, which is the concept which stands behind the idea of the 'purity of the Light' referred to above. This process of purification leaves matter (ὕλη) as dross which is formed by the servants of Heimarmene and the Sphere into the souls of men and other earthly creatures. We have the picture of the material remains of the purification process precipitating towards the center of the universe, being formed along the way by the servant of Heimarmene and the Sphere into earthly souls.

A slightly different version of this process is appended to this passage without any thought of contradiction:

Now too the Receivers (παραλήμπτωρ) of the sun and the Receivers (παραλήμπτωρ) of the moon would look at the heaven and would see the forms (σχῆμα) of the manners of motion of the aeons and the form (σχῆμα) of Heimarmene and those of the Sphere (σφαῖρα); and they would take the power of the Light, and the Receivers (παραλήμπτωρ) of the sun would prepare it and place it (aside) until they should give it to the Receivers (παραλήμπτωρ) of Melchizedek, the purifier of the Light. Their material (ὑλικόν) remains they would take to the sphere (σφαῖρα) which is below the aeons and make it into the souls (ψυχή) of man and also make it into reptile and beast and wild animal (θηρίον) and bird according to (κατά) the circle (κύκλος) of the archons of that sphere (σφαῖρα) and according to all the forms (σχῆμα) of its cycle. And they would cast them into this world (κόσμος) of mankind, and they would become

[1] *Ibid.* p. 35[1–10].

soul (ψυχή) in that place (τόπος) as (κατά-) I have (just) finished telling you.[1]

Suddenly some new figures have been introduced into the scheme, making it difficult for us to reconcile with the previous accounts, and, in fact, no reconciliation is really necessary. Rather, we have here another, more developed form of the same tradition. Now it is the function of the Receivers of the sun and the Receivers of the moon to take the power of the Light and refine it into its component parts, Light and matter. Melchizedek no longer descends into the universe, but the Receivers of Melchizedek who take the Light laid aside by the Receivers of the sun. Melchizedek in this version, though 'purifier of the Light', seems to stand apart and delegate the role of descending into the aeons to his Receivers. The material souls are cast into the innermost circle of the universe, 'this world', and are formed according to the influence of the cycles of this innermost circle. The closing words of this passage suggest an editorial link, and indeed we are not surprised to find another form of the same story immediately following.

In the versions of the myth of the descent of Melchizedek already discussed the archons play a relatively passive role in the process. Indeed, as the Light is removed from them they tend to become inert and lifeless. Book 1 ends its discussion of Melchizedek with a slightly different version of the story in which the archons resist the process by which the dross resulting from the purification process is made into the souls of earthly beings. After giving an account of the descent of Melchizedek and his taking away the purified Light, the account continues:

And as for the matter (ὕλη) of their dross, all the archons of the aeons and the archons of Heimarmene and those of the Sphere (σφαῖρα) would surround it and swallow it, and they would not allow them (i.e. the dross) to come to be soul (ψυχή) in the world (κόσμος). Thus they would swallow their matter (ὕλη) so that they would not become weak or exhausted (ἀτονεῖν) or their power cease within them.[2]

This account is repeated with little change immediately following, and we need not reproduce the remaining lines.[3] The material dross which results from the purification of the Light

---

[1] *Ibid.* p. 35[10–24].   [2] *Ibid.* pp. 36[20]–37[1].   [3] *Ibid.* pp. 37[1–14].

still contains Light, and by swallowing the dross the archons retain some Light and to that extent remain potent. This is introduced, no doubt, as an explanation for why Melchizedek must reappear periodically to extract Light from the archons.

The only discussion of Melchizedek in the second book of the Pistis Sophia is in a passing reference in which it is explained that Melchizedek came forth out of the fifth tree in the Treasury of Light,[1] a matter which receives no elaboration in the second book. Melchizedek is associated with Ieû, the Guard (φύλαξ) 'of the place of those of the right hand',[2] and the two 'Leaders' (προηγούμενος). All five of these proceed from a different tree in the Treasury and are composed of the purest Light.[3]

In the third book we find a discussion of Melchizedek's role in relation to the individual soul. In a pattern which has become familiar by now we find first a general statement about the activity of Melchizedek:

And Melchizedek the great Receiver (παραλημπτής) of the Light, who is in the place (τόπος) of those of the right hand, would seal (σφραγίζειν) that soul (ψυχή), and the Receivers (παραλήμπτωρ) of Melchizedek would seal (σφραγίζειν) that soul (ψυχή), and he would take it to the Treasury (θησαυρός) of the Light.[4]

We notice first of all the variations in spelling by which Melchizedek is designated as παραλημπτής, and his 'Receivers' as παραλήμπτωρ. From this point on Melchizedek is never again designated as παραλήμπτωρ although the significance of this is difficult to determine. Perhaps this designation παραλημπτής was originally reserved for Melchizedek and παραλήμπτωρ reserved for his 'Receivers'.

The Receivers of Melchizedek have as their task the removal of souls from the judgement of the archons or from the serpent:

The Receivers (παραλημπτής) of Melchizedek will snatch away (ἁρπάζειν) quickly (-σπουδή) the soul (ψυχή), whether (εἴτε) the serpent (δράκων) should release it or it should be, on the other hand,

---

[1] Cf. The Gospel of Thomas §19.

[2] The Light figures are also conceived of in this section as being separated from the universe of archons by a curtain. The figure of the Guard is an elaboration of an original function of Melchizedek as we shall see below.

[3] I have here given the content of the passage without quoting it. See Schmidt, *Pistis-Sophia*, pp. 194²³ – 195¹².

[4] *Ibid.* p. 291¹⁴⁻¹⁹.

subject to the judgements (κρίσις) of the archons. In general (ἀπαзαπλῶς), the Receivers (παραλήμπτωρ) will snatch it away (ἁρπάξειν) anywhere (-τόπος) it is, and they will take it to the place (τόπος) of the Middle (μέσος) before the Virgin (παρθένος) of the Light.[1]

Essentially the same thing is said of the Receivers of Melchizedek later in the third book and we need not repeat that account here.[2]

Some attempt is made to reconcile Melchizedek's function in Book I with that in relation to souls without too much success. On pp. 333^{24}–334^{10} the five archons of Heimarmene make souls by kneading the dross and dividing it into individual souls. Only those souls which are made from the sweat of the archons remain under the control of the archons. The soul which is produced 'out of the dross of the purification of the Light' is taken by Melchizedek, presumably to the Treasury of the Light. That this account is a compromise between the two functions of Melchizedek is obvious. In Book I the sweat of the archons is not given any special distinction, and it was simply placed with the breath and tears of the archons as symbols of the life force of the archons. This account smacks of hair-splitting and causes us to wonder if the two functions can in fact be reconciled.

We find a different, though more uniform, picture of Melchizedek when we turn from Books I–III and concentrate on Book IV and the Second Book of Ieû to which we now turn.

PISTIS SOPHIA, BOOK IV, AND THE SECOND BOOK OF IEÛ

Moving backwards chronologically, we come next to the fourth book of Pistis Sophia which is the earliest.[3] In this book, as well as in the Second Book of Ieû, Melchizedek is known as 'Zorokothora Melchizedek', the significance of which I shall discuss later. In Book IV we are introduced to an earlier version of the descent of Melchizedek into the aeons. This occurs in answer to a question from Mariam about how souls are taken out of the

[1] *Ibid.* pp. 324^{20} – 325^{1}.
[2] *Ibid.* p. 326^{20-6}. The only difference here is a description of the torment laid on the souls by the servants of the archons until the souls reach the Virgin of the Light.   [3] See above, p. 136.

universe.[1] First of all Jesus explains there are only two original
Light figures, Ieû and Melchizedek,[2] Ieû being the 'administra-
tor' (προνοήτος) of all the archons, and Melchizedek the
'ambassador' (πρεσβευτής) of the Lights. Both Ieû and Melchizedek descend into the world of the archons and there 'make
purification' in the midst of the archons. I quote the rest of the
passage:

And Zorokothora Melchizedek would take the purity of the Lights
which were purified in the archons and he would take them to the
Treasury (θησαυρός) of the Light. When the cipher (ψῆφος) and
also the time of their function (τάξις)[3] of their going down into the
archons would occur, they would restrict them and trouble (θλίβειν)
them, taking away the purity which was in the archons. Now (δέ) in
the hour when they should release them in the distress of their
trouble (θλίβειν), they would return to the places (τόπος) of the
Treasury (θησαυρός) of the Light. It would come to pass that when
they would reach the place (τόπος) of the Middle (μέσος), Zorokothora Melchizedek would take away the Lights and bear them above
to the gate (πύλη) of those of the Middle (μέσος) and take them to
the Treasury (θησαυρός) of the Light; and Ieû himself would return
(ἀναχωρεῖν) to the places (τόπος) of the right hand until the time of
the cipher (ψῆφος) for them to go out again should come.[4]

The differences between this account and that of Book I are
obvious. The manner of the emission of the Light from the
archons is different here in that the archons are first troubled by
Ieû and Zorokothora in some unspecified manner. As a result of
this the archons give up their 'purity'. In Book I it is the 'purity
of the Light' itself which troubles the archons, and Melchizedek
puts an end to this trouble by removing the Light. Next, we
observe the obvious difference that in this passage alone Ieû
accompanies Zorokothora into the midst of the archons and
cooperates in the collection of the Light. Melchizedek alone,
however, takes the Light into the Treasury of the Light. The
designation 'Receiver' (παραλήμπτωρ, παραλημπτής) is not
used of Melchizedek in Book IV or in the Second Book of Ieû,
just as 'Zorokothora' is not used in Books I–III of the Pistis

[1] Schmidt, *Pistis-Sophia*, p. 360²ᶠᶠ.
[2] The relevant line reads (p. 360¹²⁻¹³): 'These two (Ieû and Melchizedek)
only are the great Lights...'
[3] This translation of τάξις seems called for by the context.
[4] Schmidt, *Pistis-Sophia*, pp. 360¹³ – 361⁴.

Sophia. There is no mention made here of any 'Receivers of Melchizedek' or helping angels of any kind, and he is accompanied by Ieû only, who, if anything, is superior to Melchizedek.

A passing vignette throws some light on this older picture of Melchizedek.[1] Jesus explains in this passage that the three-faced Hecate is responsible for all lying and false swearing. Those souls which she captures remain under her control for a period of 105 years and six months after which little Sabaoth the Good and Bubastis would draw back the curtain (between the places of the right and left hands):

And Zorokothora Melchizedek looks out from in the heights, and the world (κόσμος) and the mountains move and the archons are disturbed. And he looks down upon all the places (τόπος) of Hecate, and her places (τόπος) go out and perish. And the souls (ψυχή) which were in her punishments (κόλασις) are taken and are caused to return to the Sphere (σφαῖρα) once more because they were destroyed in the fire of her punishments (κόλασις).[2]

The activity of looking upon the archons is enough to cause them to be troubled. This disturbance causes the powers subject to Hecate to give up the souls (which are at least partly Light), and these souls are sent back to the Sphere,[3] there supposedly to be reconstituted.

At the beginning of Book IV there is a prayer which serves as a bridge between Book IV and the Second Book of Ieû. Here I give a small portion of the text:

Hear me, my Father, the Father of all Fatherhood, the Unbounded (ἀπέραντος) of the Light: *aeëiwo, iaō, aōi, ōia, psinōther, thernops nopster, zagourē, nethmomaōth, nepsiomaōth, marachachtha, thobarrabau, tharnachachan*, Zorokothora, Ieû, Saboath.[4]

I do not pretend to understand the meaning of all the names presented in this prayer. The second, third, and fourth are obviously permutations on the divine name Iaô, and the last three are familiar to us from what we have already read. Enough,

---

[1] *Ibid.* p. 363[8ff]. [2] *Ibid.* pp. 363[28] – 364[6].

[3] Here I take the third masculine plural as a virtual passive, a construction very common in Coptic. See Walther C. Till, *Koptische Grammatik* (2nd ed., Lehrbücher für das Studium der Orientalischen Sprachen, vol. 1; Leipzig: VEB Verlag Enzyklopädie, 1961), §326.

[4] Schmidt, *Pistis-Sophia*, p. 353[8–12].

then, can be told about the names to question Schmidt's assumption that all of these names, including the name Zorokothora, are names for the highest deity.[1] Even though I cannot translate the names without undue conjecture, I can point out that the four names before *tharnachachan* show Aramaic- or Hebrew-like endings (*-ōth*, *-tha*, *-au*). One name shows the element *-rē*, which may represent the name of the Egyptian sun god.[2] I suggest that these names represent forms for the different names of Light figures much like the name 'Aberemtho' for Jesus used in Book III of the Pistis Sophia. The name 'Zorokothora' is a magical name for Melchizedek and within the context of prayer has a magical function. One would not be wrong in comparing these names to the use of similar magical names, say, in the Paris Magical Papyrus. The use of magical names may have been thought of as providing the one praying with direct access to the highest deity.

Zorokothora or Zorokothora Melchizedek is mentioned only twice in the Second Book of Ieû in two prayers which show similarity to the one which begins Book IV of the Pistis Sophia. I give here only the relevant portions of the prayers.

Hear me, my Father, the Father of all fatherhood, the Unbounded (ἀπέραντος) of Light who is in the ▣ of ☉: May the fifteen Assistants (παραστάτης) come, these who serve beneath the seven virgins (παρθένος) of the ☉, these who are over the baptism (βάπτισμα) of life: Astrapa, Tesphoiode, Ontonios, Sinetos, Lachon, Poditanios, Opakis, Phaidros, Odonteuchos, Diaktios, Knesion, Dromos, Euideu[ ]os, Polupaidos, Entropon. May they come and baptize (βαπτίʒειν) my disciples (μαθητής) in the water of the life of the seven virgins (παρθένος) of the ☉. And may their sins be remitted, and cleanse (καθαρίʒειν) their lawless acts (ἀνομία), and reckon to them the inheritance (κλῆρος) of the Kingdom of the Light. And if

[1] Carl Schmidt, *Gnostische Schriften in Koptischer Sprache aus Codex Brucianus* (Texte und Untersuchungen zur Geschichte der altchristlichen Literatur, vol. VIII, pts. 1–2; Leipzig: J. C. Hinrichs'sche Buchhandlung, 1892), p. 373 n. 2. This work will hereafter be cited as Schmidt, *Codex Brucianus*. Reference to the Coptic text of the Second Book of Ieû will be made to their page location in this edition.

[2] It is very possible, indeed, almost probable, that most of these names are free constructions. To the original authors who were, as we have seen, native Greek speakers in Egypt these magical words were probably formed to correspond to Semitic or Egyptian words known to them only secondarily.

you have remitted their sins and have wiped away their unlawful acts (ἀνομία), let there be a sign and let Zorokothora come and bring out the water of the baptism (βάπτισμα) of life in a single jar (ἀγγεῖον) of wine.[1]

The second prayer is longer, but very similar:

Jesus turned to the four corners of the world (κόσμος) and together with his disciples (μαθητής) cried out (ἐπικαλεῖσθαι) this prayer, saying it in the following manner: 'Hear me, my Father, the Father of all fatherhood, the Unbounded (ἀπέραντος) of Light, and cause my disciples (μαθητής) to be worthy of the baptism (βάπτισμα) of fire. And may you remit their sins and cause their unlawful acts (ἀνομία) to be cleansed (καθαρίζειν), these which have caused them to know, and these which have caused them not to know, these which have controlled them from their youth up to this day, and their slanders (καταλαλιά) and their curses and their false swearings and their frauds and their adulteries and their lusts (ἐπιθυμία) and their acts of greed, these that have controlled them from their youth up to this day. May you wipe them all away and cleanse (καθαρίζειν)[2] them all. May you cause Zorokothora Mel.[3] to come in secret and bring the water of the baptism (βάπτισμα) of the fire of the Virgin of the ☉, the judge (κριτής).'[4]

To explain the two symbols, ⊡ and ☉, employed in these prayers first, it might be pointed out that Schmidt correctly identified ⊡ as 'Treasury' and ☉ as 'Light' without, however, understanding why.[5] In seeking an Egyptian background, I found that ⊡ should be compared to the word ⌻ pr-ḥd, 'treasury', and that ☉ is the familiar determinative found in words for light such as ⌸☉, sšp, 'daylight'. These signs were probably used by the Coptic translator and not the original Greek author.

In the prayers from the Second Book of Ieû we are introduced to Melchizedek as the bearer of the water of baptism. It is perhaps surprising, but none the less true, to find that this role depends ultimately on speculation about Melchizedek in Gen.

---

[1] Schmidt, *Codex Brucianus*, pp. 107–8.

[2] Here I read ⲉⲕⲉⲕⲁⲑⲁⲣⲓⳍⲉ, the -ⲕⲁ- being lost through haplography.

[3] The meaning of the abbreviation ⲙⲉⲗ︥ can be none other than 'Melchizedek'.

[4] Schmidt, *Codex Brucianus*, pp. 109–10.

[5] See *ibid.* pp. 669–80 for a discussion of the principal abbreviations used in the Books of Ieû.

xiv. This is shown by the suggestion that Melchizedek bring out this water in a single jar of wine. We cannot imagine that this concept depends upon any other ultimate source than Gen. xiv. 18 where Melchizedek 'brings out' bread and wine to Abraham. Further, one is also reminded of Philo's interpretation of the wine:

But let Melchizedek bring forth wine instead of water, and let him give souls to drink and let him give them neat wine in order that they may become possessed of a divine intoxication which is more sober than sobriety itself.[1]

This association of the baptism of the water of life with wine is especially striking in the Second Book of Ieû when we consider that wine in Gnostic systems was often associated with ignorance, stupor, and unawareness.[2]

Melchizedek in these prayers is still a heavenly figure. Even if there is speculation on Gen. xiv. 18 in the passage referred to in the above paragraph, Melchizedek's activity of bringing wine out to Abraham cannot be expanded to a bringing down of the baptism of the water of life until Melchizedek is thought of as a heavenly figure. Hence, the passage still provides us with no clue as to how Melchizedek came to be considered such a heavenly Light figure since that conception is prior logically and chronologically to the interpretation found here. On the other hand, this conception of Melchizedek as the bearer of the baptismal waters belongs to the earliest strata of tradition in our sources.

CONCLUSIONS REGARDING THE GNOSTIC SOURCES

Can we say anything definite about the development of the figure of Melchizedek in the sources we have examined? We have seen that our earliest source, Kahle's Fragment 52, shows us that for one Gnostic community or author Melchizedek was interpreted in terms of Genesis and Hebrews, although we possess no details of that interpretation. We cannot say with certainty that Melchizedek was even considered a heavenly

[1] *Leg. All.* III. 82.
[2] See Hans Jonas, *Gnosis und spätantiker Geist*, 1: *Die mythologische Gnosis* (3rd ed., rev.; Göttingen: Vandenhoeck & Ruprecht, 1963), 115–18.

being in that fragment, though one would expect that to be the case. Speculation on Melchizedek in Gen. xiv. 18, however, was also found to be a feature of the Second Book of Ieû, but this speculation assumed already that Melchizedek was a heavenly figure. It is certain that there is no straight line of development from this early conception of Melchizedek as the bearer of the baptismal water to the final picture in Book I of the Pistis Sophia of Melchizedek as the 'Receiver' of the Light of the archons. The first evidence we have for the later view is to be found in Book IV of the Pistis Sophia in which Melchizedek in concert with Ieû disturbs the archons, causing them to give up their Light. Now Book IV is thought to stand temporally between the Books of Ieû and Books I–III of the Pistis Sophia.[1] It is not at all impossible that the myth of the descent of Melchizedek to receive the Light of the archons is dependent upon the more modest function of bringing the water of the baptism of life down to men. The relationship is difficult to imagine for us, but becomes more probable when we consider the range of ideas which surround water in various Hellenistic systems of thought.

The student of philosophy is aware that Thales, who predicted the solar eclipse of 585 B.C., considered water to be the basic principle of all things. This idea, Plutarch tells us, Thales shared with Homer, an idea which had its ultimate origins in Egypt.[2] Further, according to Hellanieus (fifth century B.C.) water and earth were the two primal substances from which all things were created.[3] For the Egyptians themselves the reason for considering water as an ultimate source for all life is to be found in the cycle of the Nile upon which the inhabitants of the

---

[1] Schmidt–Till, *Koptisch-Gnostische Schriften*, pp. xxivff.

[2] οἴονται δὲ καὶ Ὅμηρον ὥσπερ Θαλῆν μαθόντα παρ' Αἰγυπτίων ὕδωρ ἀρχὴν ἀπάντων καὶ γένεσιν τίθεσθαι.

'And they consider that Homer also, like Thales, learning from the Egyptians, posited water as the principal and origin of all things.'

For the Greek text see G. S. Kirk and J. E. Raven, *The Presocratic Philosophers* (Cambridge: Cambridge University Press, 1957), §70, hereafter cited as Kirk–Raven. It is certainly true that Homer regarded Okeanos as the source of all things. Perhaps his most famous expression of this is where Hera (*Iliad* 14, 200) calls Okeanos θεῶν γένεσιν καὶ μητέρα Τηθύν, 'origin of gods and mother Tethys' (Kirk–Raven, §9). This saying was widely repeated and commented upon. See Kirk–Raven §§11 and 14.

[3] Kirk–Raven §37.

Nile Valley depend for sustenance. Water was for them from the earliest time considered to be the element from which all life arose.[1] Hence, the idea of 'the water of the baptism of life' is quite easily understood as stemming from this association of water with life. In the last prayer studied here even fire was thought of in terms of water, whence the phrase 'the water of the baptism of the fire of the Virgin of the Light'. To the person influenced by the notion of wetness as death, as explained by Heraclitus[2] or the idea that fire is that which brings life into being as stated by Heraclitus and carried on by the Stoics, such an association of ideas is impossible. Yet for the Egyptian, as well as for many Greeks, water was the source of all life and dryness was associated with death. Mixed metaphors such as 'the water...of fire' could come about only as water was given preeminence as the primal element. The reader will recall the process by which Melchizedek takes the Light from the archons in Book I of the Pistis Sophia involves removing their power, the breath of their mouths, the waters[3] of their eyes, and the sweat of their bodies.[4] The power of the archons is stated in terms of at least two moist substances, and possibly three if the breath is here thought of as a moist vapor. The 'receiving' of the Light is thought of not in terms of darkening but in terms of drying out. As the vital liquids are removed from the archons they become lifeless and restricted to their respective orbits.

With this background it is not difficult to see how the function of bringing down the baptism of the water of life could be generalized into that of a guardian of the Light. Melchizedek is the bearer of the baptismal waters, but in the defeat of Hecate

---

[1] See Henri Frankfort, *Ancient Egyptian Religion* (Harper Torchbooks, No. 77; New York: Harper & Brothers, 1948), p. 14.

[2] For Heraclitus the soul proceeds out of water through drying. Hence, his famous dictum:

ψυχῆσιν θάνατος ὕδωρ γενέσθαι ὕδατι δὲ θάνατος γῆν γενέσθαι· ἐκ γῆς δὲ ὕδωρ γίνεται, ἐξ ὕδατος δὲ ψυχή.

'It is death to souls to become water, and death to water to become earth. Now from earth water comes, and from water, soul.'
(Kirk–Raven §232.) Note that this saying still affirms water as the origin of the soul, but on a different conceptual model.

[3] Coptic possesses a perfectly good word for 'tear', *rmÿe*, and the use of *mouyowe* here puts emphasis on the idea of water and indicates the entire fluid medium of the eye.

[4] We have reference here to Schmidt, *Pistis-Sophia*, pp. 34²³ – 35¹.

149

he also has the power of disturbing the archons by his very glance. These two older functions stand behind the first picture of Melchizedek as Receiver which we find in Book IV of the Pistis Sophia.[1] Melchizedek already possesses the essential functions required for his new role. He is a figure who descends from the upper regions into the midst of the archons bearing the water of life. He is able to disturb the archons by his glance, and in the physics of this earlier form of speculation such disturbance results in the emission of Light. Only the activity of ascending again to the upper regions bearing the captured Light remains to complete the picture. Even so, within the context of the earlier speculation Melchizedek is not allowed to exercise this new role alone. He is accompanied by the superior figure Ieû, and we may suppose that Ieû's functions in this regard are ill-defined because he gives support to Melchizedek's new role only. All of this is to say that Melchizedek in Book IV of the Pistis Sophia does not have the independent, divine role accorded him in Books I–III.

Books I–III of the Pistis Sophia, and especially Book I, show us the final picture. Melchizedek's role as the collector and purifier of the Light is quite complete, so complete in fact that in some versions of the myth Melchizedek does not descend at all but sends his own functionaries, or 'Receivers', to collect the Light. The passage of time from the earlier speculation to the later speculation is indicated by the change in the mechanics of collecting the Light. In the later speculation the very possession of the Light is what troubles the archons.[2] Book III of the Pistis Sophia applies the new role of Melchizedek to the individual soul. We have seen that although the soul is made from the material dross of the archons, that dross still contains Light.[3] It is only one further step to making Melchizedek the bearer of the individual soul, the redeemer who rescues the soul from the control of the archons and takes it above to the Treasury of the Light.

The lines of development of Melchizedek from a peripheral figure in the oldest strata of speculation in the Second Book of Ieû to a more central figure in Books I–III of the Pistis Sophia are

---

[1] *Ibid.* p. 360[2ff].
[2] See the quotation from the Pistis Sophia above, p. 138.
[3] See above, p. 142.

tangled but to a large extent recoverable. The connection of all this to Fragment 52 must remain a mystery since we do not know what kind of speculation about Melchizedek was involved in Fragment 52. Although we have succeeded to some extent in disentangling the lines of development within the Pistis Sophia and the Second Book of Ieû, we have seen that even at the earliest period of development, i.e. within the prayers of the Second Book of Ieû, Melchizedek is already considered a heavenly figure. I have shown that the speculation on Gen. xiv. 18 is to be found in the first of these prayers (Schmidt, *Codex Brucianus*, p. 108) is impossible in the absence of such a prior assumption. Therefore, we must conclude that the process by which Melchizedek is elevated from a relatively unimportant figure in Gen. xiv to a heavenly being of some kind lies outside of and prior to the Gnostic sources which we have examined. It is to the recovery of that process that we now turn in our concluding chapter.

CHAPTER 6

CONCLUSION: MELCHIZEDEK AND THE EPISTLE TO THE HEBREWS

INTRODUCTION

Up until now I have refrained from saying anything at all about the figure of Melchizedek in the Epistle to the Hebrews so that we might first understand the sources which might be useful to us in dealing with Hebrews. Chronologically, of course, this chapter belongs between Chapters 3 and 4 since the Epistle is the ideal dividing point between what I have termed the 'background sources' and the 'later sources'.[1] Interest in the figure of Melchizedek in Hebrews has, however, been only one concern of this study. The other concern is to trace the growth and development of tradition about Melchizedek, moving from a relatively minor position within the Old Testament to divine status in some materials.[2] Hence, although this concluding chapter has the function of telling the reader something about the way in which Melchizedek is used in Hebrews, it also has the function of pulling together the material which we have examined and pointing to its ultimate origin. Both as a matter of convenience and for reasons of substance which will become obvious I shall proceed to my topic through a discussion of Heb. vii. 3 and move outwards to encompass the entire range of material.

HEBREWS VII. 3

We have already seen above that Heb. vii. 3 stands behind every Christian heresy which speculated about Melchizedek, at least as far as such heresies are known to us.[3] In the modern period scholarly discussion about Melchizedek has continued to cluster often around this single verse. The text of the verse reads:

---

[1] On this division see above, Chapter 1.

[2] See my introductory remarks on this in Chapter 1.

[3] As we saw in Chapter 4 as regards the Melchizedekians, Hierakas, and the party opposed by Jerome and Mark the Hermit.

ἀπάτωρ, ἀμήτωρ, ἀγενεαλόγητος, μήτε ἀρχὴν ἡμερῶν μήτε 3ωῆς τέλος ἔχων, ἀφωμοιωμένος δὲ τῷ υἱῷ τοῦ θεοῦ μένει ἱερεὺς εἰς τὸ διηνεκές.

Without father, without mother, without genealogy, having neither beginning of days nor end of life, and being made like unto the Son of God, he remains a priest into perpetuity.

The reason for this strange interpretation of Melchizedek in Gen. xiv. 18–20 is almost universally said[1] to be because of Melchizedek's sudden appearance in Gen. xiv and his almost as sudden disappearance. He is tied to no family tree nor are his parents mentioned. No account is given of his birth or of his death. Strack–Billerbeck note that for the Rabbis what is not said in the Torah is just as important for Rabbinic exegesis as what is said, and the principle is given a Latin formulation: *quod non in thora non in mundo*.[2] Other authorities have thought of this as representing an Alexandrian principle of exegesis, making no mention of the Rabbis.[3] I do not care to enter into discussion of this point since it does not materially affect my argument, but I would point to the fact that for the Alexandrians and for the Rabbis the silence of scripture is significant. Hence it is a common claim that our verse comes from a reading out of the silence of scripture on the origin and destiny of Melchizedek.

On further consideration, however, it is quite obvious that appeal to an interpretation from silence actually tells us very little about Heb. vii. 3, as Epiphanius pointed out long ago.[4] I might illustrate my objection to this kind of interpretation by appealing to the figure of Reuel/Jethro in Exodus and Numbers.

[1] By way of example we might mention B. F. Westcott, *The Epistle to the Hebrews* (3rd ed.; London: The Macmillan Co., 1903), p. 174; C. Spicq, *L'Épître aux Hébreux*, II: *Commentaire* (Paris: Librairie l'Ecoffre, 1953), 183. Hugh Montefiore, *A Commentary on the Epistle to the Hebrews* (Harper's New Testament Commentaries; New York and Evanston: Harper & Row, Publishers, 1964), p. 119, calls the underlying principle of interpretation 'Alexandrian' (compare Philo, *Quod Det. Pot.* §178), but he also gives Rabbinic parallels. This encourages us to think less in terms of geography and more in terms of an almost universal principle of Jewish exegesis.

[2] Str.–B. III, 694f.

[3] As, for instance, does James Moffatt, *A Critical and Exegetical Commentary on the Epistle to the Hebrews* (The International Critical Commentary, vol. 15; New York: Charles Scribner's Sons, 1924), p. 92.

[4] Epiphanius, *Panarion* LV. 3. 3–8.

Here is a priest-king intimately associated with Moses who offers sacrifice and who aids Moses in matters of administration. Much more is said of Reuel/Jethro in the Pentateuch than of Melchizedek, and the connection between Reuel/Jethro and the later history of Israel is much more direct than for Melchizedek. No genealogy is given for Reuel/Jethro. His birth and death are not narrated, nor are his parents named. Further, Reuel/Jethro is directly connected with the wilderness wandering which is thematic within Hebrews.[1] Obviously the reason for the selection of Melchizedek over a figure such as Reuel/Jethro in Hebrews depends not so much upon the silence of scripture as upon more tangible tradition. Strangely enough, most commentators seem satisfied with an appeal to silence as justification for the kind of treatment Melchizedek receives in Heb. vii. 3.[2] For instance, Westcott[3] informs us that the author of Hebrews is not interested in telling us anything about the historical Melchizedek, basing his picture only on scripture's silence. Bruce[4] argues that the vagaries of the Genesis account of Melchizedek are what inspire the author to cast Melchizedek as a type of the Christ, and that if the author had been informed that Melchizedek was (as Bruce believes[5]) a priest-king of Jerusalem both with predecessors and successors in the priesthood, 'he would have agreed at once, no doubt'.[6] Moffatt, on the other hand, suggests that the author brought in Gen. xiv. 18–20 to explain an idea which he found within the text of his favorite psalm, Ps. cx.[7] According to his view, Heb. vii. 1–3 explains the expression εἰς τὸν αἰῶνα in Ps. cix. 4 (LXX).[8]

---

[1] This is very carefully discussed by Ernst Käsemann, *Das wandernde Gottesvolk: Eine Untersuchung zum Hebräerbrief* (2nd ed.; Göttingen: Vandenhoeck & Ruprecht, 1957), pp. 5–58.

[2] This remains the argument of a recent article by Walter Edward Brooks, 'The Perpetuity of Christ's Sacrifice in the Epistle to the Hebrews', *JBL*, LXXXIX (June 1970), 206–7.

[3] *The Epistle to the Hebrews*, pp. 201ff. In these pages Westcott provides us with a useful excursus on Melchizedek.

[4] *The Epistle to the Hebrews* (The New International Commentary on the New Testament, Grand Rapids, Michigan: Wm. B. Eerdmans Publishing Company, 1964), pp. 133ff.

[5] *Ibid.* p. 137. One wonders why Bruce here takes so much time to discuss the priest-kingship of Melchizedek if it has no material bearing on the Epistle. See also *ibid.* p. 136 n. 16.

[6] *Ibid.* p. 137.   [7] *Hebrews*, pp. xxxii–xxxiii and 90.   [8] *Ibid.* p. 90.

A more recent attempt to explain why Melchizedek is important for Hebrews is that of De Jonge and Van der Woude who focus on the importance of the 11Q Melchizedek.[1] They view Heb. vii. 3 as a statement which derives from a previous oral or written source that treats of Gen. xiv. 18–20.[2] They think that the verse shows a poetic character and they divide it into lines as follows:

ἀπάτωρ, ἀμήτωρ, ἀγενεαλόγητος,
μήτε ἀρχὴν ἡμερῶν μήτε ζωῆς τέλος ἔχων,
ἀφωμοιωμένος δὲ τῷ υἱῷ τοῦ θεοῦ
μένει ἱερεὺς εἰς τὸ διηνεκές.[3]

In their view we are in a position to understand this verse as referring to the angelic figure of Melchizedek which is to be found also in the 11Q Melchizedek. Against arguments which see this verse simply as speculation on the silence of Genesis, De Jonge and Van der Woude think that the author really means to say something about Melchizedek when he calls him ἀπάτωρ, ἀμήτωρ, ἀγενεαλόγητος.[4] Melchizedek is limited only by the reservation that he is ἀφωμοιωμένος...τῷ υἱῷ τοῦ θεοῦ and hence we should give full antithetical force to the δέ in this verse.

Against this view, however, I would point out that the Epistle shows no evidence of regarding Melchizedek as an angel or archangel as De Jonge and Van der Woude suppose. They claim that Melchizedek in Hebrews is both an angel and yet limited in his role so as not to be greater than Christ. One has only to remember that in Heb. i–ii the author of the Epistle shows Christ's authority over and superiority to the angels without making reference to Melchizedek. The author does not need to subordinate Melchizedek to Christ because these two figures for him are not in competition. In Heb. iii. 1–5 Christ is made superior to Moses. He is worthy of more glory as one who builds a house is more worthy than the house itself (iii. 2). Moses was faithful in the house as a servant is faithful, but Christ was faith-

---

[1] '11Q Melchizedek and the New Testament', pp. 319–23.

[2] *Ibid.* p. 319. This position as regards the poetic nature of Heb. vii. 3 is also to be found in Otto Michel's *Der Brief an die Hebräer* (11th ed., rev., Kritisch-exegetischer Kommentar über das Neue Testament, vol. xiii; Göttingen: Vandenhoeck & Ruprecht, 1960), p. 164.

[3] '11Q Melchizedek and the New Testament', p. 319.

[4] *Ibid.* p. 321.

ful as the son of the house is faithful (iii. 5). This is an example of what our author does when faced with a figure who challenges the primacy of Christ. In the case of Moses, the author may be combatting a conception of Moses as an eschatological figure[1] or as a being higher than the angels.[2] Whatever the case, the author takes great pains to subordinate Moses to Christ, and again I point to the fact that he does not do this in reference to Melchizedek. Are we perhaps to think that the author is unable to subordinate Melchizedek to Christ because of a controlling belief in the superiority of Melchizedek? There is not a shred of evidence for such a view, and such a view runs counter to all we know about the Christology of the Epistle. The phrase ἀφω-μοιωμένος δὲ τῷ υἱῷ τοῦ θεοῦ does not create subordination; it assumes subordination. The eternal Son of God is the type for Melchizedek who is the antitype. This reversal of the usual understanding of type and antitype will be discussed at length below.

I have certainly not given all of the reasons suggested by commentators as to why Melchizedek is selected by the author of Hebrews for the type of exegesis found in Heb. vii. 3, nor have I desired to do anything other than show the most usual types of solution. Even with Philo, Josephus, and the 11Q Melchizedek, the appearance of Melchizedek is far from easily understood. Yet there is a solution to the problem to which we now proceed, and Heb. vii. 3 helps point the way to that solution.

The reader will recall that in Chapter 3 we found a point of contact between Philo and Josephus which at first was not obvious.[3] Philo considered that Melchizedek possessed a 'self-taught and instinctive' priesthood, and Josephus held that Melchizedek was the first priest before God and the founder of the Jerusalem Temple.[4] I held there that Philo's position was not necessarily at variance with that of Josephus and that his idea of Melchizedek's untutored priesthood must have assumed

---

[1] This is the view of Yigael Yadin, 'The Dead Sea Scrolls and the Epistle to the Hebrews', *Scripta Hierosolymitana*, IV (1958), 40–1.

[2] Michel, *Der Brief an die Hebräer*, p. 93. Hans Windisch, *Der Hebräerbrief* (2nd ed., rev., *HzNT*, vol. XIV; Tübingen: J. C. B. Mohr (Paul Siebeck), 1931), p. 28, wonders, with some justice, how a false teaching could be countered with such a meager argument.

[3] See above, Chapter 3, p. 85.

[4] Here the reader should refer to Table 3.1 on p. 86.

something like Josephus' tradition. We may refine that observation at this point by asking what common assumption or assumptions stand behind each of these accounts of Melchizedek's priesthood. The single common assumption is that Melchizedek was the first priest of God. For Philo this means that Melchizedek's priesthood was an unlearned or instinctive priesthood, and he used the analogy of the untutored wise man (αὐτομαθὴς καὶ αὐτοδίδακτος σοφός) to explain this type of priesthood. From this Philo proceeded to consider Melchizedek as a type of the Logos. In Josephus the theme of the originality of Melchizedek's priesthood is contained in the form of a tradition that Melchizedek was the first priest ever and the founder of the Jerusalem Temple.

Where do Philo and Josephus derive the notion of Melchizedek's being the first priest? It should be obvious that neither of the two Old Testament passages which refer to Melchizedek give us any reason for such a supposition. We cannot think that the author of Gen. xiv had any such idea in mind when he set forth his account, nor does he say anything which might be construed to imply the originality of Melchizedek's priesthood. Further, such an idea is very far from the text of Ps. cx. 4 as well. Yet the reason for this supposition *is* to be found in Gen. xiv, not in the words actually used, but in the fortuitous circumstance that *Melchizedek is the first priest mentioned in the Torah*. This fact may be of little consequence to the modern reader whose critical eye tells him that the editor of Gen. xiv does not place his account where he does for the purpose of suggesting Melchizedek was the first priest in the world. For the Jewish exegete of the first century B.C., however, the fact that Melchizedek is the first priest mentioned in the Torah would be of great moment. Applying now the principle *quod non in thora non in mundo* to this datum produces the exegetical result that there was no priest at all before Melchizedek or he would have been mentioned. The fact that Melchizedek happens to be the first priest mentioned in the Pentateuch is the one fact to which the common understanding of Philo and Josephus about the originality of Melchizedek's priesthood corresponds.

Let us once again examine Josephus' statement about the primacy of Melchizedek's priesthood which is to be found in *War* vi. 438:

Now the first founder (of Jerusalem) was a Canaanite chieftain, called in the mother tongue 'righteous king', for he was just such a one. On this account he was both the first to do priestly service to God, and, having been the first to build the Temple, he also called the city Jerusalem, although it was previously called Solyma.

One finds here Josephus deriving Melchizedek's original priesthood from the meaning of the name, but this is not enough. One should ask why Josephus derives this function from a name which in itself contains no such implications. The reason is that Josephus is not deriving something new but is explaining what is to be observed in scripture, i.e. that Melchizedek was the first priest before God. I find this consistent also with what was to be found in Philo. Here I shall quote two short passages which bear upon this topic:

God has also made Melchizedek both king of peace (for that is the meaning of 'Salem') and his own priest, not having prefigured any work of his, but having made him at first a king both peaceable and worthy of his priesthood. (*Leg. All.* III. 79)

And the oracle which was laid down after the victory prayers which Melchizedek, who possessed the unlearned and untutored priesthood, made... (*De Cong.* §99)

My understanding of the priesthood of Melchizedek as having importance because it is the first mentioned in scripture is immensely clarifying when we deal with passages such as this, for we find that Philo here is not allowing his imagination to run rampant any more than is Josephus. Rather, he is making use of what seems to him to be an obvious fact of scripture, through certainly making use of it in his own characteristic way.

I mentioned in Chapter 3 that Philo, Josephus, and the Genesis Apocryphon shared the same assumption that Melchizedek received tithes from Abraham and not the other way around.[1] I showed, however, in Chapter 2 that this was not a necessary understanding of the text of Gen. xiv. 20.[2] We can now understand why this interpretation of the text came into existence and did not waver over the years. Melchizedek was not just *a* priest, he was the first priest, the progenitor of all priesthood. Abraham might well have received tribute from some

[1] See Table 3.1, Chapter 3, p. 86.
[2] See my remarks above, Chapter 2, p. 17.

other priest-king of a city, but in this case we are dealing with the one from whom all priesthood, and especially the Levitical priesthood, derives. If a tithe was given, it must have been given by Abram to Melchizedek. This is not a matter of formal interpretation or midrash. Rather, such an interpretation would occur spontaneously to an exegete. It would be unthinkable that Melchizedek should offer tribute to anyone.

We have already seen that in the Palestinian sources the Salem of Gen. xiv. 18 is taken to be Jerusalem.[1] We have also seen that some modern scholars have tried to show that this is meant in the text of Gen. xiv. 18.[2] Although I was not able to disprove this contention, I tried to give some reasons for not accepting it without some reservations.[3] Even if it were true that Jerusalem was once called Salem, it is difficult to prove that this identification was a commonplace from Jebusite times up to the time of Josephus. This is not impossible, of course, but there is no particular reason to accept that idea either. We can understand now why some wanted to call Salem Jerusalem. Since Melchizedek was the first priest of God, it would be natural to think of his place of priesthood as being Jerusalem, the one legitimate seat of sacrificial worship.[4] At this point the parallelism of Ps. lxxvi. 3 might well be taken as support for this identification, although, as we have seen, that parallelism in itself does not establish the Salem–Jerusalem equation.[5]

Let us now proceed to Heb. vii. 3 in the light of what we have found so far. It will be seen that Heb. vii. 3 recapitulates the idea of the originality of Melchizedek's priesthood which we also found in Philo and Josephus. Now we can go beyond the silence of scripture and show why Melchizedek was chosen in the first place. The silence of scripture about the life and parentage of Melchizedek is brought out by the author of Hebrews as an amplification of the concept of the originality of Melchizedek's priesthood and not as a proof of that originality. This understanding meets Epiphanius' objection that many figures in the Old Testament are without genealogy and my objection that Reuel/Jethro is a much more important priestly

---

[1] See Table 3.1, p. 86.
[2] E.g. Mowinckel, Bright, and Noth. See above, Chapter 2.
[3] See Chapter 2, pp. 49ff.   [4] Moore, *Judaism* II, 11.
[5] See above, Chapter 2, p. 49.

figure who also meets the conditions of Heb. vii. 3. The author of Hebrews has not selected just any figure without genealogy from the Old Testament; rather, the first priest on earth is not given any genealogy in the Torah, a fact which goes to underscore his originality. The absence of genealogy, the failure to mention birth and death are unimportant deficiencies for unimportant figures, but for the first priest such omissions take on significance. We are now ready to show how all of this relates to the relationship between Christ and Melchizedek in Hebrews.

MELCHIZEDEK AND CHRIST IN HEBREWS

For Rabbinic Judaism, as we have already seen, the priesthood was passed on to Abraham and to his offspring at the meeting recorded in Gen. xiv. 18–20. Already by ca. A.D. 135, the words of Ps. cx. 4 had been applied to Abraham by R. Ishmael (*t. b. Ned* 32b). The priesthood of Melchizedek, according to this view, had its outcome in the priesthood from Abraham, i.e. the Levitical priesthood.[1] We have already noted that this transition was not made without some question. In particular it was found that the wholeness required of priests was thought to be threatened by the commandment to Abraham to circumcise, resulting in the decision that circumcision of the male member did not entail ritual defilement.[2] We did not ask at the time, but do now, why it was necessary for R. Ishmael and others to derive the priesthood from Melchizedek at all. The answer seems to rest on the fact that Melchizedek was the first priest in the Torah, and since there can be but one priesthood, it is necessary to provide a transition between this original priesthood and the Levitical priesthood. The two Old Testament texts which mention Melchizedek can be reconciled in terms of Abraham so that the primary priesthood of Melchizedek is carried on forever through Abraham and his seed.

I offer the Rabbinic interpretation to show the great contrast with the interpretation to be found in Hebrews. According to Hebrews the Levitical priesthood is of an inferior order (Heb. vii. 4ff.). Indeed, it may rightly be said that Levi himself gave a tithe to Melchizedek since he was at that time in his father's

---

[1] See also *Gen. R.* (*Lech Lecha*) XLVI. 5 and LV. 6.
[2] See above, Chapter 4, pp. 119ff.

loins (vii. 9–10). The lesser (Abraham) is blessed by the greater (Melchizedek) (vii. 7). Melchizedek is without end of life, and because he has no end of life nor beginning of life, the priesthood which he possesses comes about not through priestly succession but through the very infinite quality of that life (vii. 16). Christ is a priest 'according to the order of Melchizedek' in that he is 'according to the likeness' (κατὰ τὴν ὁμοιότητα) of Melchizedek (vii. 15). Christ is 'another priest' (ἱερεὺς ἕτερος, vii. 15). Melchizedek's priesthood continues into perpetuity (vii. 3), and hence it is improper to speak of Christ being Melchizedek's successor in the priesthood. Melchizedek has no successor in the priesthood. The meaning of κατὰ τὴν τάξιν Μελχισεδέκ is expressed as κατὰ τὴν ὁμοιότητα Μελχισεδέκ, which includes the idea of recapitulation.[1] Every feature of significance in Melchizedek's priesthood is recapitulated on a grander scale in Christ's priesthood.

Just as Melchizedek is the first priest in the old order, so is Christ 'another priest' forever. We are involved here in what I would call 'antitypology'. Westcott[2] was only partially right when he said that there is no allegory involved here but only typology, by which he meant to indicate that the author of Hebrews thought of a real, historical correspondence between the two figures. This leaves unexplained the word ἀφωμοιω-μένος in vii. 3. Actually, I would hold that the author thinks of Christ as the type and Melchizedek as the antitype. We might compare a similar 'antitypology' in Heb. ix as regards the true tent. The earthly sanctuary is but an antitype (ἀντίτυπος) of the true sanctuary in the heavens (ix. 24). This antitype gives us some idea of what the true sanctuary is like, as a copy does of the original (ix. 23). One may here conveniently contrast the author's allegorizing and his 'antitypology' by noting that in ix. 9 the earthly tent is called a παραβολή of the present time. The allegorical correspondence is between two earthly entities. The 'antitypology' of the author involves taking an earthly entity and contrasting it or connecting it to its heavenly counterpart or type. The words ἀφωμοιμωένος τῷ υἱῷ τοῦ θεοῦ assure us that in Heb. vii the same scheme is operative. We gain an understanding of Christ's priesthood, the eternal heavenly priesthood, by understanding the features of the earthly per-

---

[1] See L.–S. *sub voce*. [2] *Hebrews*, p. 202.

petual priesthood of Melchizedek. Each significant feature of the antitype is to be found in its true form in the type.

We can also not avoid the suspicion that for all that has been written about the equivalency of εἰς τὸ διηνεκές and εἰς τὸν αἰῶνα,[1] in this case the author has a difference in mind. Moffatt correctly reminds us that we must give due deference to context in determining the meaning of εἰς τὸ διηνεκές.[2] This is to be remembered as we observe two similar phrases in Heb. vii:

...μένει ἱερεὺς εἰς τὸ διηνεκές. (vii. 3 of Melchizedek)

...διὰ τὸ μένειν αὐτὸν εἰς τὸν αἰῶνα... (vii. 24 of Christ)

Besides the lexical difference between the two expressions,[3] there is perhaps an unwillingness of the author to use the words εἰς τὸν αἰῶνα, which remind one of Ps. cx. 4, in regard to Melchizedek, since they should apply to Christ. However, it is necessary for him to postulate a never-ending priesthood for Melchizedek as an antitype of the eternal priesthood of Christ. He accomplishes this by using an almost equivalent expression which does not stem from Ps. cx. 4.[4]

According to the view expressed here, I would agree with Michel[5] over against Montefiore[6] that the words ἀπάτωρ, ἀμήτωρ, ἀγενεαλόγητος have to do with priestly qualifications and not with miraculous birth. We should ask what these words

[1] For example, Michel, *Der Brief an die Hebräer*, p. 164.

[2] *Hebrews*, p. 93.

[3] The phrase εἰς τὸ διηνεκές means 'perpetually' whereas the phrase εἰς τὸν αἰῶνα means 'forever'. Although the difference is not always significant, in x. 1 and x. 12 the author could not have replaced the former with the latter phrase and still have retained the same meaning. In other places, however, such exchanges could be made with no real loss of meaning.

[4] As opposed to Moffatt's view (*Hebrews*, pp. xxxii–xxxiii and 90), there is no necessity of reconciling the expression with Gen. xiv since eternal priesthood is not posited of Melchizedek in the Old Testament but the king who is made 'a priest forever according to the order of Melchizedek' in Ps. cx. 4. Rather, having assigned this eternal priesthood to the type, Christ, he must find something corresponding in his antitype, Melchizedek, and for this reason there is need for harmonization.

[5] *Der Brief an die Hebräer*, pp. 162–3.

[6] *Hebrews*, p. 119. Spicq, *L'Épître aux Hebreux*, p. 184, says too that ἀγενεαλόγητος 'suggérerait que le Christ, prête-roi par son incarnation, n'est pas une personne humaine, c'est un être supraterrestre'.

correspond to in Christ within the author's thought, and we find an answer in vii. 14:

For it is obvious that our Lord descended from Judah, concerning which tribe Moses said nothing as regards priests.

Christ, stemming from Judah, has none of the familial require-ments for priesthood under the old covenant.[1] His father is not of priestly stock, making the offspring of his father and mother ineligible for the priesthood. Nor can he trace back in his family a relationship with the priestly family. But Melchizedek too came into being as the first priest without benefit of genealogy. This corresponds, as antitype to type, to the way in which Christ has become a priest.[2]

Briefly I must state my conclusions about Melchizedek and Christ in Hebrews. Unlike Rabbinic Judaism, the author of Hebrews sees no succession in Melchizedek's priesthood. Melchizedek, as the first priest, comes to be priest with-out benefit of the hereditary process by which the Levitical priesthood was carried on. His is a priesthood superior to that of the Levites since through Abraham Levi himself paid tithes to Melchizedek. Exploiting the silence of scripture, the author shows that the priesthood of Melchizedek had no be-ginning and no end and that Melchizedek remains a priest per-petually. This priesthood of Melchizedek, however, is but the antitype of the higher priesthood of Christ, and every significant feature of Melchizedek's priesthood is recapitulated in Christ's

[1] Cf. Ex. xliv. 22; *m. Yeb.* 9: 1–2; and *m. Kidd.* 4: 5–6. Christ's mother could not be the mother of a priest since she had been first married to one not of priestly stock.

[2] It should be obvious to the reader that I consider any pagan associations of Heb. vii. 3 to be completely beside the point in this case. The misunder-standing of the words ἀπάτωρ, ἀμήτωρ, ἀγενεαλόγητος, as having reference to biology instead of to priesthood has led some to unfortunate and need-lessly complex interpretations of Hebrews. Jerome in commenting on Ps. cix reports that the official understanding of Heb. vii. 3 was that 'sine patre dicetur secundum carnem, sine matre secundum Deum'. Interestingly enough the same interpretation, as given by Theodore of Mopsuestia, is regarded as correct by Moffatt, *Hebrews*, pp. xxxii–xxxiii. The same interpre-tation is also to be found in Cyril, *Glaph.* ii. 8, and Mark's *De Melch.* §4. This is a favourite understanding of the church at the turn of the fifth century designed to counter the speculation that Melchizedek is the Holy Spirit, as we found out above in Chapter 4.

priesthood. Christ is not Melchizedek's successor, for Melchizedek, possessing a perpetual priesthood, has no successor. Rather, Christ's priesthood is of another order, a heavenly order. We pause here to point out what should be an obvious fact. The author of Hebrews has little interest in Melchizedek *per se*. He, rather than Reuel/Jethro or some other non-Israelite priest, is chosen as the antitype because he is the first priest. Any thought of Melchizedek as a divine, angelic, or heavenly being would have completely destroyed the author's scheme. 'Antitypology'[1] depends upon understanding the heavenly in terms of the earthly. Were Melchizedek also thought of as being of the heavenly regions, the 'antitypology' which the author uses so successfully would be impossible. I conclude that the Epistle to the Hebrews should not be reckoned with the literature in which Melchizedek is considered a divine or heavenly figure.

HEBREWS AND HERESY

I have already related all Christian speculation about Melchizedek as a divine being to Heb. vii. 3 in Chapter 4. Atomistic exegesis of difficult passages lends itself to unreasonable conclusions, and this was the situation in the church when isolated thinkers found in Heb. vii. 3 a figure greater than Christ to whose order Christ was subject as in the case of the 'dynamic

---

[1] By coining the word 'antitypology' I have hoped to use a neutral word which carries no particular associations of Platonism in itself. Although many of the words used by the author of Hebrews suggest a Platonism, mediated perhaps through Philo, their use does not always parallel the use in the suggested sources. The author of Hebrews seems fond of using words with such philosophical associations to present a more usual type of Christian or Jewish eschatology as C. K. Barrett has shown in his article, 'The Eschatology of the Epistle to the Hebrews', *The Background of the New Testament and its Eschatology*, W. D. Davies and D. Daube, eds. (Cambridge: The University Press, 1954), pp. 363–93, and especially pp. 386 n. 1 and 393. Where 'antitypology' is employed, the 'Platonic' scheme is altered severely in favor of a futuristic eschatology. For example, in Heb. ix the earthly tent, the antitype, is also the 'first' tent (ix. 2) whereas the true tent is the 'second' tent, access to which is closed so long as the first tent is standing. There is a chronological separation between antitype and type, the earthly tent (antitype) being first and the heavenly sanctuary being second. In relation to Christ and Melchizedek the antitype (Melchizedek) is chronologically first and the type (Christ) second.

monarchians', or when, on the basis of the words ἀφωμοιωμένος τῷ υἱῷ τοῦ θεοῦ Melchizedek was understood to be a
figure of equal rank with Christ as in the case of Hierakas or the
party opposed by Jerome and Mark. We need look no further
than Heb. vii. 3 for a bridge between Melchizedek in the Old
Testament and these heretical doctrines since, as we have seen,
the view of Christ held by each heresy determined the type of
exegesis Heb. vii. 3 would receive.

In particular, attention may be given in the future to a possible link between the speculation found in the 11Q Melchizedek and the Christian heresies which involved speculation about
Melchizedek as a divine being. Indeed, this has already been
suggested by De Jonge and Van der Woude[1] as also by Van der
Woude alone.[2] We should observe first of all that there are only
a limited number of ways in which Melchizedek could be
thought of as an angelic figure and that any two such presenta-
tions would of necessity have some features in common. Literary
parallels cannot take the place of more substantial historical
evidence in determining historical dependence or influence.
Certainly there is agreement between the Christian heretics and
the 11Q Melchizedek that Melchizedek is a heavenly figure, an
angel, or a divine figure of some sort. We cannot deny the possibility that the thought of the 11Q Melchizedek or some similar
document may have created a climate in which later Christian
heretics thought it natural to represent Melchizedek as such a
figure, but we have no evidence that such a climate existed
either. What we do have is obvious and admitted dependence
upon Hebrews, especially Heb. vii. 3, and I can see no reason
at present to conjecture unknown sources.

THE GNOSTICS

The situation may be otherwise as regards the Gnostic sources
we have examined, particularly the Pistis Sophia and the Second
Book of Ieû. We have seen the development of Melchizedek

---

[1] '11Q Melchizedek and the New Testament', p. 326.

[2] 'Melchisedech als himmlische Erlösergestalt', p. 373. We note in passing
that Van der Woude here seems to have placed the date of our Gnostic
sources previous to the Melchizedekians which is incorrect. The Books of
Ieû are perhaps to be assigned to roughly the same time, but the Pistis
Sophia is later. For a discussion see above, Chapter 5.

(Zorokothora) from the bearer of the water of the baptism of the Light to the 'Receiver' of the Light. We have, in general, been able to account for the final picture in terms of the earlier picture to be found in the prayers which mention Melchizedek. Certain items, however, I could not account for, and these may be important. In the first place, we found that even though there was some relationship between the picture of Melchizedek in the Second Book of Ieû and Gen. xiv. 18–20, the interpretation of that scripture already depended upon a conception of Melchizedek as a heavenly figure. Unlike the Christian heretics, I was unable to account for this conception of Melchizedek on the basis of Heb. vii. 3 although Fragment 52 does show at least one Gnostic writer dealing with that text. Further, unlike the Christian heresies, there is no reason to think that Melchizedek's position is determined by Christological motivations. Indeed, the Gnostic speculation about Melchizedek shows no demonstrable connection with the Christian heresies.

In the second place, a conception to be found at an early stage of the development of the idea of Melchizedek as 'Receiver' of the Light is the difficult notion of the 'time of the number of Melchizedek'[1] of Melchizedek's coming into the places of the Left hand. We cannot but be reminded that in the 11Q Melchizedek, Melchizedek is to come at the time of the last jubilee,[2] and one can imagine how that notion might have been adjusted to fit a Gnostic idea of a periodic descent of Melchizedek into the realm of the archons.

Both in the Gnostic sources and in the 11Q Melchizedek, Melchizedek is to make purification in one way or another, but the common source for this idea is the figure of Melchizedek as a priest in Gen. xiv. 18–20 and Ps. cx. 4.

I have suggested here only the possibility of a connection between the Gnostic systems studied and the 11Q Melchizedek, not the probability of such a connection. One may hope that the publication of the documents from Nag Hammadi will clarify the relationship, if any, between the two. It is quite possible that the links I have suggested will turn out to be phantoms, and on this point no verdict may now be spoken.

[1] This is the later formulation of the idea to be found in Book 1 of the Pistis Sophia. See above, Chapter 5.

[2] 11Q Melch. 1, 2, 4, and especially line 9, 'He has decreed a year of good favor to Melchize[dek...]'.

THE 11Q MELCHIZEDEK

Since I do not believe that Melchizedek in Hebrews is an angelic or heavenly figure as in the 11Q Melchizedek, it is obvious that I would not posit a direct relationship between the two. That does not mean, however, that the 11Q Melchizedek should be considered irrelevant to Hebrews, but only that it is not a direct source for Hebrews. If there is no direct relationship between Melchizedek in the 11Q Melchizedek and Melchizedek in Hebrews, there are some parallels between Melchizedek in the 11Q Melchizedek and Christ in Hebrews which, in summary form, might be listed.

1 Both Christ and Melchizedek are eschatological, redemptive figures.

2 Both are exalted in the heavens.

3 Both make atonement for sin.

4 Both overcome the forces opposed to God.

5 Both bring the promise of a new age.

Actually, these five similarities could also apply to other portions of the New Testament. Only in relation to the theme of the heavenly priesthood, and that theme is unclear in 11Q Melchizedek, is there room for more precise comparison.

Initial excitement with this aspect of the relationship between the 11Q Melchizedek and Hebrews might potentially mask more important areas of contact. Although this present work is not devoted to the topic of the relationship of Qumran to Hebrews, it would not be amiss to mention two areas in which further investigation is indicated. (1) The theme of the sabbath rest for the people of God (Heb. iv. 4, 9) is paralleled by the theme of the last jubilee in 11Q Melch. i. 2, 7, 9, this jubilee being reckoned as a sabbath of sabbath years (i.e. occurring every 49 years) and in Dan. ix. 24–7 the end of days being reckoned as the tenth such jubilee after the return from exile. In this time there will be a release for the captives (11Q Melch. i. 4–6; Heb. ii. 15). The value here is that the 11Q Melchizedek may make explicit what is only implicit in Hebrews. (2) The second value is the use of אלוהים as a virtual singular in relation to Melchizedek in 11Q Melch. i. 9–11 in the words of Ps. lxxxii. 1. This relates directly to the discussion of Heb. i. 8–9, the text of which reads:

8 πρὸς δὲ τὸν υἱόν,
'Ο θρόνος σου, ὁ θεός, εἰς τὸν αἰῶνα τοῦ αἰῶνος
καὶ ἡ ῥάβδος τῆς εὐθύτητος ῥάβδος τῆς βασιλείας σου·
9 ἠγάπησας δικαιοσύνην καὶ ἐμίσησας ἀνομίαν·
διὰ τοῦτο ἔχρισέν σε ὁ θεός, ὁ θεός σου,
ἔλαιον ἀγαλλιάσεως παρὰ τοὺς μετόχους σου.

It has been suggested that ὁ θεός in vss. 8 and 9 is a vocative addressed to the Son for the author of Hebrews.[1] This contention is, however, strongest for the ὁ θεός of vs. 8. I would not in this space attempt to resolve what amounts to a very difficult textual problem in vs. 9. What is important to say here is that the possibility of a figure other than Yahweh being addressed as θεός is enhanced by the precedent of the 11Q Melchizedek, and it is no longer possible to reject this understanding of Heb. i. 8 by a general appeal to some theological scruple against calling one other than Yahweh אלוהים as does Westcott.[2] This might be equally useful in giving a background for John xx. 28 where Thomas calls Jesus ὁ κύριός μου καὶ ὁ θεός μου.[3]

I must, however, add one word of caution here. Although I have held that Melchizedek in the 11Q Melchizedek is called אלוהים and אלוהיך in the words of Ps. lxxxii. 1 and Isa. lii. 7, this does not mean that this represents a general practice or anything other than the peculiarity of a single author. It is strongly suggestive, but we require other evidence before we can with complete certainty regard the 11Q Melchizedek's use of Elohim as forming background for the Christian practice of calling Christ θεός (whether in the New Testament or later).

I have no reason to believe that Hebrews is related to the speculation about Melchizedek demonstrated in the 11Q Melchizedek. Although there is no absolute way to rule out a relationship between Hebrews and Qumran on this point, there is no positive evidence which would necessarily lead us to posit a connection and good reasons to deny a connection.

[1] Cf. Windisch, *Der Hebräerbrief*, p. 16; Montefiore, *Hebrews*, p. 47; Michel, *Der Brief an die Hebräer*, p. 55; Spicq, *Hebreux*, p. 19; and F. F. Bruce, *Hebrews*, pp. 19–20. Spicq and Bruce attempt to relate this usage to the ancient kingship ideology whereby the king was regarded as divine, but neither show a direct connection to Hebrews. Moffatt, *Hebrews*, p. 13, does not state a firm opinion on the matter. [2] *Hebrews*, p. 25.
[3] On this see C. K. Barrett, *The Gospel According to St. John* (London: SPCK, 1958), pp. 476–7.

Heb. vii. 3 and vii. 8 implies that Melchizedek's priesthood still continues and that he is still living. At first blush this view of Melchizedek seems remarkably similar to that of the 11Q Melchizedek.[1] In the 11Q Melchizedek, Melchizedek will make atonement for the Sons of Light on the last jubilee (lines 6, 8). Further, since the text calls Melchizedek an *Elohim*, it is reasonable to assume that he is regarded as immortal. However, the theme of Melchizedek's immortality is of no importance whatsover in the 11Q Melchizedek as we have it, and Melchizedek's priestly function is never brought into connection with his immortality: Melchizedek will offer a single act of atonement on the tenth jubilee.

It is not impossible to see how a Christian writer, privy to Qumranite speculation about Melchizedek, might pattern Christ's priesthood upon that supra-mundane model. In doing so, however, it would be difficult to escape a subordination of Christ to Melchizedek similar to the subordination found in some of the Melchizedekian heresies. This subordination would conflict seriously with the view of the author of Hebrews in chapters i and ii that Christ is superior to the heavenly beings, and that in putting all things in subjection to Christ, God exempted nothing, including a heavenly Melchizedek (cf. Heb. ii. 8). To conclude that Christ is a priest according to the order of a heavenly Melchizedek would be to conclude that the author of Hebrews in chapter vii is departing from a principle he thought important enough to demonstrate in his initial chapters. It is more reasonable than this to conjecture that if the author of Hebrews had known of the speculation about Melchizedek contained in the 11Q Melchizedek, he might well have rejected Melchizedek as a type of the Christ.

I have shown above (pp. 160–4) that Hebrew's notion of a perpetual priesthood for Melchizedek is derived from exegesis of Gen. xiv. There is no need for the additional hypothesis that this exegesis was augmented by concepts similar to those in the 11Q Melchizedek. At the very least this would be to multiply hypotheses without need. Also this would point to a fundamental contradiction in the argument of Hebrews.

We are not relieved of our puzzlement about the perpetuity of Melchizedek's priesthood introduced in the Epistle to the

[1] De Jonge and Van der Woude, '11Q Melchisedek', p. 320.

Hebrews; but we can see in the Epistle that this aspect, like others of Melchizedek's ministry, held no real interest for our author apart from their connection with the ministry of Christ. If we remember that in Hebrews the movement is from Christ to Melchizedek and back to Christ, it may be argued that the most obvious source for the Epistle's belief in Melchizedek's perpetual priesthood (and the reason why the author found that perpetuity in the words of Ps. cx. 4 and in the absence of a reference to Melchizedek's death in Gen. xiv) is the author's belief in the eternal priesthood of Christ. It is entirely likely that the secondary results of this kind of exegesis as they relate to the priesthood of Melchizedek were of no interest to the author.[1]

The 11Q Melchizedek will be of increasing importance as it becomes successfully related to the major trends of Qumranite thought and history as well as to the thought and history of first-century Judaism in general.[2] One may hope that if speculation about Melchizedek as a heavenly figure was at all commonplace at Qumran that further traces of such speculation will be revealed from the material yet to be studied or published. Until such time as that occurs, the possibility, however remote, that this document represents the speculations of an isolated religionist who allowed his imagination to soar beyond the theological conventions of his community and who had no real influence on later thought cannot be dismissed out of hand.

IN CONCLUSION

I have attempted to locate the origin of Melchizedek speculation ultimately in the fortuitous circumstance that Melchizedek is the first priest mentioned in the Pentateuch. This ultimate source was already exploited by the first century B.C. since both Philo and the Genesis Apocryphon add material to the Genesis narrative in a way designed to deal with this status of Melchizedek as the first priest of God. In the Genesis Apocryphon Melchizedek is brought into connection with Jerusalem (as he is later in Josephus), and in Philo Melchizedek is honored as the possessor of an unlearned and untutored priesthood, indeed as a repre-

[1] Michel, *Der Brief an die Hebräer*, pp. 267f.
[2] Certainly this is the intent of the article by J. T. Milik, '*Milkî-Sedeq* et *Milkî-Reša'*'. See my comments on this arctile above, pp. 65–6.

sentation of the divine Logos. Hebrews, exploiting the silence of Gen. xiv, takes the unique priesthood of Melchizedek as an antitype of the eternal priesthood of Christ. Popular misunderstanding of the intention of the author of Hebrews, however, resulted in a series of heresies in the church which viewed Melchizedek as a heavenly or a divine being. Thought about Melchizedek as a heavenly being, however, was not limited to the early church. We possess one fragmentary document from the middle of the first century A.D. which deals with Melchizedek as an angelic or divine being, using of him the designation Elohim as a virtual singular. Again in the third century A.D. we find speculation about Melchizedek as a divine figure within a Gnostic sect. Although some speculation about Melchizedek among the Gnostics was probably based on Heb. vii. 3, as is shown by Kahle's Fragment 52, such does not seem to be the case for the Pistis Sophia or the Books of Ieû. Certain vague parallels between the speculation in these books and the 11Q Melchizedek were mentioned in order to suggest at least the possibility that later Gnostic speculation about Melchizedek might have had roots in sectarian Judaism, but it was held that these parallels were too weak to be any more than suggestive. For the Rabbis, Melchizedek as the first priest passes on his priesthood to Abraham and his seed, and we found only one text which suggested any eschatological role for Melchizedek. There were no Rabbinic passages for our period which suggested speculation about Melchizedek as a divine or angelic being.

It seems clear to me that by the second or third century A.D. the ultimate reason for regarding Melchizedek as important at all had all but been forgotten and that Melchizedek's importance was simply an accepted fact. This, in my view, is what set the stage for the Melchizedek legends of a later time. The reasons for assigning an important role to Melchizedek were no longer as important as that role itself. Melchizedek, even within the period discussed in this book was coming to have an independent importance, not only for the heretics, but also for those who opposed the heretics. Only within the Rabbinic materials is there actually a reduction of Melchizedek's importance in our period, and, as the legends in *Pirkê de Rabbi Eleazer* show, this reduction was not universally accepted.

I hold that the same misunderstandings which in earlier

centuries led to inordinate speculation about Melchizedek as a divine figure or as a priest of pre-Israelite Jerusalem have led modern scholars to make some of the same errors. Only when we realize that later exegesis dictated that Melchizedek was God's first priest and hence that he was of necessity the first priest in Jerusalem, or that he was even a divine priest descended from above, can we avoid these mistakes for ourselves. Our study of the Old Testament sources revealed that there was no adequate support for such ideas within the text of Gen. xiv and Ps. cx, but the later tradition which dictated these results was based not on the text but upon a lexical circumstance unrelated to the intention of the Old Testament authors. We are no closer than when we began to knowing anything of real substance about a historical figure named Melchizedek. The only solid connections between this figure and the priesthood are preserved for us only in later tradition, and we have no reason to try to push this tradition back beyond the first century B.C. On the other hand, it is hoped that we have arrived at some clarity as regards the development of the tradition about Melchizedek in the first five centuries or so of the Christian era.

SELECT BIBLIOGRAPHY

COMMENTARIES

Briggs, Charles Augustus and Briggs, Emilie Grace. *A Critical and Exegetical Commentary on the Book of Psalms*, 2 vols. (The International Critical Commentary). Edinburgh: T. & T. Clark, 1906–7.

Bruce, F. F. *The Epistle to the Hebrews* (The New International Commentary on the New Testament). Grand Rapids, Michigan: Wm. B. Eerdmans Publishing Company, 1964.

Duhm, D. Bernard. *Die Psalmen*. 2nd ed., rev. (Kurzer Hand-Kommentar zum Alten Testament, vol. xiv). Tübingen: J. C. B. Mohr (Paul Siebeck), 1922.

Fitzmyer, Joseph A. *The Genesis Apocryphon of Qumran Cave I: A Commentary* (Biblica et Orientalia, No. 18). Rome: Pontifical Institute, 1966.

Héring, Jean. *L'épître aux Hébreux* (Commentaire du Noveau Testament, vol. xiii). Paris and Neuchâtel: Delachaus & Niestlé S.A., 1954.

Kittel, Rudolf. *Die Psalmen*. 6th ed. (Kommentar zum Alten Testament, vol. xiii). Leipzig: A. Deichertsche Verlagsbuchhandlung, D. Werner Scholl, 1929.

Kraus, Hans-Joachim. *Psalmen*, vol. ii (Biblischer Kommentar – Altes Testament, vol. xv/2). Neukirchen/Moers: Neukirchener Verlag, 1960.

Manson, William. *The Epistle to the Hebrews: An Historical-Theological Reconsideration*. London and Edinburgh: Hodder and Stoughton, 1951.

Michel, Otto. *Der Brief an die Hebräer*. 11th ed., rev. (Kritisch-exegetischer Kommentar über das Neue Testament, vol. xiii). Göttingen: Vandenhoeck & Ruprecht, 1960.

Moffatt, James. *A Critical and Exegetical Commentary on the Epistle to the Hebrews* (The International Critical Commentary). New York: Charles Scribner's Sons, 1924.

Montefiore, Hugh. *A Commentary on the Epistle to the Hebrews* (Harper's New Testament Commentaries). New York and Evanston: Harper & Row, Publishers, 1964).

Noth, Martin. *Exodus*, translated from the original German by J. S. Bowden (The Old Testament Library). Philadelphia: The Westminster Press, 1962.

Oesterley, W. O. E. *The Psalms*, reprint of the 1938 edition originally in 2 vols. London: SPCK, 1953.

Schmidt, Hans. *Die Psalmen* (Handbuch zum Alten Testament, First Series, vol. xv). Tübingen: J. C. B. Mohr (Paul Siebeck), 1934.

Skinner, John, *A Critical and Exegetical Commentary on Genesis*. 2nd ed. (The International Critical Commentary). Edinburgh: T. & T. Clark, 1930.

Speiser, E. A. *Genesis* (The Anchor Bible, vol. 1). Garden City, N.Y.: Doubleday & Company, Inc., 1964.

Spicq, C. *L'Épître aux Hébreux*, 2 vols. (Études Bibliques). Paris: Libraire L'Ecoffre, 1952–3.

Von Rad, Gerhard. *Genesis: A Commentary*, translated from the original German by John H. Marks (The Old Testament Library). Philadelphia: The Westminster Press, 1961.

Weiser, Artur. *The Psalms: A Commentary*, translated from the original German by Herbert Hartwell (The Old Testament Library). Philadelphia: The Westminster Press, 1962.

Westcott, Brooke Foss. *The Epistle to the Hebrews*. 3rd ed. London: The Macmillan Company, 1903.

Windisch, Hans. *Der Hebräerbrief.* 2nd ed., rev. (*HzNT*, vol. xiv). Tübingen: J. C. B. Mohr (Paul Siebeck), 1931.

GENERAL WORKS

Bacher, Wilhelm. *Die Agada der babylonischen Amoräer.* 2nd ed. Hildesheim: Georg Olms Verlagsbuchhandlung, 1967.

Die Agada der palästinenischen Amoräer, 3 vols. Strassburg: Karl J. Trübner, 1892–9.

Baehrens, W. A. *Überlieferung und Textgeschichte der lateinisch erhaltenen Origeneshomilien zum Alten Testament* (Texte und Untersuchungen zur Geschichte der altchristlichen Literatur, vol. xlii/1). Leipzig: J. C. Hinrichs'sche Buchhandlung, 1916.

Baikie, James. *The Amarna Age: A Study in the Crisis of the Ancient World.* New York: The MacMillan Company, 1926.

Bernhardt, Karl-Heinz. *Das Problem der altorientalischen Königsideologie im Alten Testament* (Supplements to *Vetus Testamentum*, vol. viii). Leiden: E. J. Brill, 1961).

Braun, Herbert. *Qumran und das Neue Testament*, 2 vols. Tübingen: J. C. B. Mohr (Paul Siebeck), 1966.

Bright, John. *A History of Israel.* Philadelphia: The Westminster Press, 1959.

Cayré, F. *Manual of Patrology and History of Theology*, i, translated out of the original French by H. Howitt. Paris: Desclée & Co., 1936.

Cross, Frank Moore, Jr. *The Ancient Library of Qumran*, 2nd ed., rev. (Anchor Books, No. A272). Garden City, N.Y.: Doubleday & Company, Inc., 1961.

Daniélou, Jean. *Philon d'Alexandrie* (Les Temps et les Destins). Paris: Libraire Artheme Fayard, 1958.

Davies, W. D. *The Setting of the Sermon on the Mount*. Cambridge: Cambridge University Press, 1964.

de Vaux, Roland. *Ancient Israel: Its Life and Institutions*, translated out of the original French by John McHugh. New York, Toronto, and London: McGraw-Hill Book Company, 1961.

Doresse, Jean. *The Secret Books of the Egyptian Gnostics: An Introduction to the Gnostic Coptic Manuscripts Discovered at Chenoboskion*, translated from the original French by Phillip Mairet. New York: Viking Press, 1960.

Drummond, James. *Philo Judaeus or the Jewish-Alexandrian Philosophy in its Development and Completion*, II. Edinburgh: Williams and Norgate, 1888.

Dupont-Sommer, A. *The Essene Writings from Qumran*, translated from the original French by G. Vermes (Meridian Books, No. 44). Cleveland and New York: The World Publishing Company, 1961.

Dürr, Lorenz. *Psalm 110 im Licht der neueren alttestamentlichen Forschung*. Münster: Aschendorf, 1929.

Eichrodt, Walther. *Theology of the Old Testament*, 2 vols., translated from the original German by J. A. Baker (The Old Testament Library). Philadelphia: The Westminster Press, 1961-7.

Eissfeldt, Otto. *The Old Testament: An Introduction*, translated from the original German by P. R. Ackroyd. New York and Evanston: Harper & Row, Publishers, 1965.

Engnell, Ivan. *Studies in Divine Kingship in the Ancient Near East*. Uppsala: Almquest & Wiksell, 1943.

Frankfort, Henri. *Ancient Egyptian Religion* (Harper Torchbooks, No. 77). New York: Harper & Brothers, 1948.

Goodenough, Edwin R. *By Light, Light: The Mystic Gospel of Hellenistic Judaism*. New Haven: Yale University Press, 1935.
    The Politics of Philo Judaeus: Practice and Theory. New Haven: Yale University Press, 1938.

Goodspeed, Edgar J. *A History of Early Christian Literature*, revised and enlarged by Robert M. Grant. Chicago: The University of Chicago Press, 1966.

Goshen-Gottstein, M. H. *Text and Language in Bible and Qumran*. Jerusalem and Tel Aviv: Orient Publishing House, 1960.

Grant, R. M. *Gnosticism and Early Christianity*. 2nd ed. New York and London: Columbia University Press, 1966.

Gressmann, Hugo, *Der Messias* (Forschungen zur Religion und Literatur des Alten und Neuen Testaments, New Series, vol. xxvi). Göttingen: Vandenhoeck und Ruprecht, 1929.

Gunkel, Hermann. *Ausgewählte Psalmen.* 4th ed., rev. Göttingen: Vandenhoeck & Ruprecht, 1917.

The Psalms: A Form-Critical Introduction (Facet Books, Biblical Series, No. 19). Translated from the original German article to be found in vol. 1 of *Religion in Geschichte und Gegenwart* by Thomas M. Horner. Philadelphia: Fortress Press, 1967.

Gunkel, Hermann and Begrich, Joachim. *Einleitung in die Psalmen: Die Gattungen der religiösen Lyrik Israels* (Göttinger Handkommentar zum Alten Testament, Ergänzungsband zur II. Abteilung). Göttingen: Vandenhoeck und Ruprecht, 1933.

Harnack, Adolf. *History of Dogma*, vols. II–III (bound as one vol.), translated from the original German by Neil Buchanan. New York: Dover Publications, 1961.

Jérôme, J. 'Der geschichtliche Melchisedech-Bild und seine Bedeutung im Hebräerbrief.' Unpublished doctoral dissertation, Freiburg University, 1927. N.V.

Johnson, A. R. *Sacral Kingship in Ancient Israel.* Cardiff: University of Wales Press, 1955.

Jonas, Hans. *Gnosis und spätantiker Geist*, vol. 1: *Die mythologische Gnosis.* 3rd ed., rev. Göttingen: Vandenhoeck & Ruprecht, 1963.

Käsemann, Ernst. *Das wandernde Gottesvolk: Eine Untersuchung zum Hebräerbrief.* 2nd ed. Göttingen: Vandenhoeck & Ruprecht, 1957.

Kees, Hermann. *Das Priestertum im Ägyptischen Staat vom Neuen Reich bis zur Spätzeit* (Probleme der Ägyptologie, vol. 1). Leiden: E. J. Brill, 1953).

Kistemaker, Simon. *The Psalm Citations in the Epistle to the Hebrews.* Amsterdam: Wed. G. Van Soest, 1961. N.V.

Klausner, Joseph. *From Jesus to Paul*, translated from the original Hebrew by W. F. Stinespring (Beacon Paperbacks, No. 115). Boston: Beacon Press, 1961.

Kosmala, Hans. *Hebräer-Essener-Christen* (Studia Post-Biblica, vol. 1). Leiden: E. J. Brill, 1959.

Laqueur, Richard. *Der jüdische Historiker Flavius Josephus: Ein biographischer Versuch auf neuer quellenkritischer Grundlage.* Giessen: Münchow'sche Verlagsbuchhandlung (Otto Kindt Wwe.), 1920.

Milik, J. T. *Ten Years of Discovery in the Wilderness of Judaea*, translated from the original French by J. Strugnell (Studies in Biblical Theology, No. 26). London: SCM Press, 1959.

Moore, George Foot. *Judaism in the First Centuries of the Christian Era*, 3 vols. Cambridge, Mass.: Harvard University Press, 1927–30.

Mowinckel, Sigmund. *He that Cometh*, translated from the original Norwegian by G. W. Anderson. New York and Nashville: Abingdon Press, 1954.

Psalmenstudien II: *Das Thronbesteigungsfest Jahwäs und der Ursprung der Eschatologie*, photomechanical reproduction of the original Oslo edition of 1921–4. Amsterdam: P. Schippers Verlag, 1961.

The Psalms in Israel's Worship, 2 vols. translated out of the original Norwegian and revised by D. R. Ap-Thomas. Oxford: Basil Blackwell, 1962.

Noth, Martin. *Die Israelitischen Personennamen im Rahmen der gemein-semitischen Namengebung* (Beiträge zur Wissenschaft vom Alten und Neuen Testament, series 3, vol. x). Stuttgart: W. Kohl-hammer Verlag, 1928.

The History of Israel, translated from the original German and revised by P. R. Ackroyd. New York: Harper & Row, Publishers, 1960.

Poulssen, Nick. *König und Tempel im Glaubenzeugnis des Alten Testaments* (Stuttgarter biblische Monographien, No. 3). Stuttgart: Katholisches Bibelwerk, 1967.

Quasten, Johannes. *Patrology*. III, *The Golden Age of Greek Patristic Literature from the Council of Nicaea to the Council of Chalcedon*. Westminster, Maryland: The Newman Press, 1960.

Reid, Richard. 'The Use of the Old Testament in the Epistle to the Hebrews.' Unpublished Th.D. dissertation, Union Theological Seminary in New York City, 1964.

Ringgren, Helmer. *The Faith of Qumran: Theology of the Dead Sea Scrolls*, translated from the original Swedish by Emilie T. Sander. Philadelphia: The Fortress Press, 1963.

Sanders, James A. *The Psalms Scroll of Qumran Cave 11* (Discoveries in the Judaean Desert of Jordan, No. 4). Oxford: The Clarendon Press, 1965.

Schlatter, D. A. *Die hebräischen Namen bei Josephus* (Beiträge zur Förderung christlicher Theologie, vol. XVII/3). Gütersloh: C. Bertelsmann, 1913.

Schreiner, Josef. *Sion-Jerusalem – Jahwes Königssitz: Theologie der heiligen Stadt im Alten Testament* (Studien zum Alten und Neuen Testament, vol. VII). Munich: Kösel-Verlag, 1963.

Schröger, Friedrich. *Der Verfasser des Hebräerbriefs als Schriftausleger* (Biblische Untersuchungen, No. 4). Regensburg: Friedrich Pustet Verlag, 1968.

Schürer, Emil. *The Jewish People in the Time of Jesus*, translated from the original German by John Macpherson, edited and abridged by Nahum N. Glatzer (Schocken Paperbacks, No. 8). New York: Schocken Books, 1961.

Shutt, R. J. H. *Studies in Josephus*. London: SPCK, 1961.

Stork, Hellmuth. *Die sogenannten Melchizedekianer mit Untersuchungen ihrer Quellen auf Gedankengehalt und dogmengeschichtliche Entwicklung* (Forschungen zur Geschichte des neutestamentlichen Kanons und der altkirchlichen Literatur, vol. VIII/2). Leipzig: A. Deichert, 1928. N.V.

Strack, Hermann L. *Introduction to the Talmud and Midrash* (Harper Torchbooks, the Temple Library, No. 808L). Translated from the original German by Elaine Lustig and Bernard Cole. New York and Evanston: Harper & Row, Publishers, 1965.

Strack, Hermann L. and Billerbeck, Paul. *Kommentar zum Neuen Testament aus Talmud und Midrasch*, 4 vols. Munich: C. H. Beck'sche Verlagsbuchhandlung, 1922–8.

Von der Osten-Sacken. *Gott und Belial: Traditionsgeschichtliche Untersuchungen zum Dualismus in den Texten aus Qumran* (Studien zur Umwelt des NTs, vol. 6). Göttingen: Vandenhoeck & Ruprecht, 1969.

Von Rad, Gerhard. *Old Testament Theology*, 2 vols., translated from the original German by D. M. G. Stalker. New York and Evanston: Harper & Row, Publishers, 1965.

Wilson, R. McL. *Gnosis and the New Testament*. Philadelphia: Fortress Press, 1968.

Wolfson, Harry Austyn. *Philo: Foundations of Religious Philosophy in Judaism, Christianity, and Islam*, 2 vols. (Structure and Growth of Philosophical Systems from Plato to Spinoza, No. II). Cambridge, Mass.: Harvard University Press, 1947.

Wuttke, Gottfried. *Melchisidech der Priesterkönig von Salem: Eine Studie zur Geschichte der Exegese* (*BZNW*, vol. v). Giessen: A. Töpelmann, 1927.

ARTICLES

Albright, W. F. 'Abram the Hebrew: A New Archaeological Interpretation', *BASOR*, CLXIII (October 1961), 36–54.

Allegro, J. M. 'Fragments of a Qumran Scroll of Eschatological Midrašim', *Journal of Biblical Literature*, LXXVII (September 1958), 350–4.

'Further Messianic References in Qumran Literature', *Journal of Biblical Literature*, LXXV (September 1956), 174–87.

Altaner, B. 'Die Schrift ΠΕΡΙ ΤΟΥ ΜΕΛΧΙΣΕΔΕΚ des Eustathios von Antiocheia', *Byzantinische Zeitschrift*, XL (1940), 30–47.

Avigad, N. 'The Palaeography of the Dead Sea Scrolls and Related Documents', *Scripta Hierosolymitana*, IV (1958), 56–87.

Bandstra, A. J. 'Heilsgeschichte and Melchizedek in Hebrews', *Calvin Theological Journal*, III (April 1968), 36–41.

Bardy, G. 'Melchisédech dans la tradition patristique', *RB*, XXXV (October 1926), 496–509, and XXXVI (January 1927), 25–45.

Barrett, C. K. 'The Eschatology of the Epistle to the Hebrews', *The Background of the New Testament and its Eschatology: Studies in Honor of Ch. H. Dodd*, W. D. Davies and David Daube, eds. Cambridge: The University Press, 1954, pp. 363–93.

Barton, G. A. 'A Liturgy for the Celebration of the Spring Festival at Jerusalem in the Age of Abraham and Melchizedek', *Journal of Biblical Literature*, LIII (March 1934), 61–7.

Batdorf, Irvin W. 'Hebrews and Qumran: Old Methods and New Directions', *Festschrift to Honor F. Wilbur Gengrich*. Leiden: E. J. Brill, 1972, pp. 16–35.

Beek, M. A. 'Hasidic Conceptions of Kingship in the Maccabean Period', *The Sacral Kingship: Contributions to the Central Theme of the VIIth International Congress for the History of Religions* (Rome, April, 1955) (Studies in the History of Religions, Supplements to *Numen*, vol. IV). Leiden: E. J. Brill, 1959, pp. 349–55.

Benzinger, Immanuel. 'Zur Quellenscheidung in Gen. 14', *Vom Alten Testament: Karl Marti zum 70. Geburtstag*. Karl Budde, ed. *BZAW*, vol. XLI). Giessen: Alfred Töpelmann, 1925, pp. 21–7.

Braun, Herbert. 'Qumran und das Neue Testament: Ein Bericht über 10 Jahre Forschung (1950–1959) – Hebräer', *Theologische Rundschau*, XXX (June 1964), 1–38.

Burrows, Millar, 'The Meaning of 'ŠR 'MR in DSH', *Vetus Testamentum*, II (July 1952), 255–60.

Carmignac, Jean. 'Le Document de Qumrân sur Melkisédeq', *Revue de Qumrân*, VII/3 (December 1970), 343–78.

Coppens, J. 'Les apports du Psaume CX (Vulg. CIX) à l'idéologie royale israélite', *The Sacral Kingship: Contributions to the Central Theme of the VIIIth International Congress for the History of Religions* (Rome, April 1955) (Studies in the History of Religions, Supplements to *Numen*, vol. IV). Leiden: E. J. Brill, 1959, pp. 331–48.

Cross, Frank Moore, Jr. 'The Development of Jewish Scripts', *The Bible and the Ancient Near East: Studies in Honor of William Foxwell Albright*, G. Ernest Wright, ed. (Anchor Books, No. 431). Garden City, N.Y.: Doubleday & Company, Inc., 1965, pp. 170–264.

Daube, David. 'Participle and Imperative in I Peter', *The First Epistle of St. Peter*, Commentary by Edward Gordon Selwyn. 2nd ed. London: Macmillan & Co., Ltd, 1964, pp. 467–88.

De Jonge, M. and Van der Woude, A. S. '11Q Melchizedek and the New Testament', *NTS*, XII (1965–6), 301–26.

Delcor, M. 'Melchizedek from Genesis to the Qumran Texts and the Epistle to the Hebrews', *JSJ*, II (December 1971), 115–35.

du Toit Laubscher, F. 'God's Angel of Truth and Melchizedek', *JSJ*, III (October 1972), 46–51.

Emerton, J. A. 'Melchizedek and the Gods: Fresh Evidence for the Jewish Background of John X. 34–6', *JTS*, n.s. XVII (April 1966), 399–401.

'Some New Testament Notes', *Journal of Theological Studies*, XI (April 1960), 329–36.

'The Riddle of Genesis XIV', *VT*, XXI (October 1971), 403–39.

Fisher, Loren R. 'Abraham and his Priest-King', *JBL*, LXXXI (September 1962), 264–70.

Fitzmyer, Joseph A. 'Further Light on Melchizedek from Qumran Cave 11', *JBL*, LXXXVI (March 1967), 25–41.

'Now this Melchizedek...', *CBQ*, XXV (July 1963), 305–21.

'The Use of Explicit Old Testament Quotations in Qumran Literature and in the New Testament', *New Testament Studies*, VII (July 1961), 297–333.

Flusser, David. 'Melchizedek and the Son of Man', *Christian News from Israel* (April 1966), pp. 23–9.

Gammie, John G. 'Loci of the Melchizedek Tradition of Genesis 14: 18–20', *JBL*, XC (December 1971), 385–96.

Goshen-Gottstein, M. H. 'Linguistic Structure and Tradition in the Qumran Documents', *Scripta Hierosolymitana*, IV (1958), 101–37.

Hardy, E. R. 'The Date of Psalm 110', *Journal of Biblical Literature*, LXIV (December 1945), 385–90.

Horton, F. L. 'Formulas of Citation in the Qumran Literature', *Revue de Qumrân*, VII/4 (December 1971), 505–13.

Hunt, Ignatius, O. S. B. 'Recent Melchizedek Study', *The Bible in Current Catholic Thought*, John L. McKenzie, S.J., ed. New York: Herder & Herder, 1962, pp. 21–33.

Jefferson, H. G. 'Is Psalm 110 Canaanite?', *JBL*, LXXIII (September 1954), 152–6.

Jenni, E. 'Das Wort 'ōlām im Alten Testament', *ZAW*, LXIV (June 1952), 197–248.

Johnson, A. R. 'The Psalms', *The Old Testament and Modern Study*, H. H. Rowley, ed. (Oxford Paperbacks, No. 18). Oxford: The Clarendon Press, 1961, pp. 162–209.

Kahle, Paul. 'Das palästinische Pentateuchtargum und das zur Zeit Jesu gesprochene Aramäisch', *ZNW*, XLIX (1958), 100–16.

Kutscher, E. Y. 'Dating the Language of the Genesis Apocryphon', *JBL*, LXXVI (December 1957), 288–92.

'The Language of the Genesis Apocryphon: A Preliminary Study', *Scripta Hierosolymitana*, IV (1958), 1–35.

Landes, George M. 'The Material Civilization of the Ammonites', *The Biblical Archaeologist Reader*, II (Anchor Books, No. 250b). Garden City, N.Y.: Doubleday & Company, Inc., 1964, 69–88.

Michel, Otto, 'Μελχισεδέκ', *Theological Dictionary of the New Testament*, vol. IV, Gerhard Kittel, ed. Translated from the original German by Geoffrey W. Bromily. Grand Rapids, Michigan: Wm. B. Eerdmans Publishing Company, 1967, pp. 568–71.

Milik, J. T. '*Milkî-Sedeq* et *Milkî-Reša*' dans les anciens écrits juifs et chrétiens (I)', *JJS*, XXIII (Autumn, 1972), 95–144.

Miller, Merrill. 'The Function of Isa. 61_{1-2} in 11Q Melchizedek', *JBL*, LXXXVIII (December 1969), 467–9.

Mowinckel, Sigmund. 'General Oriental and Specific Israelite Elements in the Israelite Conception of the Sacred Kingdom', *The Sacral Kingship: Contributions to the Central Theme of the VIIIth International Congress for the History of Religions* (Rome, April 1955) (Studies in the History of Religions, Supplements to *Numen*, vol. IV). Leiden: E. J. Brill, 1959, pp. 283–93.

Noth, Martin. 'Jerusalem und die israelitische Tradition', *Gesammelte Studien zum Alten Testament*. Munich: Chr. Kaiser Verlag, 1957, pp. 172–87.

'Gott, König, Volk im Alten Testament', *Gesammelte Studien zum Alten Testament*. Munich: Chr. Kaiser Verlag, 1957, pp. 188–229.

Roberts, C., Skeat, T. C., and Nock, A. D. 'The Guild of Zeus Hypsistos', *HTR*, XXIX (January 1936), 39–88.

Rowley, H. H. 'Melchizedek and Zadok (Gen. 14 and Ps. 110)', *Festschrift für Alfred Bertholet zum 80. Geburtstag*, Otto Eissfeldt, Karl Ellinger, Walter Baumgartner, and Leonard Rost, eds. Tübingen: J. C. B. Mohr (Paul Siebeck), 1950, pp. 461–72.

'Zadok and Nehustan', *JBL*, LVIII (June 1939), 113–42.

Sanders, J. A. 'Dissenting Deities and Phil. 2_{1-11}', *JBL*, LXXXVIII (September 1969), 279–90.

'Outside the Camp', *USQR*, XXIV (Spring, 1969), 239–46.

Schmid, Herbert. 'Melchisedech und Abraham, Zadok und David', *Kairos*, VII (February 1965), 148–51.

Simon, M. 'Melchisédech dans la polémique entre juifs et chrétiens et dans la légende', *Revue d'Histoire et de Philosophie Religieuse*, XVII (1937), 58–93.

Smith, Robert Houston. 'Abram and Melchizedek (Gen. 14, 18–20)', *Zeitschrift für die Alttestamentliche Wissenschaft*, LXXVII (February 1965), 129–53.

Spicq, C. 'L'épître aux Hébreux, Apollos, Jean-Baptiste, les Hellénistes et Qumrân', *Revue de Qumrân*, I (1958–9), 365–90.

Stoebe, Hans-Joachim. 'Erwägungen zu Psalm 110 auf dem Hinter-grund von 1. Sam. 21', *Festschrift Friedrich Baumgärtel zum 70. Geburtstag, 14. Januar, 1958* (Erlanger Forschungen, series A, vol. x). Erlangen: Universitätsband Verlag, 1957, pp. 175–91.

Vajda, Georges, 'Melchisédec dans la mythologie ismaélienne', *Journal Asiatique*, ccxxxiv (1943–5), 173–83.

Van der Woude, A. S. 'Melchisedech als himmlische Erlösergestalt in den neugefundenen eschatologischen Midraschim aus Qumran Höhle XI', *Oudtestamentische Studiën*, xiv (1965), 354–73.

Winter, Paul. 'Note on Salem-Jerusalem', *Novum Testamentum*, ii (April 1957), 151–2.

Yadin, Y. 'A Note on Melchizedek and Qumran', *Israel Exploration Journal*, xv (1965), 152–4.

'The Dead Sea Scrolls and the Epistle to the Hebrews', *Scripta Hierosolymitana*, iv (1958), 36–55.

INDEXES

MODERN SCHOLARS

HEBREW WORDS AND PHRASES

GREEK WORDS AND PHRASES

SUBJECTS

116493